MGM British Studios:
Hollywood in Borehamwood

MGM British Studios:
Hollywood in Borehamwood

Celebrating 100 Years of the Film Studios of Elstree/ Borehamwood, 1914-2014

by Derek Pykett

BearManor Media

2015

MGM British Studio: Hollywood in Borehamwood
Celebrating 100 Years of the Film Studios of
Elstree/Borehamwood, 1914–2014

© 2015 Derek Pykett

For information, address:

BearManor Media
P. O. Box 71426
Albany, GA 31708

bearmanormedia.com

Typesetting and layout by John Teehan

Front cover image courtesy of Stephen Scott
Back cover photograph by Sandy Wright

Published in the USA by BearManor Media

ISBN—1-59393-883-7
978-1-59393-883-3

For Ruth, Willow, and Lucy—
the lights of my life.

Table of Contents

Acknowledgments

Many people have contributed towards the production of this book by providing me with help, support, suggestions, and invaluable information. They have made this long overdue story of MGM British Studios possible. They are:

My Dad and my whole family to whom I shall always be eternally grateful, and without their continuous support nothing I have done would have been possible.

Luke Pykett, my younger brother, who has helped me throughout with the compiling of photographs and research.

Ruth Potter, my beautiful fiancée, for staying by my side during the writing of this project, and for helping me in the collecting together of important material.

Olivia de Havilland, Kenneth Hyman, Rod Taylor, Nicolas Roeg, and Virginia McKenna, who generously gave of their time and wrote me the Forewords.

Paul Welsh and Bob Redman of Elstree Screen Heritage for their help and knowledge, and for also inspiring me to write this book about one of the great film studios of England.

Colin Beardmore, a mind of filmic information and who always came forward with contacts of important MGM film personnel.

My special and dear late friends, Cecelia and Michael Ripper, who continuously inspired me to write more film books.

Brian Holland, a first-class friend and his lovely family, who are always endlessly kind and supportive and encourage me in whatever I do.

Nick and Sandy Wright, and beautiful baby daughter Jasmine, close friends whom I know that I can always rely on, both privately and professionally.

Simon Flynn, Sally-Anne Ryan, Andrew Thirlwall Potts, Theresa Doyle, Michael and Karmellah Howlett, Danny R. Fulce, Ian Tyler, Martin Killeen, and Elmar Podlasly, who have always been true friends to me, and have made my life a brighter place for it.

Marianne Stone, John Harris, June Randall, Francis Matthews, Bryan Forbes, Trader Faulkner, Douglas Slocombe, Brian Clemens, Joss Ackland, Terry Pearce, Peter Sasdy, Katharina Kubrick, Brook Williams, Norman Mitchell, Michael Ripper, Geoffrey Bayldon, Lance Percival, Vera Day, Ron Moody, Kelvin Pike, Freddie Francis, Alan Hume, Sir Sydney Samuelson, Michael Winner, Ian Carmichael, Richard Gordon, Paul Wilson, Jane Asher, John Cairney, Ray Harryhausen, Ken Taylor, Peter Copley, Paul Scofield, Ernest Borgnine, Honor Blackman, Freddie Young, Vincent Ball, Christopher Challis, Michael Gough, Bill Maynard, Janette Scott, Donald Sinden, Keir Dullea, Gary Raymond, Murray Melvin, Oswald Morris, Ronnie Maasz, Martin Benson, Betta St. John, Gerry Fisher, Nosher Powell, Ronald Neame, James Fox, Geoff Glover, Dennis Fraser, Phyllis Townshend, Jimmy Devis, Tim Hutchinson, Robin Vidgeon, Peter Newbrook, Renee Glynne, Sally Jones, Neil Binney, Danny Shelmerdine, Roy Walker, Stuart Cooper, Trini Lopez, Angela Allen, Peter Mullins, Douglas Wilmer, Keith Blake, David Minty, Frank Elliott, Hugh Harlow, David Wynn-Jones, Elaine Schreyeck, Laurence Payne, Pamela Carlton, Herbert Smith, Malcolm Vinson, Terry Ackland Snow, Pamela Francis, Geoffrey Helman, Jack Lowin, Jimmy Dawes, Stephen Scott, Douglas Adamson, Graeme Scaife, Les Ostinelli, Trevor Coop, Patrick Macnee, Brian Taylor, Peggy Spirito, Brian Johnson, Sir Ken Adam, James Sharkey, Christopher Neame, John Richardson, Gilbert Taylor, Ivor Selwyn, Ian Gregory, Sheila Whittingham, Derrick Sherwin, Jill Hyem, Bob Jordan, Jack Cardiff, Brian Cobby, Nick Danziger, Danny Danziger, Ken Holt, Donald Fearney, Bob Pearson, Roger Garrod, Derek Smith, Neil Thompson, Rory Flynn, Michael Sellers, Dennis Lloyd, Frances Russell (British Society of Cinematographers), The Guild of British Camera Technicians, British Film Institute, Pegasus Entertainment, British Library Newspapers (Colindale, London), and Borehamwood Library. To all of the above, my sincere thanks, and I shall always be eternally grateful.

Photographs courtesy of: John Harris, June Randall, Francis Matthews, Trader Faulkner, Brian Clemens, Michael Ripper, Olivia de Havilland, Kelvin Pike, Alan Hume, Pamela Francis, Paul Wilson, Ray Harryhausen, Gerry Fisher, Rod Taylor, Geoff Glover, Dennis Fraser, Phyllis Townshend, Tim Hutchinson, Kenneth Hyman, Peter Mullins, David Wynn-Jones, Herbert Smith, Stephen Scott, Graeme Scaife, Virginia McKenna, Brian Taylor, Robin Vidgeon, Keith Blake, James Sharkey, John Richardson, Ian Gregory, Sheila Whittingham, Jack Cardiff, Geoffrey Helman, Bob Jordan, Rory Flynn, Roger Garrod, and Neil Thompson.

My eternal thanks to the many actors and technicians who gave of their time to share their memories with me, particularly Stephen Scott (son of Elliot Scott), who not only shared his memories but also allowed me to look through his fathers many MGM British production designs and some of those of Alfred Junge.

Finally, a big thank you to Olivia de Havilland, (who worked at MGM in both Britain and Hollywood during their golden eras), for her kind correspondence.

Foreword
by
Olivia de Havilland

How I wish I could summon up an entertaining anecdote about my experiences while shooting *That Lady*, *Libel*, and *Light In The Piazza*, the three motion pictures that I filmed at MGM British, Borehamwood. Alas, none rises to the surface of my memory.

What I do recall, however, is that the MGM Borehamwood lot was compact, attractive, rather intimate in character, and immaculately maintained. Since its staff was of a high order, too, I enjoyed working there.

In contrast, my impression of the MGM Studios in Culver City, California, is of a huge, sprawling, somewhat disorganised maze of structures through which I only just managed to find my way when sent there by David Selznick for special Melanie photo sessions. This, of course, was during the filming of *Gone With The Wind*, which, though released by MGM, was shot at the nearby Selznick International Studios.

Derek Pykett's book on MGM British is indeed an interesting project, and a valuable contribution to film lore.–Paris, France. Films at MGM British: *That Lady* (1955), *Libel* (1959), and *Light In The Piazza* (1962).

Foreword
by
Kenneth Hyman

To me, a studio is a studio, whether you're in Hollywood or England, but MGM British was a fine studio. Wonderful. The management were professional and very co-operative. It was an efficient factory. Excellently run. It was a joy working there. Happy Times.

I remember that Sidney Lumet was taken with working in England, and particularly with working at MGM Borehamwood, where he directed his film *The Hill*. Sidney was an actor's director but believed in the spontaneity of a single take. Rehearsals at MGM British beforehand, though, were very important to him.

When we blew the chateau up for the film *The Dirty Dozen,* we did of course get lots of complaints from people who lived quite near to the MGM Borehamwood studios, but it was a one off. We only had one go at it. The chateau had cost quite a lot to build. So, all I can say is, thank Christ the cameras were working.–Henley-on-Thames, Oxfordshire. Films at MGM British: *The Hill* (1965), and *The Dirty Dozen* (1967).

Foreword
by
Rod Taylor

I have nothing but happy memories of MGM Borehamwood, a wonderful studio. My first visit to work with dear friend Maggie Smith and an impressive cast, as you know, on *The VIPs* was to open the door of an enormous sound stage to find myself in a two-storied replica of the interior of Heathrow Airport, one of the biggest and best sets I've ever seen.

I also had a very satisfying professional time working with director Jack Cardiff on *The Liquidator* and keeping as fit as possible to keep up with Trevor Howard's demands to accompany him to the busy bar on the lot, between scenes.

Jack Cardiff and I actually did three movies together at MGM British, and the greatest thing about those three pictures was the crews. The humour from the electricians and grips (usually the same blokes on each picture) made for some hilarious days while still being the best technicians one could wish for. Nothing was too much of a problem for them in the studio or on location (except interfering with tea breaks).

The executive family at MGM Borehamwood was comfortable, too, in their lack of interference. We were there to create a good movie, and they were happy to help us do it.

I really do feel warm and sentimental with my memories of MGM Borehamwood.–Beverley Hills, California. Films at MGM British: *The VIP's* (1963), *The Liquidator* (1965), *Young Cassidy* (1965), and *The Mercenaries* (1968),

Foreword
by
Nicolas Roeg

MGM British was my film school. It was my training ground, and people had permanent regular jobs at that studio, which is quite extraordinary in the movie business. It was considered a more upmarket studio to work at than others, and it did have a sort of snobbism about it, because of its connection with America, and Hollywood.

The big bosses had a sort of attitude, which went something like, "We need to make this picture. It is an investment in our prestige." Quite brilliant really.

It was certainly a very grand studio but had a sort of factory atmosphere about it, and you knew your place.

Part of the magic, though, of working at MGM British was that it was quite a secretive working environment. There was very little gossip on or off the set, and if you did hear anything about any extra curricular activity, it was never mentioned outside the studios gates. So, when you entered MGM (Borehamwood), you were very privileged to be a part of it, but you didn't take anything out with you at the end of the day. No-matter what you'd seen or heard.–Notting Hill, London. Films at MGM British: *The Miniver Story* (1950), *Calling Bulldog Drummond* (1951), *Knights Of The Round Table* (1953), *Bhowani Junction* (1956), *Tarzan's Greatest Adventure* (1959), *Jazz Boat* (1959), and *Casino Royale* (1967).

Foreword
by
Virginia McKenna

I remember the two films I worked on at MGM Studios, Borehamwood, with the greatest pleasure—for professional and personal reasons. It was a first-class studio.

The Barretts of Wimpole Street starred Jennifer Jones and Bill Travers. Bill and I were to marry the following year. So, it was very special to be working there. The wonderful John Gielgud played Mr. Barrett in that film—an example to us all of courtesy, patience, and perfect timing.

One day on set at MGM Borehamwood I shall always remember involved a scene supposedly in the street in a snowfall. Vernon Gray and I had a clandestine meeting in the street, and showers of "snow" descended on us from high in the studio ceiling. Suddenly it all came to a halt, and a producers meeting was urgently called. It seemed that the crew up aloft were suffering from intense heat and were asking for supplies of cold drinks to be winched up to them. At first, this wasn't forthcoming, but when it was realised the men were in earnest, action was taken, and we all watched as refreshments were hoisted aloft. I thought it was quite funny, but I expect the producers were counting the cost of time lost!

The Wreck of the Mary Deare at MGM British was a highlight for me. I had only one scene, but it was with Gary Cooper. How lucky could one be? He was the least "starry" person one could imagine. Quietly spoken, modest, charming, and generous in the way he acted with me.

This was all a very long time ago, but some memories don't fade with age. Perhaps they improve, like good wine!–Dorking, Surrey. Films at MGM British: *The Barretts Of Wimpole Street* (1957), and *The Wreck Of The Mary Deare* (1959).

Introduction

The very first time I drove through Elstree in December 2005, I was shocked to discover that there were no film studios. The truth being in fact that there was only ever one in Elstree itself, and that was the Danziger Brothers Studios, or New Elstree Studios as it was known, and that had closed some forty years previous. Of the other five studios that existed, and the two of which that still remain today (all of which being known, at sometime or another, as the film studios of Elstree) these could and can actually be found in neighbouring Borehamwood.

It has been said over the years that the studios adopted the word Elstree for "snob value" since Elstree had and still has a better reputation than Borehamwood. In reality, however, back in the early twentieth century, when the first film studios were constructed in Borehamwood, the now quite large town was nothing more than a rural hamlet, whilst Elstree village was a well-known and somewhat ancient watering hole (dating back before Roman times), so it was therefore natural for the studios to adopt the more established name.

Elstree, in terms of film industry then, was actually Borehamwood. It became known as the "British Hollywood" because outside of Hollywood it was, in its heyday, the single most concentrated center of film and television studios anywhere in the western world.

Before you read on, however, it is important for me to point out the brief history of the six studios of Elstree/Borehamwood and their various name changes. I do this to help you, the reader, not to get confused, as the studios will be mentioned in their several incarnations throughout this book.

The first moviemakers arrived in Borehamwood in 1914, when the original film studio was erected on Clarendon Road. The facility was called Neptune Studios, and its stage was entirely devoid of any windows, making it the first "dark stage" outside of Hollywood. In the years what followed Neptune would change its name several times, firstly to Blattner, then Rock, and then to British National. It was during its period as a film

1

studio that various stars appeared in movies there, including George Formby, Old Mother Riley (Arthur Lucan), and Deborah Kerr, who appeared in *Love On The Dole* (1941), which launched her career.

In the mid 1950s, Douglas Fairbanks Jr. appeared in 160 half-hour television programmes at the studio, and the now classic 1950s television serials, *The Scarlet Pimpernel*, *William Tell* and *The Invisible Man* were also produced on its stages.

In 1960, Lew Grade's ATV purchased the studios, and with him in charge, thousands of programs were created, including *Emergency Ward 10*, *The Morecambe And Wise Show*, and *The Muppet Show*.

The BBC took over from ATV in 1983 and continued the run of television successes: *Top Of The Pops*, *Grange Hill*, *Holby City*, and the popular soap *EastEnders*, which started its run at the studio in 1985. Today, the studio is known as the BBC Elstree Centre.

The second and longest serving film studio to open in Borehamwood is the now named Elstree Film Studios on Shenley Road. It opened its gates for the first time in 1926, and over 500 major motion pictures have been made there, including box office hits such as *The Dambusters* (1954), *Moby Dick* (1956), *Look Back In Anger* (1959), *Murder On The Orient Express* (1974), *Star Wars* (1977), *The Empire Strikes Back* (1980), *Raiders Of The Lost Ark* (1981), *Return Of The Jedi* (1983), *Indiana Jones And The Temple Of Doom* (1984), and *Indiana Jones And The Last Crusade* (1989).

Charlie Chaplin called the Elstree Film Studios on Shenley Road the "home of British cinema," and that studio launched the screen careers of Charles Laughton, Ray Milland, Laurence Olivier, Stewart Granger, Richard Todd, and a pre-*Gone With The Wind* Vivian Leigh.

In the 1960s, the Elstree Film Studios on Shenley Road also produced television productions, and four of the better known were *The Avengers*, *The Saint*, *The Human Jungle*, and *Randall And Hopkirk (Deceased)*.

Like its predecessor, the Elstree Film Studios on Shenley Road also had several name changes, these included British International Pictures (or BIP), Associated British Picture Corporation (or ABPC), and EMI-Elstree Film Studios.

Sadly, this studio, even though it still exists today, has had a very checkered past, including many attempts to close its gates permanently, resulting in part of it being sold off to Tesco in 1996, leaving much of the original site (including where *Star Wars* was filmed) buried beneath a giant shopping superstore.

Gate Studios was the third studio to be built at Borehamwood. It surfaced in 1928 on Station Road and was the closest studio to Elstree Railway Station. Its original name on opening was Whitehall Studios. The H.G. Wells science fiction film, *Things To Come* (1936), was partially shot there, as were *Amazing Quest Of Ernest Bliss* (1936) with Cary Grant, *London Melody* (1937), and the comedy classic *Old Mother Riley Joins Up* (1939).

In 1947, the studios was purchased by the J. Arthur Rank Organisation, and it was then renamed Gate Studios.

Several features were made there during this period, including *Decameron Nights* (1953), *Innocents In Paris* (1953), and probably the most famous movie to come out of the studios, *Odette* (1950) with Trevor Howard.

Gate Studios was also used for experimental work. In 1953, Max Bygraves starred in *Harmony Lane*, a support film made in Technicolor 3D.

Film production ceased at Gate Studios in 1957, and after many attempts to save the building, it was sadly demolished in 2006 to make way for housing.

When the British & Dominions Imperial Studios opened on Elstree Way in 1929 its future looked good. Its life was cut short, however, by tragedy in 1936 (see chapter 1).

The two final studios to rise up are the ones featured in this book: MGM British Studios and the Danziger Brothers New Elstree Studios, which was born out of MGM British (see chapter 4).

Sadly, nothing remains of either of these studios today, as I discovered when I moved to the area to be with my fiancé, Ruth, in 2005.

We actually lived just off the Edgwarebury lane to the south of Elstree, in the shadow of the Edgwarebury Hotel and Stanley Kubrick's former home on Barnet Lane.

The Edwarebury Hotel (a regular haunt for me and Ruth) was location to many an Elstree movie, including Hammer's *The Devil Rides Out* (1967) and the Terry-Thomas/Alistair Sim comedy, *School For Scoundrels* (1960), which featured the now disused tennis court behind the hotel in a major sequence.

I'm hoping that in writing this book about the studios MGM British and Danziger Brothers that it will help in keeping their memories alive,

The fact is that MGM British produced some of the biggest movies made in the United Kingdom, and just a small mention in books here and there just isn't good enough.

Paul Welsh, on the other hand, does deserve credit here. His weekly column in the *Elstree & Borehamwood Times* and his tireless work, along with Bob Redman of Elstree Screen Heritage have certainly helped to make sure that MGM British is never forgotten. It was they in fact that probably inspired me to write this.

To some though (in the business) MGM British was most definitely in the Golden Era of British cinema and studios. For others (in the business), it was the finest studio this country ever had—the absolute *crème de la crème*. This is its story, as told to me through the eyes of the people who knew it best.–Derek Pykett, Chorleywood, Hertfordshire

The Rise of MGM British

On February 9, 1936, disaster struck in the form of an old enemy of the film studios… fire.

The result of which was nothing less than devastating, and sadly the British & Dominions Imperial Studios that had played host to a number of important movie productions, including *The Private Life Of Henry VIII* (1933) with Charles Laughton, and *The Private Life Of Don Juan* (1934) with Douglas Fairbanks, was burnt to the ground.

The sad irony of the fire was that, at the time, the local brigade were based at BIP Studios next door, under the leadership of the studio manager, who was reported to be terrified of fire. Terrified or not, the blaze lasted for eight hours with fourteen brigades being called to the scene, but to no avail, as all six sound stages were completely destroyed and the damage was estimated at £500,000.

One of the creators of British & Dominions, producer Herbert Wilcox, watched the fire with his wife, Anna Neagle, from their home at the top of Deacons Hill Road.

Future MGM British grip, Jimmy Dawes, was among the many others to bear witness to the blaze. "My father was a stagehand at British & Dominions, and I remember quite clearly the night it burnt down. I was just a kid, but I remember my mother shouting me and my brother out of bed, and we all watched the fire through our bedroom window. We lived on Shenley Road at the time, quite close to the studios. The flames went right up. There was nothing left of the studios the next day, just twisted metal. It's funny, though, because nearly all the workers from British & Dominions ended up at MGM British."

Sir Ronald Neame, producer/director, was also in Borehamwood that fateful night. "On the night in question, long after we'd gone to bed, the phone rang. It was my next door neighbour, Hector Coward, the manager of British & Dominions Studios, which ran alongside BIP. He sounded distraught.

"Look out of your window." he said.

At the time, I was living in Radlett, Hertfordshire, a short distance from Borehamwood, and I was working at the time at BIP. The night sky was lit with a great red glow.

"What is it?" I asked.

"It's the studios… not yours, but mine! My bloody car won't start! You've got to get me there, fast!"

I immediately pulled on some clothes, and we both jumped into my new car, reaching Elstree/Borehamwood in record time. The flames were already bursting through office windows and one of the stages and part of the roof were well on their way to collapsing.

Joe Grossman, the studio manager, who had given me my first job and was by this time a little larger round the middle, was in charge of the BIP Studios fire brigade. He and some of his men had run out six hoses and were valiantly fighting the inferno, but alas, there was little water pressure—certainly not enough to reach the flames. Talk about a piss in the ocean! Joe was frantic, shouting orders left, right, and center, to no avail.

My God! I thought. *We ought to be filming this.* At that moment, I ran into Jack Cardiff, a young colleague cameraman, who would become an internationally famed cinematographer of *The Red Shoes* and *The African Queen*. Together, we broke into the camera room at BIP, and in no time had the equipment set up in front of the burning building, but the camera we had was newly designed and I didn't know how to use it.

"Jack! For heaven's sake, lace up this wretched thing!" I shouted over the commotion.

I was scared stiff the fire might go out before we started filming. Joe's hoses still weren't functioning, but the real fire brigade had arrived.

Jack looked at me in dismay. "I can't do it! Oh, my God, what can we do?"

Then, we noticed a young lad standing nearby—the clapper boy on my currant production.

"Hey, Bob! Can you load this camera?" I asked.

"Of course," he said rather cockily.

"In a couple of minutes, we were shooting away like crazy. I operated, Jack pulled focus, and Bob lugged the equipment. We got some of the best fire footage I have ever seen—in black and white, of course.

"That night, February 9, 1936, the studios of British & Dominions was completely destroyed, and they were never rebuilt, but BIP Studios survived.

"The following day *The Daily Express* sent a photographer down to Borehamwood to get pictures of the charred remains. After watching the footage we had shot, the reporter stated, it was 'a masterpiece of realism.' We became temporary heroes."

Oscar-winning cinematographer, Jack Cardiff, also had memories of the Elstree/Borehamwood fire. "It was like a mad dream because there were girders and things falling down and flames everywhere. We gasped and ran back. The firemen ordered us out because they thought the film would explode. By that time, the other stage had caught fire and was blazing. Ronnie Neame and me, midst all this excitement, went all over the place photographing the fire. It was my first bit of publicity in a very peculiar way because the next morning it was quite loudly proclaimed in the newspapers, 'Terrible Fire Destroys Film Studio,' and the story went something like, 'Mr. Ronald Neame and his tripod carrier, Jack Cardiff, got shots of the fire.' As if I was his slave, I thought, *tripod carrier*! But I realised any publicity is better than no publicity. That was my first mention in a paper."

It wasn't long though before another film studio rose out of the ashes of British & Dominions. Amalgamated Studios, as it was originally called, was built just prior to the Second World War. Its location to British & Dominions was further along Elstree Way (to the north) and on the opposite side of the road.

During the war, when BIP Studios was contributing to the war effort, Amalgamated Studios were requisitioned by the Government and the huge sound stages were used for the construction of Halifax bombers, and because of this, parts of the original building were extensively damaged by air raids.

MGM actually first came on the scene when they purchased the freehold of the studios in 1944. Later that year, the company started to convert all the property that the Government was able to release, from an aircraft factory back to the filmmaking facility it had originally been intended to be.

Apart from the normal reconstruction, it was found necessary to strengthen existing roofs so that the considerable weight of overhead lights and other technical equipment needed for color films could be carried without possible risk.

At the same time, it was decided that because of proposed big productions the roofs should be raised to give a higher working area. Therefore, three of the existing sound stages had their roofs raised by 18 feet, while another one was rebuilt and repaired for the cost of £71,000. The total bill for reconstructing the studios eventually ran into over £1,000,000.

In a bid to cut down on costs, MGM started to rent studio space to independent producers, and several films were completed under this arrangement in 1947 and early 1948, including interiors for *Brighton Rock* and *The Guinea Pig* (the latter to be the first cinema movie to use the word 'arse'). Films would sometimes be on production in one stage as builders were busy at work reconstructing others.

With the reconstruction and change-over from aircraft factory finally finished in June 1948, MGM was about to embark on its first major motion picture production. So, then began a new era.

In the summer of 1948, MGM (Borehamwood) commenced production on *Edward My Son,* directed by George Cukor and starring Spencer Tracy and Deborah Kerr. It was filmed entirely at the studio, and despite the fact that Deborah Kerr would be nominated for an Oscar for her performance, the film itself was a box office flop.

Deborah Kerr later recalled in an article in the *Borehamwood & Elstree Post*, "*Edward My Son* was, of course, for me a great experience—working with the unique Mr. Tracy and the famous and talented George Cukor. My performance was no doubt aided by the old age make-up, which took hours to put on and even more painful hours to peel off! But the new MGM Studios had a very good make-up department. The studio itself was rather barn-like and large but ran very well and the dressing rooms were very comfortable. It was never as cosy a studio as Shepperton or Pinewood and somehow did not have the personality of the latter two."

Spencer Tracy was considered something of a problem actor for MGM as he had a drink problem often resulting in binge sessions. He was also tormented by inner demons, and was a deeply troubled man in his private life, completely unlike his screen image. It was also written into his contract that he would finish work at 4 p.m. each day. So, regardless of which scene they would be filming at the time, he would look at his watch, put on his coat, and waved goodbye.

Supporting actor Finlay Currie was paid £100 a day for his (uncredited) part in the production and, Ian Hunter, £5,000 for seventeen days work. Laurence Naismith, who would later appear in famous British films, such as *A Night To Remember* (1958), doubled for Spencer Tracy in one or two of the scenes.

Cinematographer on the movie was Freddie Young, who would become MGM British Studios resident director of photography. "MGM British was a fine studio, but I always thought that it was never used to its full advantage. The first film I photographed there was *Edward My Son*, which was a very good picture. George Cukor directed that. We were doing long takes on that movie, around a thousand feet in one take, on a crane where it moved around the whole sequence. Bits of sets had to slide away for the crane to go through and all that sort of thing. George would shoot everything ten times whether or not he was satisfied. Its funny because some directors don't know anything about the camera at all; some always want to look through the camera, and some never look through the camera. They just talk to the actors. George Cukor never looked through the camera, but he knew exactly what he wanted."

Freddie Young was born in London in 1902. In a career that lasted some sixty years, photographing his first film in 1928, he would go on to win three Oscars for his work with David Lean on *Lawrence Of Arabia* (1962), *Doctor Zhivago* (1965), and *Ryan's Daughter* (1970). Because of his role of importance at MGM British Studios, in 1996 he unveiled a plaque on the studio site. He passed away in 1998.

Another resident at the studio was German born production designer Alfred Junge, who would work on some of the studios finest and biggest productions.

Born in Gorlitz, Germany in 1886, Junge's, first movie working as a production designer was the German film *Das Alte Gesetz* (1923).

Before joining MGM British in 1948, he had worked on ten films with Michael Powell between 1934 to 1947, winning an Oscar for his work on the Powell/Pressburger classic *Black Narcissus* (1947). Junge died in London in 1964.

Now that the production of *Edward My Son* was in full swing, and with the studios fully reconstructed and equipped with modern facilities, MGM purchased another 90 acres of land to use as a back lot, and MGM British finally became one of the best-equipped and most modern studios in Europe.

It was also at this time that the American company had even bigger ambitions. In 1949, it was decided that the British Studios should produce large-scale, top-budget productions that would make the studio in Elstree Way the most important production center outside Hollywood. The programme ahead was lavish and extensive, and by mid 1949 MGM in Borehamwood was employing 376 technicians, 96 construction workers, and 230 clerical staff.

In the autumn of 1948, Elizabeth Taylor sailed to England to make *Conspirator* at MGM British. Her handsome leading man was thirty-seven-year-old Robert Taylor, who played the role of a British Army Officer who was a communist agent, and Elizabeth played the part of his wife. It would be her first adult role.

Robert Taylor later admitted that during a bedroom scene with Elizabeth in which he had to kiss her passionately, he had to tell the lighting cameraman, Freddie Young, to shoot him from the waist up, because he had an erection.

Playing the supporting role of Joyce in the film was a young, Honor Blackman. "I was loaned by Rank. It was, however, one of the most horrific films I've ever made. The director, Victor Saville, was a bastard. He was hated by the crew, as well, and someone actually did drop a lamp which just missed him—unfortunately. I regarded it as one of those films on which the director has to have a whipping boy. I was it. He obviously couldn't whip Elizabeth or Robert, who were big stars, and Wilfrid Hyde-White wouldn't notice if he tried to whip him anyway, so I was it. Elizabeth and Robert Taylor, though, were perfectly professional, although neither of them was inspired."

Also appearing in the film was child actor, Janette Scott. "I was about seven years old, and cast in a small part as one of 3 or 4 children living in a house in Wales, I think. Anyway, I do remember going on location to Wales for a week or so before returning to MGM Borehamwood to shoot interiors—all to no avail since all the scenes were cut in the final version and I think all that remained was a quick shot of us children around a breakfast table sitting with Elizabeth Taylor and Robert Taylor entering the room.

"I don't think Robert Taylor spoke to us children at all—a lesson for my later career—I always made a point of being friendly to 'small part players.' Shortly afterwards, in fact, across the road at ABPC Studios while filming my first starring role in the movie *No Place For Jennifer*, I gave lifts into London each night for a week to a young actress. I was in a nice big chauffer driven car with my Dad and there was loads of room. The actress was playing a cigarette girl in the film *Laughter In Paradise* being made on the next set. Her name was Audrey Hepburn.

As a seven-year-old, I wanted to say something nice to Elizabeth Taylor, so I said how much I enjoyed her performance in *Black Beauty*. 'It wasn't *Black Beauty*, it was *National Velvet*,' she responded. I was dreadfully embarrassed, and she turned away, and that was that. On reflection, I realise how very young she must have been, perhaps playing an adult role for the first time, perhaps being a little insecure herself, so I don't blame her for keeping her distance.

"The director, Victor Saville, I do remember was very disliked by the film unit. He was loud and rude, and on one unforgettable afternoon, after he'd finished shouting at one of the crew, there was an almighty crash and one of the large arc-lights fell from one of the gantries to within inches of where he sat in his director's chair. Did it fall or was it pushed? Nobody knew."

Shortly after filming was complete, Robert Taylor left for Rome to make the MGM film, *Quo Vadis* (1951) with Deborah Kerr. She later recalled, "Robert was a dear man. Always very correct and professional. He was though quite shy really, most unassuming, and I think as a private person his incredible good looks were more of a burden than an asset to him."

No sooner had Elizabeth Taylor and Robert Taylor moved out of MGM British than Greer Garson and Walter Pidgeon moved in to make the sequel to *Mrs Miniver* (1942) entitled *The Miniver Story* (1950). It bore little resemblance to its predecessor, however, and proved to be a flop.

Making his film debut at MGM British in *The Miniver Story* (as Toby Miniver) was James Fox. "I was fortunate enough to work at MGM Borehamwood in the 50s. The studio as I remember it was staffed by US and British. I believe that Miss Irene Selznick was casting at that time.

"When I worked later at their Hollywood studios, I recall MGM British in the 1950s was a facsimile of that."

Unwisely, Walter Pidgeon stayed around at the studios to star in their next production, *Calling Bulldog Drummond* (1951). It was hoped to be the beginning of a series of movies, but the film's failure at the box office stopped that.

In 1950, Michael Powell worked at the studio for the first and last time, when he filmed part of his movie, *The Elusive Pimpernel*, there with David Niven.

Appearing briefly in the film was actor Peter Copley. "I remember walking to the studios from Elstree/Borehamwood Station on a sunny but dull and dusty morning to film my tiny role in a Powell/Pressburger picture and thinking, MGM doesn't fit into this loosely spread out suburb."

Prior to the opening of MGM British, Les Ostinelli, had joined the camera department. "In 1946 after demob [demobilization], I signed a contract with David Cunningham of MGM London films at Belgrave Square, as camera operator in Special Effects; matte photography and optical/projection printing being my designation, to commence January 1947.

"Despite being newly built in 1938-1939, the studios at Borehamwood were undergoing major construction work. The roofs of all stages were being raised by 18 feet.

"The camera department was Freddie Young, Skeets Kelly, Chris Holden, Dave Mason, and Les Wheeler who dealt with the administration. Les Smart was the loader and did any hand tests. Bunny Franke was second unit and effects cameraman. Later arrivals included Kelvin Pike and Nic Roeg.

"We awaited the delivery of four brand new Mitchell cameras, equipped with Bausch and Lomb lenses, which were immediately replaced with Taylor Hobson Cooke Special Panchros II, which had to be calibrated. This was done in Camera Maintenance, part of the Studio Engineering building, the heads of which were Bill Williams and George Merritt. Both were ex Denham Studios.

"Percy Head, Pattern Shop; Jack Ramsey, Props; Davis Boulton, Stills; Dora Wright, Production Office; Frank Clarke, Editing; Bob Carrick, Sound Editing; DP Field, Sound Maintenance. My boss was, of course, Tom Howard, head of Special Effects.

"Initially, I was housed in No. 4 building waiting for the assembly of Matte Painting frames and camera pedestal set in concrete.

"The first of two optical printers were in a room adjacent to the matte room, and were based on designs from MGM Culver City, with extra modifications such as mechanical wipe head with Polar screen light control.

"Eventually the studios were ready for use, the interiors for the Boultings *Brighton Rock* being the first, followed by *While I Live* in which I did my first two optical and matte shots, using an Eymo Camera mounted at height which tracked down at speed to replicate a body falling from a cliff top. The other shot on the floor was a tied down bi-pack camera to double in a missing section of the set.

"The first MGM picture was *Edward My Son* for which I photographed the titles and a matte shot of putting Spencer Tracy in a long shot.

"This was the start of the long 10-foot takes, and in one shot 'props' missed their cue whilst moving the sofa out. It had been seen on film moving out of shot. To save an expensive retake, the optical printer was lined up to eliminate the sofa moving, this took three of us, with the aid of a metronome, to do all the moves, pan, tilt and zoom in sync.

"In 1950, some 140 matte and model shots done for the epic *Quo Vadis* were completed in 3-strip Technicolor. A Ruby and Emerald shot entailed twelve runs through a Bell & Howell Camera. Doug Adamson assisted me on the Matte painting photography."

Douglas Adamson had also joined the camera department early on. "I first went to MGM British in 1950 to work for four days on a film called

The Miniver Story, and ended up staying for twenty years. The studio was a magnificent place. The best studios in Europe. We even had our own fire engine, and grew our own vegetables for use in the canteen.

"We also had a farm on the back lot, and after lunch on a nice day we would wander up there, and I remember on one fine day they were shearing the sheep, which were eventually sold to a farmer in Wales.

"One other thing I do recall is that the art department at MGM British were quite frightened of Alfred Junge. He had been a U-boat commander in the war, or something like that."

James Sharkey, who would later become a noted theatrical agent, worked at the studios from 1946 to 1949. "I had lived in Borehamwood since 1934, when my parents moved from their home in Philadelphia PA (USA). They were in no way connected to the film business. My father was in the hosiery industry. However, we were always surrounded by movie people. We lived first in Clarendon Road (which runs down one side of the old Rock Studios, now BBC Elstree), and then by the opposite gates, in Eldon Avenue (which runs down the other side with 'The Red Lion' pub on the top corner).

"During lunch hours, the main road, Shenley Road, was always lively with the 'crowd artists' and minor players going to and from the BIP Studios and 'The Red Lion', and the restaurant next to the studio gates, in their various period costumes. Some used to sneak into the locally notorious club, The Cock and Hen, never to be heard of again!

"Often we children would be recruited to appear in movies made at the Rock Studios, which were at the bottom of our playing field. When I was six, I was picked out to sit on a bench with Sandy 'Can You Hear Me, Mother?' Powell. I didn't say anything but just stared at him as he became more and more discomforted by my presence.

"It was not unusual for local women, and sometimes out-of-work men, to earn a few pounds doing crowd work in the years before the war. The village was not a wealthy area and with the depression many of the men from the North East stayed in the village, and found work in the hosiery factory which my father had brought over from the States to help get on its feet, the Dufay photographic company, and the film studios, which were the only real sources of constant or casual work.

"I never got inside the studios until I was chucked out of grammar school just after the war ended and had to get a job. I got one through a friend of my parents. They said I should take it, as it would be a good first step into the business I had always longed to be in.

"It was at the BIP Studios, with a demolition firm, and my first job on my first day was to break up the cement around the support pillars in the main studio with what I believe to be an iron mallet and a sort of large chisel.

"The job lasted three days until my mother saw my bruised and bloody hands, burst into tears, and gave me two eggs for my tea—quite a sacrifice in those days of austerity after the war!

"Rubbish jobs followed, but my luck changed when I met the niece of Anna Neagle, a certain Miss Robertson, whom I met through the local amateur theatrical group. She lived near her aunt and Herbert Wilcox on Deacons Hill; very smart! Suddenly, I felt that I was moving closer to my ambition. I was already well-known in the Village (as it was then still a village) through my stage work with The Borehamwood Players; things were looking up.

"On my way home one evening, a close neighbour who was working in the Amalgamated Studios, as it then was, stopped me and asked me if I was working at the moment. I replied that I wasn't. He said they were looking for an assistant in one of the departments and, if I was interested, he would speak to the Head of Department and arrange for me to meet. He said it was the Stills Department. I had no idea what that was, but even if it was this department I wanted the job. I got it.

"Through the main gates, the Administration and Production Offices were on the left as you passed the Gate House on the right. The Stills Department was situated some way back from the main sound stages, near all the other departments (builders, carpenters, painters, etc).

"At that time, there was no actual back lot at the studios, and everything seemed to be in something of a flurry.

"I started work at the studios in late 1946 in the Stills Department as dark room assistant and one of my primary jobs was glazing the prints. The dark rooms were up two flights of stairs on the right. There was a large door with a red light above it and, when you went through that, there was another door with a flashing red light. No one was allowed to enter while the lights were flashing and work was going on. There were two dark rooms within, the larger of which contained the printing machines and the developing, fixing and washing tanks. Off that room was a smaller one, with a very large enlarger.

"The Glazing Room, to the right of the Dark Rooms, contained three large revolving drums, onto which the prints were fed. There was a large table along one wall to lay out the prints for inspection. The drums had to have constant attention during glazing, to ensure they did not come out with any blemishes, and had to be polished each day before use.

"Each day, the photographs shot the day before had to be delivered to the Head Office and Production Office in the main building.

"On the left on the main staircase there were three more steps which led to the Retouching Room and the Studio, where all the stars came for their publicity portraits. There was also an office for 'the governor'—oh, and the loos.

"It was a very quiet yet very hectic place, too. The team consisted of the head stills photographer. This was Davis Boulton, and I do remember that he was held in very high esteem by everyone, especially the stars.

"Then there were the two lady 'retouchers' beavering away at their screens. Although they were two of the best in the business, some of the female stars never seemed entirely satisfied with their work. I remember Sonia Dresdel on *While I Live* sending back three times her set of retouched proofs with ink lines and dots all over them. The ladies were in despair and felt very upset. One of them grumbled that if they touched the negatives any further she would look younger than beautiful Carol Raye, who was the star of the movie.

"The member of the team whom I remember best was a real cockney cheeky chappy called Joe. It was he who had charge of the dark rooms—and me. He was also the one who spent a lot of time on the sets taking production stills and general publicity stills. The main man scrutinised everyone before presenting them to the front office, the director, production office, and, of course, if they included any images of the leading artists, they had to approve too.

"I was totally movie-struck over those years and was fortunate enough to be the one to deliver the proofs to the various departments and on the stages or to the dressing rooms. So, I got to know some of the crews and some of the artists quite well. One person I particularly liked was Irene Howard. She was the sister of Leslie Howard and was the casting director for the MGM movies when the studios changed hands. She was always chatty and, however busy she was, I had to sit down opposite her while she was going through the proofs and we would chat.

"Sometimes when I was delivering to the unit on set I would arrive just as the stage was settling down for a take and I was able to watch the action.

"Before MGM took over the studios, I worked on several independent productions, including *While I Live* with Carol Raye, Sonia Dresdel, and a wonderful old character actor called Tom Walls. There was also an actress called Patricia Burke. When I subsequently became an actor, I co-starred with her, along with Michael Denison and Dulcie Gray, in *Let Them Eat Cake* at London's Shaftesbury Theatre in the mid-50s.

"There followed *Idol of Paris* starring Beryl Baxter, with a bevy of other beautiful young women and a distinguished cast of British theatre actors. Naturally, I spent as much time as I could on the stage and around the dressing rooms! I fell deeply in love with Patti Morgan, who was not really an actress, but a 'beauty queen' from, if I remember correctly, Australia.

"Anna Neagle starred in *Spring In Park Lane* opposite Michael Wilding, who was later married to Elizabeth Taylor, who also starred with Robert Taylor in *Conspirator*. Peter Graves was one of the co-stars and became a close friend of my wife and I in the 1950s.

"Somewhere along the line, I remember being in the portrait studio while Richard Attenborough was being photographed in full make-up including blood for *Brighton Rock*.

"When my theatrical ambitions grew too strong, I left the studios to join the Watford Theatre Repertory Company, and the staff at MGM, as a farewell gift, had the carpenters' department make me a beautiful wooden make-up box, which I still have and cherish, although naturally, never use."

Highly regarded cinematographer, Gilbert Taylor, photographed his first film *The Guinea Pig* at MGM British. "When MGM was presented to us, it had the advantages of new equipment for fast clean air changes. Improved spotting for spot rails to use maximum space. First class service at all grades in production. Good restaurants. Unlimited overtime."

Jimmy Dawes, one of the finest grips in the movie business, started his long career at the studios. "When I was a kid, my mother appeared as a film extra in movies made at Borehamwood. Well, everyone who lived in Borehamwood worked as a film extra, even the cats and the dogs. I even did some extra work myself, as a kid. You got a guinea a day.

"When MGM British opened in 1948, I started on days as a stage-hand. Then they started a night shift, building sets, striking sets, etc. (construction) to keep up with the daily filming. So, I did that for about eighteen months. Five or six nights a week.

"I worked as a grip at the studios from it opening in 1948 to it closing in 1970. It was a great studio. Simply great. The best studios around. It was better than any of the English studios. It had good workers. Good skilled people. But because America had the whip hand, we could go three or four months on flat money.

"When I wasn't being a grip, I would work again on construction. Because you had to work between filming jobs. You worked bloody hard too.

"I was grip on *Edward My Son* with Spencer Tracy. He was a nice bloke. He used to speak to everyone. He'd make a habit of it, in fact, and go around the studio.

"I briefly worked at the Gate Studios up the road. We used to have to stand on top of the building and if we saw a train coming we'd press a button which would be heard in the sound studio below. Basically they'd have to stop filming every time a train passed because of the noise. The film I worked on was *Odette* with Trevor Howard."

The youngest person to join the studio was teenager Peggy Spirito. "When I worked in the studios, I was known as Peggy, even though my real name is Maggie Spirito Perkins. However, there were too many Margarets in the film business, so I was christened Peggy by them.

"I was brought up in the 1930s, when money came out of your mums purse and not a hole in the wall, and a 'Big Mac' was something you put on when it rained. Those were the days. Cinema I remember in the 1930s was very popular, and I loved going to see the movies just as much as the next person.

"I began working at MGM British Studios, Borehamwood, as a junior Girl Friday in the late 1940s. My first experience there was working with Freddie Young's camera department. He was Mr. Young then, and all his crew wore ties and shirts. Nowadays on films no one wears a tie or a shirt. I was really privileged though to be at MGM at this time, but also fascinated by cameras, let alone good-looking camera crew. I learned much about filmmaking, because it was an overall education working at MGM. It was my University, if you like. They had every department that you can think of. It was fabulous. The film cameras were really interesting in those days, too. Technicolor had just come in with Jack Cardiff. I also learned a lot about lighting, watching Freddie Young, as he was a perfectionist. Skeets Kelly was his camera operator, and being a junior Girl Friday, I could watch them at work and take all of this knowledge in. One of my main jobs with them was to write letters. I also learned though how to play poker and throw dice in the crew room—which was great fun. Putting bets on horses for the crew was another of my jobs. But don't tell anyone that.

"Several films were being made when I started at MGM. One was *The Guinea Pig*, a Boulting Brothers film with Richard Attenborough. A lovely man. I fell in love with him. I used to watch him all starry eyed. One evening, in fact, after watching him film a major scene, I ran to the bus stop rather late to catch my 107, but sadly it went without me. However, as I arrived at the bus stop, the most embarrassing thing happened to me—I felt my knicker elastic go, and you can imagine, my knickers fell down. So, I quickly stuffed them in my handbag, and stood there bum freezing cold. At that very moment, a big car stopped right next to me, and a voice said, 'Do you want a lift sweetie?' It was Richard Attenborough. My mouth dropped open. I couldn't believe it. So in I get into his wonderful Rolls, legs crossed tightly, as my mother always told me—as innocent as a kitten—and he drove me all the way to my front door. Anyway, the next day on the set I thanked him for the lift home, and he said, 'I've got a present for you'. He gave me two tickets for *The Way Ahead*, a play he was appearing in the West End.

"I had some truly lovely times at MGM, and met some gorgeous people. Spencer Tracey was another one I met there. These people were such big stars in those days, and had such charisma. Spencer Tracy was wonderful for that. I was so lucky to be able to observe them. Elizabeth Taylor was another star I met there. She was very young then, and very beautiful.

"Another film being made when I started at MGM was Edward Dryhurst's *While I Live*. Now that was an interesting film, as it had a lot of special effects. Tommy Howard was the main special effects man at MGM British, and he was truly superb at his job.

"They also used to use me from time to time for make-up tests, and try some costumes out on me. Another thing they would do is stand me in front of back projection to try it out, and it would look like I was in the desert, etc. It was very clever, and very popular in the old days of films.

Hitchcock's *Capricorn*

The career of the now legendary film director, Alfred Hitchcock, played an important part in the history of the film studios of Elstree/Borehamwood.

Born on August 13, 1899, in Leytonstone on the eastern edge of London, young Hitchcock left school at the age of fourteen and worked as a clerk for in-house magazine, *Henley Telegraph*. He also took evening classes in draughtsmanship and drawing at the University of London.

In 1919, these skills enabled him to get a job as a title card designer with the American production company, Famous Players-Lasky, when it began making films in a converted power station in Islington.

This was bought and taken over in 1924 by Michael Balcon's Gainsborough Pictures, and the building was then named Gainsborough Studios.

Balcon allowed Hitchcock to work at an array of jobs for his company. These included, set designer, scenario writer, editor, and as the assistant director to Graham Cutts, who was then Gainsborough's top director.

In 1925, Hitchcock was given his own directorial assignments with *The Pleasure Garden* and *The Mountain Eagle*, both of which were filmed in Munich as part of a co-production between Gainsborough and the German producer Erich Pommer. Neither film, however generated much attention.

It was not until the release of his third film, *The Lodger,* filmed at Gainsborough Studios in 1926, that both the critics and public took notice of Hitchcock.

In 1927, Hitchcock left Gainsborough and headed for Borehamwood and the larger British International Pictures Studios (BIP), and his new contract with them made him the highest paid director in Britain. He was also assigned at BIP to direct Britain's first talking picture, another sign of his status, and *Blackmail* (1928) proved that such regard was richly deserved.

It was just prior to the filming of *Blackmail* that Ronald Neame started work at BIP Studios. He was sixteen years old. "It was a typical English winter day in late 1927 and heavy rain was falling on the corrugated roof of Elstree's BIP Studios. It was noisy, but this was of no consequence because the four features being made were silent. The studios structure was large, divided down the middle lengthwise by a thin, non-soundproof wall. This, then, was my first working day in a movie studio. I was a messenger boy, a tea boy, a callboy, a you-name-it boy.

"I was assigned to a thriller called *Toni* starring theatre matinee idol Jack Buchanan. I was probably overeager, because someone on the crew sent me to fetch the 'sky hook.' It seems Elstree had only one of these much sought after, complicated pieces of equipment, and we, on the *Toni* set, were scheduled to use it in the afternoon. I was told that the 'sky hook' was on *The Farmer's Wife* set. This film was being shot on the other side of the dividing wall, and was forbidden territory. But I had been told to get the 'sky hook' and this I was determined to do.

"Somewhat timidly, I slipped through the door of the dividing wall and wound my way through a number of farmyard sets towards a lighted area at the far end. Then, I discovered why this production was so special. The director, busy rehearsing his actors, was the rather plump twenty-seven-year-old Alfred Hitchcock.

"It only took a few moments for me to realize that this was a man in complete control. For several minutes, I forgot the 'sky hook' and watched the great director at work. Then, I came sharply down to earth and approached Jack Cox, Hitchcock's cameraman. This kind man let me down gently."

"What's your name?" he asked.

"Ronnie Neame," I replied.

"And this is your first day here?' he asked.

I nodded.

"Well Ronnie, you've been given a sort of initiation. You see, there's no such thing as a sky hook. They've been pulling your leg. Why don't you go back to your set and tell them it was sold last week because nobody was using it!"

"This fictitious hook turned out to be a blessing in disguise. Because of it, I was able to watch Hitchcock at work, and I met Jack Cox, someone I would work with again, when I replaced his assistant cameraman on Hitchcock's film *Blackmail*.

"*Blackmail* would, of course, go down in history as one of the most important productions filmed at Elstree. It had started like all other movies of that time, as a silent film. Just a few weeks before completion, however, we began to hear rumours that John Maxwell, head of British International Pictures, was considering the addition of sound. Talkies had recently arrived in Britain from Hollywood, and Maxwell wanted to be the first to make one in England. In preparation, a large property room and a plaster shed were hastily converted into sound stages. The original writers, Charles Bennett, who had written the stage play, and Ben Levy, were brought in to write dialogue to replace titles used in the silent version.

"Hitchcock must have had more than a hint of what was about to happen. Instead of completely dismantling the sets as we finished shooting on them, he had them 'pack struck' so they could be quickly reassembled.

"Most of the footage already shot on *Blackmail* could be transferred to the new version. We had fortunately used motorized cameras, which ran at twenty-four pictures a second, the essential speed required for talkies.

"Once we began shooting on the primitive sound stages, we had dozens of seemingly unsolvable problems. Jack and I, with our noisy camera, were installed in a sealed soundproof booth with a large glass window for the camera to shoot through. When it was necessary for the camera to track, two men had to push the booth backwards and forwards on rails. They also had to pivot the booth if we had to pan more than three feet to avoid filming the frame of the window.

"The members of this now new sound department at Elstree thought that they were the most important people on the set, and perhaps they were; after all this was the first "talkie" [shot there]. The difficulty was, that unless the microphone, an enormous contraption, was practically touching the top of the actor's head, the sound was unusable. Also, the mike and its cumbersome boom cast heavy shadows on the walls of the set, wreaking havoc with Jack Cox's lighting.

"Hitchcock, however, took all of this in his stride. Rather than create another level of anxiety, he resolved it. Technical problems brought out his gift as an innovator. I don't think anything ever ruffled him, not even the heat on the set. Dressed in his invariable black suit, white shirt, and dark tie, he never seemed to perspire, even though the rest of us, also in suits and ties, were dripping.

"Adding to these technical problems was our leading lady, Anny Ondra. She was not British and spoke with a heavy Czechoslovakian accent, which didn't of course matter for the silent version. To overcome this problem, Hitchcock devised the first form of "dubbing." British actress Joan

Barry was engaged to be Anny's voice. They rehearsed the dialogue together to get in synch. When it came to the shoot, Joan stood just outside frame, with a separate microphone, and as she spoke the lines, Anny mouthed them.

"On one of many good days associated with *Blackmail*, the Duke and Duchess of York visited the set (the Duke became King George V1, after his brother Edward abdicated and the Duchess became our Queen Mother). Hitchcock and the Duchess went into the sound booth, while the Duke joined Jack Cox and me in the camera booth. I saw Hitchcock ask the Duchess to take off her hat in order to wear earphones as she and the Duke waved at each other.

"Without doubt, Hitchcock was a cinematic genius. But he had a penchant for practical jokes that were more cruel than funny. The brunt of his humour on *Blackmail* was Harry, the prop man. Hitchcock used part of the set, a gas bracket with a live flame, to heat up a coin with a pair of pliers. After the coin was hot he dropped it on the floor and asked a passing Harry to pick it up.

"His practical jokes went beyond the crew. He invited Sir Gerald de Maurier, one of England's most important actors, to a dinner party at the Café Royal in Regent Street, along with 200 other guests. Sir Gerald was told that the evening was a fancy dress party. The poor man arrived in Shakespearian garb. To his embarrassment, and Hitchcock's shear delight, everyone else was in formal evening attire.

"There was also another surprise courtesy of Hitchcock that same evening. During desert, the restaurant door opened and in walked a naked girl who crossed the room and sat down on Gerald's lap.

"Hitchcock preferred to work late at the studios, never finishing before eleven p.m., and more often than not, we were still working at midnight. At about eight p.m., the unit would break for supper, and Hitchcock would head for his favorite pub, 'The Plough,' in Elstree village, where he ate an excellent meal."

Hitchcock remained at BIP during the early part of the 1930s. His films included a suspense thriller, *Murder* (1930), an adaptation of a successful West End play, *Juno And The Paycock* (1930), and *Number Seventeen* (1932).

By the time he made *Jamaica Inn* at BIP Elstree in 1939, both Hitchcock and his star Charles Laughton were big names, both in the UK and in the US, with Hollywood promising even greater careers.

Laughton had actually started his distinguished film acting career at BIP Elstree appearing in the silent movie *Piccadilly* (1929), before winning an Oscar for Best Actor for his performance in *The Private Life Of Henry V111* (1933) filmed at the adjacent and doomed British & Dominion Studios.

Laughton later recalled in an article that was printed in the *Borehamwood & Elstree Post*, "BIP Elstree launched many a famous career. We all remember it with fondness, despite its restaurant, which was the worst there ever was!"

Jamaica Inn would not stand up as one of Hitchcock's favourites. It was, in fact, a film that he didn't really want to make, but Charles Laughton had persuaded him to direct the costume epic. Hitchcock was unhappy, and even though the film was a box-office hit, it remained one of the films he wished he hadn't been associated with. He left for the US shortly after its completion.

It was after a very successful stint in Hollywood that Hitchcock returned to the UK in 1948 with his own production company, Transatlantic Pictures, which was founded to enable him to make films in Britain. Of the company's two movies, however, *Rope* (1948) and *Under Capricorn* (1949), only the latter was made on English soil, and the studio Hitchcock chose to shoot the film was the recently opened MGM British, Borehamwood. Hitchcock later confessed in an article which was printed in the *Borehamwood & Elstree Post*, "I did *Under Capricorn* because Ingrid Bergman liked it, and wanted to do it. From that, I learned that it was better to look at Ingrid than to listen to her."

The film turned out to be Hitchcock's least favourite, as from the onset he had struggled to adapt Helen Simpson's 1937 novel into what would become a sprawling costume drama.

Jack Cardiff, joined the production as cinematographer. "They built a huge composite set of the entire mansion that is mentioned in the original novel. It filled the largest stage at MGM British Studios. Hitchcock also decided that he wanted the picture to be shot largely in one-reel takes. He'd done a similar thing when filming *Rope*. It wasn't that every single shot was ten minutes, but every few shots were ten or eight minutes long. For this we used an electric crane, which could travel in any direction without having to lay tracks.

"One of the stars of the film, Joseph Cotton, told me that he was terrified of this bloody great crane, and said that he could always feel this huge monster sneaking up behind him and was terrified that he was going to be run over.

"I remember while filming a rather passionate scene between Ingrid Bergman and Michael Wilding, Hitchcock suddenly let out a howl of pain, and then in the most gentle tone said, 'Please move the camera a little to the right, as you've just run over my foot.' An x-ray later revealed that the camera's weight had broken Hitchcock's big toe.

"We usually rehearsed these long takes in a day, and then shot the next day. I had to light all of the sets we'd be using in one go. The noise, of course, was indescribable, with this electric crane rolling through sets with whole walls opening up, and furniture being whisked out of the way by frantic prop men.

"The most incredible take we did was when the camera ended up in a dining room with eight people sitting at a long Georgian table. Hitchcock wanted a shot of the guests, looking down the table, then to track in to a close-up of Ingrid Bergman at the far end."

These ten-minute takes did cause the end film to have one or two minor mistakes, one of which is quite early on in the movie. It happens as the characters gather for a dinner party. As the camera tracks backwards across the dining room, the dining room table is pushed into the path of the camera as it comes into view, but unfortunately the candlestick are still shaking violently.

James Sharkey, who was working in the stills department at the time, recalled being on the set of *Capricorn*. "I've never walked on to a movie set where the feeling of tension was so intense and so quiet before a take. A ten minute take that is."

The star of the picture, Ingrid Bergman, hated the long shots. Hitchcock later said of this in an article that was printed in the *Borehamwood & Elstree Post*, "I hate arguments and I try never to lose my temper. One evening I walked out of Ingrid's dressing room while her back was turned on me. She had lost her temper over those long shots. Later on someone called me to say that she hadn't noticed my departure and was still complaining twenty minutes after I'd gone."

Jack Cardiff, remembered Hitchcock's method of work. "Practically all of Hitchcock's energies were spent on pre-production. Everything was worked out in detail, every page timed. If a page was just a few seconds off, everything would have been off. For instance, once the script was finished, he would never touch it and never change it on set. He would stick to it completely.

"During a ten minute take, he would have his back to the set, aimlessly looking down at the floor. Then, after a scene was shot, if the camera operator was happy with the take, he would accept the whole reel. He hardly ever watched the rushes of the day's work. From the moment he had drawn pictures of the camera setups, he had the picture all firmly in his mind.

"Hitchcock was no fool. He never shouted on set. If he had any fault to find with people he'd let the front office handle it. He was an extraordinary man."

Les Ostinelli worked with Jack Cardiff on *Capricorn*. "My claim to fame in the movie business was certainly lining up that massive crane for those long takes in Hitchcock's movie. He was a wonderful director, and what amazed me most about him was that he knew, without even looking through the camera, whether he was happy with a shot."

Someone else who was lucky to see Hitchcock at work was the young, Peggy Spirito. "The ten minute takes really fascinated me. The continuity girl had to time very carefully to give the grip the cues, because as the cameras moving walls have to be moved out of the way. They would shoot a take in a day, and God help anyone who blew it.

"Alfred Hitchcock was a very quiet man. Very unassuming. Got on with his work. No messing about. He appreciated people who knew what they were doing. Fools were not tolerated. You certainly couldn't bum your way in those days if you didn't know anything. You really had to be in the know."

Playing a small uncredited role in the movie was actor, Martin Benson. "Hitchcock was a genius, without doubt. The master filmmaker. I was lucky to work with him in the early part of my career."

Martin Benson, also took time to remember MGM British Studios. "My abiding memory of MGM Studios at Borehamwood is the sound. As you approach the space suddenly clears. There is nothing between you and the massive rumble which shakes the history of the cinema. The MGM lion stands—as did the studio itself—for everything that was oversized. A big voice, a big studio, big pictures. You really did hear the roar of the lion when you entered those huge gates, and a frisson of excitement tingled the spine."

Sadly *Capricorn* would be Hitchcock's only film at MGM British. A movie that ended up going over budget and dying at the box-office.

Hume Cronyn, who worked with Hitchcock to adapt the screenplay recalled the legendary director predicting the failure of the film before they had completed shooting. "I remember one day when we were working in the studio, Hitchcock suddenly said, 'This films going to be a flop,' and he disappeared. Now this wasn't like him. It really wasn't. It was like a temperamental outburst, and that haunted me."

The finished film would see the end of Hitchcock's company, Transatlantic Pictures, after making just two movies.

Hitchcock later said of *Capricorn* in an article that was printed in the *Borehamwood & Elstree Post,* "I should never have done it. I should also never have tackled a costume picture. It would be my last."

In his autobiography, *Vanity Will Get You Somewhere,* Joseph Cotten referred to the film as, "Under Corny Crap."

After the completion of *Under Capricorn,* Hitchcock stayed in the UK to shoot his next picture, *Stage Fright* (1950). He would also remain in Elstree/Borehamwood, but instead of filming at MGM, he returned to BIP Studios, or the now newly renamed Associated British Pictures Corporation (ABPC).

Stage Fright, however, would be Hitchcock's last picture at the studios, as upon his return to Hollywood, he would only return to the UK to film on one more occasion.   The movie in question was *Frenzy* (1972), and even though he had planned to shoot interiors at the studios in Borehamwood, it ended up being shot at Pinewood Studios instead.

Paul Wilson, who worked at MGM British in the 1950s, would later be camera operator on *Frenzy.* "Hitchcock was easy to work with, and lots of fun. We would often find him asleep in his director's chair between takes."

Finally, it is only fair that, Ronald Neame, should have the last word on Hitchcock. "In December 1979, Alfred Hitchcock received the Man of the Year Award from the British American Chamber of Commerce and I was asked to present it to him.

"He was very old and frail in a wheelchair when I approached him for a quick word before the ceremony."

"Hitch, it's Ronnie, do you remember me?" I asked.

"Smiling tentatively, he placed his hand on my arm. 'Of course I remember you Ronnie. You're one of my boys.'"

His extraordinary life ended within four months.

The Lion Roars
in Borehamwood

"ROYAL VISIT TO ELSTREE STUDIOS. Queen and Princess Margaret see *The Magic Box* filmed." This was the headline on the *Borehamwood & Elstree Post* dated March 22, 1951.

The article by *Post* reporter, Larry Signy, went on to state that the inhabitants of Borehamwood, immune as they are to the sight of glamour and spectacle from the film studios, turned out in force to welcome the Queen (later the Queen Mother) and Princess Margaret, on the first Royal visit to the studios of Elstree/Borehamwood since 1928.

On their arrival at 11 a.m., the Queen, who wore a petrel blue corded silk loose coat and dress, with a silver fox stole, and Princess Margaret, in a coat and dress, with a silver fox gentian blue velvet tight-fitting full-skirted coat with a high fur collar and hat to match, were received by executives of Associated British Pictures Corporation Ltd.

After introductions, they proceeded to the immense sound stage 2, where *The Magic Box* was being made. The film was being produced for the Festival of Britain about the life of William Friese-Greene, a film camera pioneer of the motion picture industry.

They were then introduced to the movies director, John Boulting, and stars of the film, Robert Donat and Maria Schell.

While the Queen took time to speak to cameraman, Jack Cardiff, Robert Donat showed Princess Margaret a copy of the original camera used by Friese-Greene.

After this, the Royal party then seated themselves in front of a set designed by John Bryan, depicting Freise-Greene's laboratory, and watched rehearsals and final shooting of a scene between Robert Donat as the film camera pioneer and Maria Schell as his first wife. With the scene safely "in the can," all eyes once again turned to the Royal visitors.

Janette Scott, a twelve-year-old actress at the time (playing the part of Ethel, Friese-Greene's eldest daughter in the movie), handed a bouquet of yellow tulips, lily of the valley, and orchids to the Princess.

When all the presentations were finally completed and a shortened 20-minute version of the film had been shown, the Royal visitors departed at 12.30.

Afterwards, Miss Maria Schell, told the *Post* reporter, "There were so many things that I wanted to say to the Queen, but when she spoke to me I could only smile."

The producer of *The Magic Box* was Ronald Neame. "The movie was specially made for the Festival of Britain (1951), and the plan was to cast as many British stars in cameos as was possible.

"We particularly wanted Laurence Olivier, but needed him to work for practically nothing. 25 guineas a day to be exact. Anyway, we got him, and fifty of the best names in British cinema followed. There was actually only one actor who turned us down—Alec Guinness.

"The completed film was screened at the Festival on September 18, 1951, and received good notices."

On May 8, 1952, the *Borehamwood & Elstree Post* reported:
"TRAGEDY AT FILM STUDIOS
Workman's Death Fall"

It happened after the filming of a television drama, *The Accused*, at the Gate Studios. One of the workmen, whilst dismantling scenery rigging, slipped and hurtled to the concrete floor below.

Later in the year, at the same studio, another workman was injured when a piece of scenery fell on him.

MGM British had started 1952 with the return of Robert Taylor. He was to star in the epic adaptation of Sir Walter Scott's classic *Ivanhoe*. Supported by Elizabeth Taylor, Joan Fontaine, Emlyn Williams, and George Sanders, Robert would portray a Saxon knight fighting and loving his way through medieval England.

No expense was spared on this production, as three years of historical research had taken place beforehand.

Fifty interior sets were constructed on the studios stages, as well as a complete replica of Torquilstone Castle erected on the studio lot. The castle was one of the most striking film sets ever, carefully aged to give it the patina it would have had in the twelfth century. This was then surrounded by a ten-foot moat, flooded with 170,000 gallons of water.

Douglas Adamson worked in the camera department on the movie, and recalled a funny incident. "We were shooting a fight scene in which some soldiers had to fall off the battlements. We had three cameras rolling, needless to say, one stuntman fell badly and lay writhing and groaning on the ground. The assistant director shouted, 'Cut. Get some first aid!' The director, Richard Thorpe, shouted, 'Keep rolling!' and then turned to the camera operator and said, 'Did you get that in close-up. It was better than acting.'

"I continued to work on many other movies at the studio, and feel very proud to have been an MGM man."

Ivanhoe cost MGM £1,200,000 to make, but it did live up to expectations at the box office, and this encouraged studio chiefs to undertake other important productions.

Freddie Young who was cinematographer on *Ivanhoe*, later said of its star, Robert Taylor, "Taylor was quiet, almost shy, but a good professional actor."

It would be during the early part of the 1950s that top ranking Hollywood stars would become commonplace around MGM Borehamwood. Clark Gable in *Never Let Me Go*, Glenn Ford in *Time Bomb*, and Gene Kelly in *Invitation To The Dance*.

The latter made in 1952 was Kelly's directorial debut, and he was remembered by members of the crew for his enthusiasm for perfection, yet the movie was shelved by MGM and wasn't released until 1956.

In order to construct the many sets required for these big-budget pictures, the studio was carrying a stock of stores (timber, paint, etc.) worth in excess of £80,000 pounds.

In 1953, John Ford, arrived at the studio to direct *Mogambo* with Clark Gable, Ava Gardner, and Grace Kelly.

Gable had just turned down a role in *Quo Vadis*, so he certainly wasn't going to let *Mogambo* slip him by.

A large part of the movie was shot on location in Africa from November 1952, with the cast and crew arriving at MGM British to film interior shots in January 1953.

Ford was a rough, gruff, and abusive director of Westerns, whose rude and uncouth manner on the sets could not be ignored. He often referred to Grace as "Kelly" and bellowed at her when she recited her lines. He was, however, just as demanding and cruel to Ava and Clark, who walked off the set one day and refused to talk to him.

Having recently started work at the studios, Kelvin Pike, joined the production as clapper/loader. "On the film *Mogambo*, Grace Kelly wouldn't talk to anyone. Clark Gable on the other hand was very down to earth, very friendly. I remember though that Ava Gardner and Grace Kelly would never see eye to eye. There was some sort of tension/friction between them. Ava Gardner though had a rough side to her, whereas Grace Kelly was very posh, very superior.

"I recall a quite funny occasion on *Mogambo*. We had on the sound stage a little hut, a little cabin for quick changing. Ava Gardner went in there and stripped off, looked up, and saw dozens of electricians looking down at her. 'You bastards', she shouted. She wasn't lost for language, I can tell you. Frank Sinatra was married to her at that time, and he visited the studios several times during the shoot."

Kelvin Pike, took time to remember the MGM Studios. "It was a delightful place. Very big, with lots of facilities, and a complete engineering department, which was amazing. It had a wonderful back lot with a farm on it, and when we were not working we would go and have a walk around the farm. The studio also had a permanent camera crew. I can also remember that they could raise the roof of a whole sound stage, so that they could get the big lamps in. It was very Hollywood style.

Another thing I recall, though, is that electricians were always treated very badly on film sets in the early days. They were on the rough end, I would say, treated like shit, and I remember once offering to help some out as they were having difficulty, and I was told not to interfere, as I worked in a different department. Totally ridiculous."

Mogambo featured a young Donald Sinden in an early supporting role. He later recalled, "When we arrived at MGM Borehamwood in 1953 to do the studio work on *Mogambo*, Clark Gable received £750 pounds a week apart from his salary—I don't know what that was—as his living expenses. I was being paid £50 pounds in total! However you look at it, there is a discrepancy there.

"During the filming, though, I spent a great deal of time with Gable, and found him to be a splendidly professional actor."

Filming was completed in April 1953, none too soon for Gable, as he disliked the English climate and found London very dull. The final budget for the movie was 1,000,000 pounds.

Ava Gardner stayed on to appear in the next MGM picture, *Knights Of The Round Table*. Robert Taylor returned as the lead, with strong support from Mel Ferrer and originally George Sanders.

Frank Westmore, the famous Hollywood make-up artist, was brought in to work on the film. "It took me a week to exchange even 'Good morning' with George Sanders. I confess, I hated poor George, really hated him. When we were introduced, he could spare only two fingers of his right hand to shake mine."

Sanders, however, left the film shortly after shooting began. He had suffered a nervous breakdown. A replacement was quickly found, rising young British star, Stanley Baker.

Once again, Kelvin Pike, was clapper/loader on the film. "We had to shoot an army of soldiers for *Knights of the Round Table* coming down the banks of a valley, with trees on either side. When we looked at the rushes at the end of the day, right behind the army was a double decker bus coming along a road, which nobody had noticed. So, we had to re-shoot."

Nicolas Roeg, joined the camera department prior to filming. "Assistant camera jobs at MGM British were advertised in trade papers within the business at that time. This was the early 1950s. So, I went along and was interviewed by the chief loader, Les Smart. I then met Freddie Young after Les had approved me. At that time, I was only working in a film cutting room in Wardour Street, and so to follow that with an assistant camera job at MGM was marvellous.

"Freddie Young was very distant at that time. I reckon, though, that he was just very well defined because he was head of the camera department. He was very nice though. A very decent chap."

Nicolas Roeg recalled his early days at MGM Borehamwood. "If you went into the restaurant—the canteen—and you were a clapper boy, you would get some strange looks. You were not banned, but… you see every department had their own seats in the canteen, and if you sat in any other departments seats, you would be instantly moved back to your own department."

During filming of *Knights Of The Round Table*, Nicolas Roeg recalled a funny incident. "Freddie Young was lighting a scene and saw that Alfred Junge, the production designer, had painted in a black area above a chair. I remember Freddie saying, 'What's this?'

"And one of the art department said, 'It's a shadow. Mr. Junge has painted in a shadow.'

"So, anyway, Alfred Junge, was called to the set, and Freddie said to him, 'Alfred, we do a shadow with lighting, not with paint.' So there proceeded a sort of clash between the camera and the art department. But I thought personally that painting in a shadow was a very daring thing to do."

On June 25, 1953, the *Borehamwood & Elstree Post* reported:

"KING ARTHUR'S MEN STRIKE TWICE IN STUDIO DISPUTE"

The story centred around 250 crowd artists who were striking for a second time over a wage dispute. The extras had asked for a guinea a day increase, on the two guinea minimum they were being paid. The problem was quickly resolved, and King Arthur's Knights returned to work.

The budget for the completed film came in at £750,000, and when released made a favourable profit. It was also the first MGM film to be released in Cinemascope with six-track stereophonic sound.

Stewart Granger arrived at MGM Borehamwood at the end of 1953 to make *Beau Brummell*. He was one of Britain's top post-war stars before leaving for Hollywood to seek further fame and fortune.

Granger was no stranger to Borehamwood, though, having started his career as an extra there in the 1930s at the BIP Studios.

By the time he came to work at MGM British, he was known to be a "difficult" star and continued to prove this on each new film. He later said in an article that was printed in the *Borehamwood & Elstree Post*, "One was arrogant, because one was not proud of, very often, what one was doing."

The lighting cameraman on *Beau Brummell* was Oswald Morris. "I knew and liked Stewart Granger, but he was difficult. He had a bent bridge on his nose which he knew showed up if photographed from one side. So we had to shoot his other profile or full face. Even the sets were built to allow for this."

Kelvin Pike, who was clapper/loader on the production, remembered a different Granger. "I recall that he had his breakfast brought on to the studio floor every morning, without fail. Anyway, a member of the crew complained about his special treatment, and Granger overheard. So from then on, every morning, Granger made sure that breakfast was brought on to the studio floor for the crew, too. He was a good man really."

Cinematographer, Oswald Morris shares his memories of MGM British. "My memory of this studio can best be summed up as equivalent to the Rolls Royce in the car industry—it was quite simply the very best.

"Ben Goetz, a true blue MGM stalwart of many years standing in California, was in charge. He was a very clever business man.

"One of his first acts as head of the studio was to take the cream of the industry and put them under lucrative contract as heads of the various departments. That really paid off. When you think, Freddie Young (head of camera department); Alfred Junge (head of production design).

"Goetz also hired George Catt as Estate Manager. He supervised the entire grounds, including the back lot. A flock of sheep were purchased to keep the grass under control. He kept the grounds around the stages neat and tidy and sold cut flowers grown on the lot. No other studio attempted anything like this.

"MGM British pictures were scripted, cast, and packaged in Culver City in California, including the producer, and transported to Borehamwood. It was all very upmarket, and the films were of MGM quality.

"MGM had a strict policy of style for their movies, and when I was first hired to photograph *Beau Brummell* for them, Ben Goetz made their position quite clear to me.

"They believed that their 'stars' put 'bums on seats' so to speak and should look at their best in all their movies. They believed that audiences went to the cinema to escape the hum-drum of daily life and that all their movies should have happy endings. It was further made clear that when shooting 'day for night' on exteriors (turning sunlight into moonlight by the use of filters on the camera lens) the result should show the actors quite clearly. The result however was more like a blue day! And finally, never mention or produce 'kitchen sink' photography in their presence.

"If you knew your job they were a dream company to work for, but impostors were given short shrift."

Returning to MGM Borehamwood for the third time to play Lady Patricia in *Beau Brummell* was Elizabeth Taylor. Kelvin Pike took time to remember her. "She was smashing to work with. When she heard a carpenter on the film wasn't being paid his overtime, she called the producer on to the floor and said that we would all stop working until the man was given his full money. They listened, of course. She was a very powerful woman though, but all the stars were powerful in those days."

Gene Kelly, after his unsuccessful previous MGM British picture, returned to the studios to star in (but not direct) *Seagulls Over Sorrento* (1954). The movie was actually directed by the famous Boulting brothers, Roy and John.

Paul Wilson worked as assistant camera on the film, and shared his early memories of the studios. "In my sixty years plus in the film industry, working my way up (on 112 movies) from clapper boy to director of photography, and a freelance at that, so I am pretty sure I have worked in all of Britain's studios that were open during the period 1942 to 2003. Without reservation I would say MGM Borehamwood was the best of them all in terms of facilities.

"MGM's magnificent back lot was the largest in the country. You could stand in many parts, turn through 360 degrees and see nothing but grass and trees, with sheep wandering about with their coats branded MGM. Their presence was something to do with taxes, I believe.

"It also had a fabulous camera-engineering and maintenance department, second to none. The same quality was to be found in their electrical and construction departments.

"MGM British was most certainly a taste of Hollywood, as it had been built in the Hollywood style."

Betrayed (1954), a wartime story about the Dutch resistance, starred Lana Turner, Clark Gable and Victor Mature.

Appearing in the film, in his first and only Hollywood role, was British actor Ian Carmichael. "I had a very good part in *Betrayed*. A tip-top light comedy juvenile role written by Ronnie—later Sir Ronald Millar, but it was MGM. So it had an American director, with very big American stars, and I never got a look in. It was the star system, of course. They never did the reverse shots, I had no close-ups, and they gradually whittled my part down.

"I remember vividly my only scene with Lana Turner. She was ill in bed in a hospital, and I went in to take her some flowers. I was standing at the end of the bed talking to her, and it was either shot from over my shoulder or close up on Lana Turner.

"This was my only experience with MGM."

Betrayed was Clark Gable's last picture for MGM after twenty-four years under contract with the company.

It was also at this time that MGM were boasting that they had "more stars than there are in heaven" under contract.

The loss of Gable was therefore a blow, but not a fatal one, as his star quality was already on the wane.

By 1954, MGM Borehamwood was beginning to rent studio space, and so Warwick Film Productions moved in to make four movies. The first being part of the Tay Garnett directed picture *The Black Knight*. Alan Ladd was the star, an actor who had a problem about his height, or lack of it.

Harry Andrews appeared with him in the above film, and recalled, "Alan Ladd was easy to work with and quite charming, but had a great inferiority complex about his lack of inches. Consequently, one had to be certain not to stand too close to him, and I always managed to sit for conversations."

Ivor Selwyn worked for Warwick Films at MGM British as second assistant editor. "Warwick made American influenced movies for Columbia Pictures. I actually worked on three films for them—*Odongo* (1955), *Zarak* (1956), and *Fire Down Below* (1957).

"They were utter crap—most of my studio days were spent on rubbish—I only count *The Cruel Sea* (1953) at Ealing and *A Night To Remember* (1958) at Pinewood as good movies.

"MGM Borehamwood was influenced by the parent complex at Culver City. The studio was strikingly newish and very smart. The stages had tin helmets; the original design failed to provide sufficient height! The management was pleasant and the site employed newer technology. The restaurant and separate canteen were excellent, and it had a large 'lot' with a small farm with sheep, and a big Kew Gardens-type greenhouse. On Friday afternoons in the summer, we workers could buy a very large   bunch of flowers for only 2/6d (50 pence in old money). This was a popular activity, as the assistant was a very friendly, beautiful girl!

"*Zarak* was an immense production. We used the entire Spanish cavalry. Yakima Canutt did all the battle scenes, and, sadly, a stuntman was killed. I also recall Irving Allen, the boss, asking his colleague, Cubby Broccoli, 'How much are we paying the horses?'

"On *Fire Down Below,* the largest crowd scenes were shot in the studios. The picture was apparently so expensive that it caused Warwick Film's demise.

"While I was working at MGM, I remember David Niven visited to show us his new Bentley, and Yul Brynner and Jack Lemmon (a marvellous pianist) gave lunchtime concerts. On another day, I spent twenty minutes chatting to Ingrid Bergman whilst we were both stuck waiting outside the sound department.

"You may gather that I enjoyed working at MGM, but some of the more permanently employed editing crew were not so friendly."

On September 30, 1954, MGM British hit the headlines in the *Borehamwood & Elstree Post*:

"MGM STUDIO MAN ON 500 POUNDS BAIL

Accused of Stealing 55,000 feet of Film"

The man who was described by the paper as the head of the camera department at MGM was, in fact, responsible for purchasing film negatives from Kodak. The man appeared in court accused of stealing film which was valued at £561.

Then on October 21, 1954, the following headline appeared in the *Borehamwood & Elstree Post*:

"MAN IN FILM CASE FOUND DEAD"

Not the same man as previously, but obviously connected, was due to appear in court on a charge of receiving three lengths of film, the property of MGM British Studios. He was found dead in a gas-filled room at his home.

The courtroom verdict: the man had taken his own life while the balance of his mind was disturbed.

Olivia de Havilland's first visit to the studios was to appear in the Terence Young movie *That Lady* (1955).

Making his screen debut in the film was actor, Paul Scofield. "I very much enjoyed working at MGM, and have distinct memories of driving my car there from Sussex in the early mornings.

"They were happy times, and I am more than grateful for them. Sadly, though, I have hazy recollections of the actual studio, but know that I was more than content with the working conditions.

"In retrospect, I have no negative feelings whatsoever. After all I was lucky to have the job."

John Harris was camera operator on the movie. "MGM British was a lovely studio to work in, and always very well-run. It was, of course, designed by Hollywood, so it was very modern."

The *Ivanhoe* castle (still standing on the back lot) was used again when another legendary Hollywood name, Errol Flynn, came to the studios to make his last swashbuckling adventure, *The Dark Avenger*.

Flynn had actually visited Borehamwood two years previous to appear in *The Master of Ballantrae* (1953) at the ABPC Studios.

Getting her first job as continuity on *Ballantrae* was, Pamela Francis. "I was called down from the production office because the actual 'continuity' girl on the film had fallen sick. So, they asked me to take over. To be honest though, I hadn't a clue what I was doing.

"By that time, and its quite sad to say, but Errol Flynn was a bit of an old drunk. Well past his best. I used to think he was gorgeous, but he wasn't by that time."

During production of *The Dark Avenger* at MGM British, Flynn was visited at the studios by his parents, who lived nearby at that time in St. Albans, Hertfordshire.

A local journalist also had the pleasure of taking Flynn to visit Hatfield House in Hertfordshire, where Elizabeth I was told that she was Queen of England. In the library, Flynn was shown a letter written by Elizabeth, and when he returned to the set of his film at MGM, he recited the document, word for word. Flynn apparently had a photographic memory.

Drinking quite heavily at that time, though, Flynn could often be spotted during lunch hours at The Red Lion, directly across from the

ABPC Studios (now a McDonalds). This was the place where actors so-cialized. It had a public bar to the right, and the lounge was to the left, and this is where all the famous actors used to go and eat.

Though drinking, Flynn always made sure that it never interfered with his work, and he was looked on by his fellow actors as an absolute professional.

Christopher Lee, then a supporting actor, never forgot the day he had a sword fight with Flynn in *The Dark Avenger*. "I was savaged by Er-rol Flynn. It was the first time I'd met him, and I don't think there was anything personal in it.

"In the film, I was playing an officer in charge of French soldiers, required to interfere with Errol's plans. We had enormous broadswords, but he was encased in gloves and I had bare hands. It was a four and a half minute duel. Errol threw himself into it, but he slipped and with the maximum possible zing struck me a shrewd blow on the little finger of my right hand, and nearly cut through it. 'Oh F**k!' exclaimed Errol, as it bled like a fountain. It remained bent, forever."

Clapper/loader on the movie was Kelvin Pike. "Flynn was nice. Great fun. He was one of the crew, and mixed in very well. He was a heavy drinker, but it never ever got in the way of his work, like it did with other actors. I would say it relaxed him."

MGM British continuity girl at this time was, Elaine Schreyeck. "I got to work with Errol Flynn, whom I had adored when younger as Robin Hood. *The Dark Avenger* was originally known as *The Black Prince*. Flynn himself was no trouble at all to work with. Sadly, though, he did like his drink, and you could smell it on his breath. But it hon-estly never got in the way of his performance. He was very professional on set, and knew every one of his lines. One strange thing that struck me about him was his enormous hands. I've never seen hands quite so big in my life."

By 1955, Flynn, was fifteen years past his peak as a movie star. His co-star in *The Dark Avenger*, Peter Finch, said at the time in an article that was printed in the *Borehamwood & Elstree Post*, "I realised after a weeks shooting that I was in a very crumby picture."

The film went almost unnoticed, and is rarely seen today. Four years and six forgettable movies later, Flynn, was dead at age 50.

The mid 1950s saw studio space rented for the first 'B' picture to be produced at MGM British. A turkey of its day entitled *Fire Maidens From Outer Space*.

Continuity girl, Renee Glynne, worked on the film. "It was a terrible movie directed by Cy Roth. Truly dreadful. We would probably love it now, though. It'd be a cult classic.

"The MGM British studios where we shot this masterpiece of cinema was big and orderly. Custom built. Proper gates. Proper gatemen. A big restaurant and hundreds of corridors. It was very efficient. Very superior.

"I remember while working there, Janet Leigh, who was appearing in another movie, making a fuss of my newborn baby. Shortly after this, she had Jamie Lee Curtis."

At this time, ABPC Studios was having many successes at the box office, including *The Dam Busters* (1955), and *Rob Roy: The Highland Rogue* (1953), which was produced by Walt Disney, who also made a flying visit to the Borehamwood studios during production.

ABPC, though, was about to welcome into its studios one of its biggest productions yet, the John Huston motion picture, *Moby Dick* (1956).

Before the movie had gone into production, it had caused a few problems. On July 1, 1954, the *Borehamwood & Elstree Post* reported:

"STORM OVER STUDIO BACKCLOTH"

Local residents had complained that a huge tank backed by a frame to carry backcloths and skycloths was "ruining their view." The tank, the biggest in Europe, built for *Moby Dick,* cost around £40,000. One resident complained, saying "It looks like a gigantic hoarding, and completely blocks the view from a large number of houses."

On March 24, 1955, residents complained again, this time about studio noise, as jet engines were being used to create waves for *Moby Dick.* One housewife said, "The noise is deafening. When the engine starts up it is difficult to get my children to sleep." Another resident described it as "a racket."

Angela Allen, who had worked as continuity on previous Huston pictures, *The African Queen* (1950), *Moulin Rouge* (1953), and *Beat The Devil* (1954), joined *Moby Dick* at ABPC. "They built a tank at the studio especially for the film, and this is where they filmed certain scenes, and all the model work. This model work, though, went on for months, because Moby Dick used to get broken and carted off the hospital. So, we would have nothing to do. Just sit around.

"They used to have this clocking in system at Elstree (ABPC), and I used to get so angry, because if we were not working, we'd have to sit around. In fact, I remember once kicking this clock. I was a bit of a rebel like that. Anyway, we used to sit around for hours, doing absolutely nothing, because the Moby Dick model wasn't there. So I called up John Huston, and he said, 'Go home kid.' The crew couldn't believe that I'd called him, but I'd already done three films with him.

"John Huston was incredibly charismatic. You could also make suggestions to him. He would have taken them from anybody. He would always listen. He might not use all the ideas, but he would listen. John could also get his crew to do anything. He had that charm, you see.

"*Moby Dick* had a lovely cast. Gregory Peck was charming. Orson Welles, at that time, was fine. He learned his lines. He got on well with John Huston. He was very talented, but dissipated in a way. Very sad. The casting of Richard Basehart was actually my suggestion."

Angela Allen recalled working at ABPC. "I remember Elstree Film Studios (or ABPC) as having a sort of factory atmosphere, especially with the clocking in and out. The studio was also not known for making the best pictures. They were quite cheap, and would have the cheapest things. But when we went there with *Moby Dick,* it was probably one of the biggest things they'd done.

"Elstree (ABPC) was a strange sort of place. The back lot was very minimal, because you were hemmed in by the surrounding housing estates. There really wasn't much there, to be honest. It wasn't my favourite studio. It wasn't pretty to look at, and the whole atmosphere about it was cheap and tight. I also didn't find it to be a very creative place, as regards the management."

Double Oscar-winning cinematographer, Freddie Francis, also worked on *Moby Dick.* "My main job on the film was actually filming all the live whaling stuff. It took about three months. I also did the tank stuff at Elstree (ABPC), though. In fact, I nearly killed myself on that picture, as I was on the tank doing all the special effects things there, and also operating on the other special effects on the floor. I loved working with John Huston, though. We got along very well indeed. I had a lot of luck with John."

On October 6, 1955, the *Borehamwood & Elstree Post* reported:
"FINED FOR ASSAULT AT FILM STUDIOS"

A court fine of £1 with £5 costs was imposed on an electrician of MGM Studios, Borehamwood, who admitted assaulting a fellow worker.

The electrician was said to have been working on Gantry No. 2 when he spat on his fellow worker, who was working below him. A fight then broke out on the studio floor, with the fellow worker getting severely kicked in the groin by the electrician, making him unable to work for five days.

The electrician was dismissed from the studios, and later said that he was accused unjustly of spitting on his fellow worker.

In 1956, Ealing Studios was sold to the BBC for £300,000, and the company moved to MGM Borehamwood.

The films made under the Ealing banner at MGM included *The Man In The Sky* (1956), *The Shiralee* (1957), *Davy* (1957), *Nowhere To Go* (1958), and *Dunkirk* (1958).

The latter starred John Mills and Richard Attenborough, and Douglas Slocombe (cinematographer), who would later work for Steven Spielberg, photographed part of the movie. "The MGM British Studios were quite beautiful. They were superbly designed in the Hollywood style, and extremely lavish, with first-rate equipment and a great wealth of lamps. It also had an enormous back lot, much bigger than any other British studio.

"I worked on several films there, including shooting the model sequences for Leslie Norman's movie *Dunkirk*, were we had a huge water tank built inside one of the sound stages."

After the release of *Dunkirk,* a lady came to the gates of MGM several times asking to see whoever made the movie. She believed that she had recognized her dead husband on the Dunkirk beaches shown in the picture, but refused to accept that those scenes had actually been filmed in Norfolk.

The Man Who Never Was (1956), directed by Ronald Neame, was based on one of the greatest deceptions planned against the enemy during the war. Montagu, a British naval intelligence reservist, devised an idea code named "Operation Mincemeat.: If he could absolutely convince the Germans that the anticipated Allied invasion of Europe would begin in Sardinia rather than Sicily (the obvious route), they would deploy their defending troops to the wrong location.

To achieve this, false information would have to fall into German hands by way of a messenger—a Royal Marines officer drowned at sea. For this, Montagu and his team needed to find the suitable body of a young man.

Montagu also had to create false documents that would serve as undeniable proof to the German High Command. These papers would then be placed in an attaché case chained to the wrist of the corpse.

The decision was made to jettison the body from a submarine off Southern Spain and currents were studied to establish exactly where it would be guaranteed to float ashore, with British Intelligence knowing that the Spaniards would pass information on to German agents.

Darryl Zanuck was financing this fascinating picture, which was to be partly shot at MGM British. He also insisted that Clifton Webb be cast in the role of Montagu.

It is also interesting to note that in one scene the voice of Winston Churchill is heard. An unknown actor, who did a wonderful impersonation of the great man, was hired. Soon, however, this unknown would become known to all—Peter Sellers.

According to director, Ronald Neame, his star, Clifton Webb, had a wonderful sense of humor. When relaxed, a lot of his conversation revolved around his mother, Maybelle.

Oswald Morris was cinematographer on the movie. "Arthur Ibbetson, who was my camera operator on the picture, one day asked Clifton, 'How's Maybelle?' 'Oh don't talk about mother. You'll never guess what's happened. She's been at the gin again. I'd locked it up. I promise you, I hid the key. Mother found it. I don't know what I'm going to do with her.'"

"None of us ever saw her. For all we know, she could have been a Mrs. Bates-type character from the film *Psycho*. But Clifton was very fond of her."

The Man Who Never Was had an excellent script, and it received good reviews, many finding the story, based on fact, compelling.

It also has scenes that are deeply moving, particularly the very end sequence, which takes place beside the grave of the dead soldier, who was used in the deception. Here we see Ewen Montagu, decorated for his part in deceiving the Germans, place his own medal on the young Soldier's grave.

The Good Companions (1956), a musical, shot mainly at ABPC and partly at MGM, starred Janette Scott in a leading role. "It was my first musical. I was seventeen years old. Tony Martin was on the next stage making a film with Vera-Ellen called *Let's Be Happy* (1957).

"Tony Martin was married to Cyd Charisse at that time, and for many years to come. That fact, however, did not stop him trying to date me. Since I had virtually grown up in the studios, though, there was no shortage of people around ready to protect me from wolves like him.

"Errol Flynn was another—much past his prime, but trying to sit next to me in the studio exec dining room, but finally warned off by studio bosses."

Robert Taylor returned to MGM British in 1956 to appear in *The Adventures Of Quentin Durward*. Based on the Sir Walter Scott novel and co-starring Kay Kendall, Robert Morley, and Wilfrid Hyde-White, it was an action story set in fifteenth century France, with some location work done in that country.

Robert Taylor was reported to have said at the time in an article that was printed in the *Borehamwood & Elstree Post*, "It has been my good fortune to make several pictures here in the British Isles, and there is nothing quite so beautiful as an English summer. The countryside is so very green."

Working as scenic artist on the film was, Peter Mullins. "I worked under Alfred Junge, who was art director. A very famous art director, whose claim to fame was having worked on the original *Cabinet of Dr. Caligari* (1920). He was a very solid man with absolutely no sense of humor, and used to walk around in a black overcoat wearing a black homburg hat. To be honest, he looked very much like an Austrian waiter. He wasn't much fun, but he was very, very clever."

Peter Mullins shared his early memories of MGM Borehamwood. "MGM British to me was like a big, big factory. Well organized, with very good departments and very good people. It was very, very professional, but because I was only young I found it a little bit overpowering."

Stewart Granger and Ava Gardner teamed up next for *Bhowani Junction* in 1956. Though both were unhappy at the time under contract to MGM, they very much enjoyed making the film under the direction of George Cukor.

James Sharkey, who had worked at MGM British previously in the stills department, almost returned, this time in an acting role. "I was suggested by casting lady, Irene Howard, to George Cukor for a major role in *Bhowani Junction*. I auditioned for him in London, and was then called for a screen test at MGM Borehamwood. They had whittled down the choice to two; my friend Francis Matthews and me. Francis got the role. However, Cukor told me that mine was the better acting test, though Francis had the better features under a turban. That's show business for you!"

The part of Ranjit was indeed played by Francis Matthews, who shares with us his experiences of working on the picture. "It is now almost forgotten that the great MGM created a huge studio in Elstree/Borehamwood, and helped to turn those places into the English equivalent of Hollywood. It was the center for visiting American movie stars who were brought over to play the leading roles, while most of the supporting roles were played by British actors. This made it an immensely impressive place to work, and it was where I first set foot on a film set.

"Needless to say, for a twenty-five-year-old actor straight out of 'Rep' this was all a stunning and exciting experience. As well as the overwhelming thrill of suddenly being in this incredible studio, I would find myself working in the close company of Ava Gardner (then the top female star in the world) and Stewart Granger.

"I was soon to become very familiar in fact with that great studio, and lunching in the restaurant with Ava and Jimmy Granger became a 'head-turning' exercise, because you were surrounded by many of the great Hollywood names. Stars, directors, producers, writers, make-up artistes (many of whom were brought over at the stars' command!)

"To give a flavour of just how 'high-powered' was the surrounding atmosphere there, on my dressing-room floor, a walk along the corridor took you past (in this order): Robert Taylor, Kay Kendell, Ava Gardner, Stewart Granger, Claude Rains, as well as, on other floors, the cream of the finest British character actors.

"Taylor and Kendall were working on another big film *Quentin Durward,* and the huge sound stages were full of activity. The whole place alive with artistes dressed either in armour or chain-mail or Saris and Dhotis.

"The producer of *Bhowani Junction* was Pandro S. Berman, a tiny, dark, sharp-eyed man with a rapid vocal delivery. The director, George Cukor, was slow, watchful, with a heavy lower lip and pronounced lisp. I recall he made an extraordinary remark when I was cast: 'Our acting man in Hollywood has seen your test and tells us you are a good actor!' They were his very words, the sort of comment I could not possibly invent, and I wanted to say, 'Couldn't you make up your own minds?' but I didn't! I was just happy to be cast as fourth lead opposite Ava Gardner in one of MGM's most ambitious projects. It was certainly unusual casting, particularly as my only work had been Repertory and an aborted West End play.

"My part in the film was Ranjit, and the location shooting took place in Pakistan. On my first day, Cukor told me, 'I'm sending you to Amritsar. I don't want you to act a Sikh, I want you to be a Sikh. Ranjit is very religious, like a Goddam Catholic, but I don't want you to be boring. You're gonna meet the Gurus at the Golden Temple to learn about their religion. Your Sikh advisor will go with you.'

"This was loading me with the daunting possibility of rapidly transforming into a 'method' actor, yet there was something stimulating about Cukor's fervour for total authenticity.

"Ava Gardner, the female star of the film, was then the queen of Hollywood, billed in her previous film, *The Barefoot Contessa* (1954), as 'The World's Most Beautiful Animal' and indeed she was the most effortlessly ravishing woman I had ever seen, which is hardly news, yet she managed to convey the air of a carefree young girl. I had suddenly entered the world of true glamour. Her easy friendliness mixed with unashamed sexuality was fairly devastating. After my first brief meeting with her, I watched her sway away, probably open mouthed.

"On one of my first days, I arrived at the location fifteen minutes after my 'call' because make-up had been dragging their heels, and I was told that there was no point in me turning up not prepared. The scene I faced when I finally arrived taught me a principle I have followed ever since.

"Cukor himself was waiting by my caravan, clutching his usual rolled-up script. He grabbed my arm in a vice like grip (to which I was to become accustomed!) and thrust me into a chair incandescent with rage. 'Who the f**k do you think you are? You are late! You have kept your Director and your leading lady, to say nothing of an entire film crew, waiting around unable to work. How dare you!'

"I tried to tell him that I was following make-up's instructions, but to no avail. 'Don't give me that actor's crap, you little shit. You are responsible to me and no-one else. When your call is nine o'clock you be on that set at nine o'clock, and I don't care if you're bollock naked. Now get your goddam ass ready to work.' He was absolutely right of course, and over fifty years later I have never again been late on set.

"It should be said here that, no matter what the daily apprehension and criticism to which he subjected me, Cukor was a superb director with an enormous emotional input to every scene, and meticulous attention to detail.

"It is also worth recording his greatest put-down for me. The camera was on me for a simple reaction to Lionel Jeffries lascivious leering at Ava. I needed only to notice, react, look up at Ava, and exit—what we call 'No Acting Required.' We got up to about six 'takes' with Cukor grumbling, 'I don't believe it. It's not real. Get it in your mind,' and calling 'Cut' even in the middle of what I was trying to do.

"Finally I said, 'I'm sorry, sir. Maybe the problem is I've never done a film before, only Theatre?'

"He muttered, 'Yeah, yeah, yeah,' then walked back to the camera shouting, 'Stand by!' There was a moment, and then he suddenly strode back to me, grabbed my arm, as usual, and said, 'What you're doing would be pretty goddam crappy on the stage too, yer know!'

"Ava began to become very protective of me and gave me lessons in how Hollywood stars behave. 'When he is being a bastard you should walk off the set and not come back till be apologizes. What can they do?

Re-cast? It would cost them a fortune. Anyway he'll respect you more if you stand up to him.'

"Needless to say I never walked off, but that was the last time that I tolerated that kind of professional cruelty.

"I realize I have said very little about our male star, Stewart Granger. That is because, apart from the occasional distant contact on the set, he was not 'one of us.' Also whenever he had a spare moment on location he would be off on an elephant with his stand-in-cum-side-kick, to shoulder rifles and kill things; the cliché macho, tough guy, Hemingway syndrome indulged in by many big stars.

"One day at the Unit Hotel, Cukor collared me in the corridor and said, 'I'm having Ava moved to another Hotel. You're distracting her from her work!' I can't imagine what he meant since no actress could be more punctual, perfect on her lines, and less troublesome than Ava. She was always inclined to burn the midnight oil and drink a great deal of vodka, and demonstrate her Flamenco to the Covent Garden porters at 3 a.m., but she hardly needed lessons from me in that.

"Ava moved into a large apartment in Kingston House, on the south side of Hyde Park, close to Kensington where I was renting a top-floor room in my old friend William Franklyn's house, and so we did see a lot of each other 'after hours.'

"After one very late night, she insisted I take her to meet my parents, in Surbiton of all places. Surbiton is the quintessential suburb, stuck in the south London sprawl, and my parents lived in a smart but very ordinary semi-detached house there, so I hardly thought it was Ava's 'speed.' 'For God's sake, I'm a farm girl from North Carolina,' she said. So long-suffering, Eddie, her driver, took us to Hook Road. It was 1am.

"My father in his dressing gown, dragged from sleep and thinking something was very wrong, was not a pretty sight and had only the vaguest idea who Ava was, but my mother had given herself time to titivate and rushed downstairs fairly overwhelmed. Ava behaved as if she were my girlfriend, and was so utterly different from her pampered grandeur at the studios, but then she was always a very different person when we were privately together.

"She insisted my parents come to the studios to watch us shooting our love scene, and, on the day, had a studio car sent for them, seated them by the camera crew, and treated them like visiting royalty. Even Cukor managed to be a little more tolerant of me after he met them. There's nothing like an old Yorkshire couple to bring inflated egos down to earth!

"Shot in huge close-ups that love scene, when I saw the rushes the following day was quite stunning, but then the lighting-cameraman was the great Freddie Young, a multiple Oscar winner. Sadly, it ended up on the cutting-room floor after a Hollywood preview where the 'form-fillers' thought Ava should not be seen kissing a Black man! Quite apart from this being a revelation of the then deep-rooted race prejudice in America, the fact that I was a White man playing the part of an Indian seems to have passed right over their heads. The last, and most relevant, scenes of my role suffered the same fate because they said they knew nothing, and cared less, about the history of the British in India…

"Cukor returned to MGM Borehamwood several weeks after completion, under pressure, to shoot a totally altered ending, cutting half an hour from the two-hour epic, and turning the last scenes into nothing more than a vapid Hollywood love story between the two stars, which decimated both Master's story and Cukor's faithful work. These are the background machinations that the critics, who gave the final film short shrift, could never know.

"At the post-synching session I had to attend, to re-record new dialogue covering the changes, the great Cukor was in tears. 'They have ruined my picture!' he said."

Production designer, Sir Ken Adam, who would later work on the *James Bond* movies, came to MGM British to design part of Mike Todd's *Around The World In 80 Days* (1956). "I have nothing but the fondest memories of MGM Studios, Borehamwood. There was a great atmosphere with modern stages and workshops and everything very well laid out.

"I practically started my career there, designing the London and French settings for *Around The World In 80 Days*, for which I received my first Oscar nomination.

"Cyril Graysmark, their resident construction manager, took me under his wing and I learned a great deal from his professionalism.

"Then there was Alfred Junge, one of the greatest designers, who was under contract to MGM, and who kept a fatherly eye on what I was doing.

"MGM at that time still had a permanent special effects department, which came in useful when in 1957 I designed John Ford's *Gideon's Day*. There was an important scene with Jack Hawkins in an office at Scotland Yard overlooking Westminster Bridge. I opted for a miniature with moving traffic rather than back projection or a painted backing and it was rather realistically executed by the MGM special effects department. John Ford was delighted with it and staged all the action favouring the bridge, but sadly disaster struck, when buses, trucks, and all the traffic crossing the bridge jolted and jerked to a stand-still. They were attached to a never-ending canvas belt ,which, due to the heat of the lighting, had stretched and jammed. I thought I would be fired on the spot, but John Ford decided to shoot all the reverses first giving the special effects department time to replace the canvas with a leather belt, resulting in the traffic moving better.

"Altogether, I must have designed seven films at MGM British, and it was, without doubt, my favourite studio, until I settled down at Pinewood for the design of the *Bond* films."

Sir Ken Adam, also took time to remember the ABPC Studios. "I was not very fond of that studio, since they were very tight with money and I always had a battle with their budget. But in all fairness, I designed two of my most important early films there. In 1957, Jacques Tourneur's *Night Of The Demon* with Dana Andrews, which has since become a cult film, and then in 1960, Ken Hugh's *The Trials Of Oscar Wilde*, the color version with Peter Finch, for which I received the 1962 Moscow Film Festival Prize for Best Art Direction.

"So, in hind sight, when the chips are down, the construction department at ABPC always came up with the goods."

On May 2, 1957, the *Borehamwood & Elstree Post* reported:
"FIRE EXPLOSION ROCKS HOUSES NEAR STUDIO
Station Road Gardens Ablaze"

A violent explosion had rocked houses in Borehamwood when fire broke out at the Gate Studios. Flames from the fire that apparently started in a film vault shot out and set fire to the fences in nearby houses. Fireman who saw smoke and flames billowing high above the studios were at the scene in two minutes.

In the vault was found 600-weight of nitrate film and 120 gallons of petroleum spirit in 29 drums that were well ablaze.

On July 11, 1957, the following sad report appeared:
"FILM STUNT MAN DIES"

A middle aged stuntman died during an audition for *The Moonraker,* which was to be shot at the ABPC Studios. He was being auditioned for the part of a horseman at Radnor Riding School on Allum Lane, Elstree, when he collapsed after kneeling down to rest. It was reported that the man from Kensington had died of natural causes.

The Boulting Brothers (Roy and John) returned to MGM Borehamwood in 1957 to film their comedy *Lucky Jim* with Terry-Thomas and

Hugh Griffiths. The star of the movie was Ian Carmichael. "There was trouble with *Lucky Jim*. The first fortnight of filming we were on one set—the big quadrangle in the university—and it was on the large stage at MGM. The director of the film (Charles Crichton) I personally found intimidating. Whereas the Boultings always whispered in my ear, he was apt to stand behind the camera and shout, which I didn't like very much.

"The production company was working through British Lion, who were distributors, and the Boultings happened to be on their board, and they (the Boultings) were not happy with the daily rushes.

"After two weeks, British Lion, who had the power to do so, sacked the director, and on the following Monday morning, John Boulting was in the director's chair.

"It was a ten-week schedule, of which two had gone, and John was hamstrung inasmuch as we were already in production. There was also terrible trouble with actor Hugh Griffith, who hadn't liked the changeover and who was a pal of the original director.

"Generally speaking, it was a right old bloody mess."

When Ian Carmichael appeared in this film, he was thirty-seven, playing a twenty-four-year-old, and Terry-Thomas, who was forty-six, was actually a year older than Hugh Griffith, who was playing his father.

Special Effects titan Ray Harryhausen visited MGM British in 1957 to work on the film *7th Voyage Of Sinbad*. "We needed to use the blue screen stages at MGM to do the travelling matte work on the film, and at that time this studio was the world's leading travelling matte experts. It was a fine studio, just like the big ones in Hollywood. I was there for two weeks, and sadly, never returned again."

Don Chaffey's *A Question Of Adultery* (1958), mainly shot at the ABPC Studios, had one scene shot at MGM British. This sequence featured actor Trader Faulkner as a Flamenco Dancer. "The film starred Julie London and Anthony Steel, and because I could dance Flamenco, I had to dance their orgasm, which obviously you could not show on screen in 1958!

"The producer, Raymond Stross, said when I had finished the sequence, 'Trader, if you can screw like you dance, your marriage will either last a very short time because you'll die of exhaustion, or you'll live to be a very wicked old man.' Well, I'm still here in my eighties, so it must be the latter."

In 1958, Ingrid Bergman visited MGM British to appear in the tear-jerker, *The Inn Of The Sixth Happiness,* with Robert Donat. It tells the story of Gladys Aylward (Bergman), a missionary in war-torn china, and her efforts to save a school of orphans.

For the movie, a huge Chinese set was built on the back lot at MGM Borehamwood, the largest film set ever constructed in Europe up until that time, costing a $250,000.

On April 17, 1958, the *Borehamwood & Elstree Post* reported:

"NO STATEMENT ON LOSS OVER FILM STRIKE"

Production of the $4 million *The Inn Of The Sixth Happiness* was held up for a day and a half when 500 workers stopped work in a dispute arising when outside labour was brought in to carry out certain jobs. A spokesman of the studios declined to say how much the stoppage had cost the moviemakers.

The film would turn out to be Robert Donat's last picture. He'd been a sick man for many years, and during filming, he suffered a brain haemorrhage. However, he returned to the studios, confined to a wheelchair, and manfully struggled through. On the final day of shooting, he was so ill that his lines had to be written on idiot boards, which were held up just off camera.

In the scene in which he is saying goodbye to Gladys, Donat delivers his lines as though he was prophesying his own death. "I fear we shall not see each other again." A few days after filming had been completed, Donat was dead.

During production of *The Inn Of The Sixth Happiness*, Richard Gordon, was shooting his horror movie, *Corridors Of Blood*, at MGM.

"King of Terror" Boris Karloff was the star, with Christopher Lee and Adrienne Corri playing supporting roles.

The movie tells the story of Dr. Thomas Bolton (Karloff), an eminent London surgeon, who believes that "pain and the knife are not inseparable" and experiments with drugs to create an effective anaesthetic. After a failed demonstration—the patient awakens while being cut—Bolton is disgraced and suspended from the hospital. Worse, he falls in with Resurrection Joe (Christopher Lee), grave robber and sometime murderer.

Although Boris Karloff could play this type of role in his sleep, he still managed to make it look new.

Producer Richard Gordon remembers the filming, and working with its star. "A problem beyond our control occurred when MGM changed management in the midst of production, and the new guys were not interested in financing 'little' pictures, like ours. They were also not interested in releasing it... for the time being. We had no way, therefore, of getting anybody else to put up the money to reimburse MGM to take over the film, so it languished for a while until MGM, in one of their other, later management changes, came back to the idea of forming a secondary unit to release pictures of this type. The film, however, was shelved for four years, finally getting released in 1962.

"Karloff wasn't happy with *Corridors*, but it doesn't alter the fact that he was one of the most courteous, friendly, gentlemanly, and good-natured people I've ever worked with—or met! He was the perfect gentleman, and a typical Englishman—the garden, cricket, the 'country squire'—part of the Hollywood 'English Colony'.

"Like so many, though, who were as professional as Karloff, he could become intolerant with those on the set who were not—who were not pulling their weight. So, there were moments with him when there was tension on the set. He was, shall we say, not tolerant of people stumbling around, not knowing what they were doing, or telling him to do something that was patently wrong—he didn't have any time to waste.

"I felt that his greatest strength as an actor was that if he accepted a role, from the moment he signed on, he treated it as a professional and would give the best possible performance; he never walked through a part; it wasn't his nature. He felt a very strong obligation towards his employers; if he was taking their money, they were entitled to their money's worth.

"Away from the set, he was a very private person, and some people have been, for whatever reason, looking for a 'dark side' of Boris Karloff. A 'dark side', which may very well have been there, but was certainly not evident to those who actually knew him.

"Boris Karloff, was, without doubt, a very dedicated actor, very much appreciative of the success that he had. He felt an obligation to audiences, as well as producers. He believed that if people paid to see him, he owed them the best of his ability. I think he'd be very surprised—and grateful— for the continued interest in his life and career so long after his death."

Playing Karloff's son in the movie was actor, Francis Matthews. "My dressing room neighbors this time were Ingrid Bergman and my hero, Robert Donat. I was still very star-struck and used to go and watch the great Bergman working on the huge Chinese set built on the back lot.

"In the movie in which I was appearing, we had Boris Karloff. I had, in fact, just completed a film for Hammer, *The Revenge Of Frankenstein*, with Peter Cushing, and was then immediately asked to appear with Boris.

"Working with Peter had been a joyous experience. A happy, funny man, and a consummate professional. I was to find exactly the same relationship with Boris. Isn't it therefore strange that the two most celebrated exponents of 'Horror' should both be equally charming, jolly, disciplined, and great company.

"Boris was immensely popular with the entire crew and cast, playing practical jokes and enjoying the latest scandals and gossip. At the time there was a Test (Cricket) Series in England (can't recall our opponents), and I had a portable Radio on set to keep track of the scores. Boris and I spent every spare moment bent over that Radio.

"At the end of each day's filming Boris did a running joke of offering to sweep up the mess created by the day's work (there was always a lot of broken glass and blood and gore!) At the end of shoot party, the crew got their own back on him by gifting him a huge studio sweeping brush, which we had all signed.

"As a young actor I was fortunate to cut my filming teeth with two of the profession's great gentleman."

Actress, Betta St. John, also appeared in the movie. "I disliked the title, but remember it as a comfortable, happy production. The studio (MGM Borehamwood) made you feel like a star, and you had fresh flowers in your dressing room each day, which had been grown on site. We also had a good director in Robert Day. Boris Karloff was a most professional and lovely gentleman, and it was always a pleasure to work with Francis Matthews."

Geoff Glover was assistant camera on *Corridors Of Blood*. He recalled, "I was a very young man when I worked on the Boris Karloff film. He was very professional though, but I think that he probably only did the movie to pay his bills, as at that time he was definitely in his twilight years.

"MGM British, where we shot the film, was always my favourite studio. Apart from it being the nearest studios to my home, I also found it to be the best laid out. In fact, one of the pleasures of working at MGM was that the camera equipment was the best maintained of all the studios. This was much do to the then head of the camera department, Les Smart.

"Les ran a tight ship and also acted an unofficial and unpaid employment agent for camera crews long before answering and booking services came into being. Any production manager or producer when looking for a crew would always phone Les first.

"Not surprisingly, the walls of Les Smart's office at MGM were covered with postcards from all over the world often telling Les when they were going to be available again. Then, at the beginning of each year the walls were cleared so to start again."

Several other films were shot at MGM during the later part of the 1950s, including *The Doctor's Dilemma* with Dirk Bogarde and Leslie Caron; *Ice Cold In Alex* with John Mills, Anthony Quayle, Sylvia Syms, and Harry Andrews (partly shot at MGM); and *Tom Thumb* with Russ Tamblyn in the title role. This film also brought together two of Britain's top film comedians, Peter Sellers and Terry-Thomas. Both were at the height of their comedy careers and provided the comic relief as a couple of villains. The movie itself proved to be a great success.

Ken Holt worked in the special effects department on the movie. He shared his memories of MGM Borehamwood. "Apart from meeting my wife, my other special memory from working at the studio is when we won the special effects Oscar for *Tom Thumb*. It was, in fact, the second Oscar for my boss, Tom Howard.

"MGM British was a great studio, the best in Britain. It had a very good atmosphere, and everyone mixed well, and was at a top standard at their jobs.

"I treasure my time working there."

On May 22, 1958, the *Borehamwood & Elstree Post* printed the following report:

"FIRE AT FILM STUDIO

Fireman Saved a Major Disaster"

Firefighters fought a large blaze in one of the five large stages at ABPC Studios, caused by either a cigarette end or an electrical fault in the studio lighting system.

On the stage, a large set had been erected for *The Man Within* starring Anita Ekberg and Jack Palance.

Then, on September 4, 1958, the *Borehamwood & Elstree Post* reported the following:

"FILM STAR'S PARKED CAR DAMAGED"

Burt Lancaster's chauffeur-driven car was damaged when another car ran into it, when it was stationary in Elstree Way near the junction with Shenley Road, Borehamwood.

Lancaster was not in the car at the time of collision. He was filming *The Devil's Disciple* at ABPC Studios with Kirk Douglas and Laurence Olivier.

The driver of the other car, which was extensively damaged, was injured, but not seriously.

1958 also saw John Osborne's successful stage play, *Look Back In Anger*, filmed at ABPC Studios with a cast headed by Richard Burton, Mary Ure, and Claire Bloom. On its initial cinema release in 1959, however, it was not an instant commercial success, but it did find its audience in later years.

During 1958, MGM British did some work on the epic *Ben Hur*, including building sets and props, most notably the famous chariots, and doing screen tests. The actors who auditioned for parts included Robert Shaw, Michael Gough, Christopher Lee, Nigel Davenport, Edward Judd, Nigel Green, Bernard Miles, Michael Hordern, Guy Rolfe, Andre Morrell, and Lionel Jeffries.

Actor, Laurence Payne, recalled the auditions. "William Wyler came to MGM Borehamwood to cast, and a lot of actors turned up to audition for him. It was quite an overpowering experience, as the studio itself was larger than life, a perfect setting in fact for one of Hollywood's biggest directors.

"I went up for the part of Joseph, and had about four minutes in front of the camera, with Wyler looking on, intensely.

"Later, Willie told me that he gave me the part because of the way I smiled when I read my lines. He was though a wonderful director and fantastic to work with."

The Safecracker, directed by Ray Milland, was the next movie to be shot at the studio, and Angela Allen was continuity. "Well the crew more or less directed the movie, as technically, Ray Milland, wasn't very good. But he was a charming man. Extremely nice. Very sweet. But I think that he should have just stayed with acting, rather than directing.

"In fact, when I first went to work in Hollywood, he heard that I was working at Universal, and he cycled all the way from his end of the building just to see me. I was quite flattered. The crew said, 'We've never heard of a star making a special journey to see the script girl.' He was a truly lovely man, though."

Angela Allen gave her first impressions of working at MGM British. "MGM was modelled on the Hollywood studios. It was very luxurious, and had a wonderful back lot. The stages were also bigger and better than anywhere else, and the facilities were excellent."

When Lana Turner arrived at Borehamwood to film *Another Time, Another Place* (1958), her lover, Johnny Stompanato, followed.

During production, Stompanato suspected Lana of having an affair with her leading man, Sean Connery, and so confronted him on the set at MGM. Waving a gun, the jealous Stompanato told Connery to stay away from Lana. Connery responded by landing a right to Johnny's nose, knocking him helplessly to the floor.

Shortly after, back in the US, Stompanato met his end at the hands of the frightened teenage daughter of Lana Turner (Cheryl Crane). He was stabbed to death.

Tarzan swung his way into MGM in 1959 in *Tarzan's Greatest Adventure*. The camera operator was Nicolas Roeg. "This was one of my brushes with a second feature. The producer was Sy Weintraub. He was a real character, and for some reason was on the set for the entire shoot. He would say, 'F**k the film, just get the shots. Let's not go into any sort of thinking about it. He swings from a tree. What's the time?'

"I said to Sy one day, 'You're finishing Tarzan off aren't you, calling it his greatest adventure?' He said, 'What are you talking about? Are you teaching grammar or something?' Sy was a really amusing guy."

Robert Taylor returned to Borehamwood in 1959 to make his last film under contract to MGM for some twenty five years. The picture was a thriller, *The House Of The Seven Hawks*.

Sadly, though, Taylor's career was already in decline, and twelve mediocre movies later he died in 1969 after a long battle with cancer.

Some work was also done on *The Wreck Of The Mary Deare* (1959), Gary Cooper's penultimate movie at MGM British, which also starred Charlton Heston, Virginia McKenna, and Michael Redgrave.

It was during this production that Redgrave learned of his Knighthood in Her Majesty's Birthday Honours. In kindness, the crew and cast gave Redgrave a congratulatory note.

A number of well-known actors were suggested for various roles in *The Wreck Of The Mary Deare,* including Donald Pleasence and Lionel Jeffries for the role of Mr. Petrie, (which actually went to Alexander Knox), and Peter O'Toole and Patrick Allen for the part of Higgins, (which went to Richard Harris).

Actor Geoffrey Bayldon appeared in *Libel*, the next movie to be shot at MGM Borehamwood, with Olivia de Havilland back at the studio appearing alongside Dirk Bogarde.

Geoffrey Bayldon recalled his role in the movie. "The late Robert Shaw and myself shared a scene. For some reason, though, we only got the pages of the script that we were appearing in, and unfortunately it didn't tell us who was playing what. So, we looked at it and knew immediately that Robert would play the toughie, as he always did, with a slight edge, and I would play the more gentle character.

"The director was the extremely good—Anthony Asquith—and we all met at MGM to do our scenes with the star of the film, Olivia de Havilland. Upon seeing me and Robert, Anthony Asquith said, 'I'm so pleased to see you, Robert.' Never mentioned me. He continued, 'Robert, you are so right for this, I saw you recently in a production of *The Long And The Short And The Tall*, and the way you played your character, it had that edge, kindly edge, that I knew you were exactly what I wanted.' Well, me and Robert looked at each other quickly, thinking, *Shit, we've been learning the wrong parts*—and we had, but we quickly adjusted.

"Also in the cast of *Libel* was Joyce Carey, who I'd worshipped as part of the 'Coward' set-up. Whenever you met her, though, she would introduce herself, offering her hand, 'Joyce Carey…?' as though it was a question. So, you'd reply, 'No, I'm Geoffrey Bayldon.' She was gorgeous, though. Olivia de Havilland was very pleasant, too."

MGM British was next visited by Bette Davis and Alec Guinness for the making of *The Scapegoat* (1959). Miss Davis didn't hold fond memories of the experience. She later said in an article that was printed in the *Borehamwood & Elstree Post*, "The director cut my part to shreds, so much so that my final appearance in the movie made no sense whatsoever."

Miss Davis wasn't too thrilled with her co-star either. "Alec Guinness is an actor who plays by himself, unto himself. In this picture, he plays a dual role, so at least he was able to play with himself."

Herbert Smith was camera operator on the movie. "Alec Guinness I'd first worked with at Ealing. So, he was an old chum. He was a lovely man, though, and very talented but very private away from work.

"The film was directed by Robert Hamer, who had a marvellous brain, but sadly drank too much. I worked on his last movie a year later at Elstree Studios (ABPC) called *School for Scoundrels* with Ian Carmichael and Terry Thomas. It was quite upsetting to see other people directing Hamer's work for him, because he was unable to do it himself, due to drink. Sometimes they'd find him in the gutter, when he was supposed to be on set. Very sad."

In the late 1950s, Alfred Junge stepped down as production designer at MGM British, and his role was taken by, Elliot Scott.

Elliot's son, Stephen Scott (now a noted 'production designer' himself) recalls, "My father was at MGM Borehamwood at the start, and he was there when it closed. He was first a draughtsman working for production designer Alfred Junge, who did all the early MGM stuff. My father then graduated to become production designer there in about 1956.

"The MGM studios, as a complex, was very large. It had a huge back lot, and all the facilities you needed.

"Funnily enough, I was an extra in *The Barretts Of Wimpole Street* at MGM. My father was art director on it. I got paid £5, which was a lot of money then.

"I also remember my father borrowing our pair of kitchen scissors to put on the set of the film *Lucky Jim*. When I visited the set, I found it quite amusing to see them."

Art Director, Terry Ackland-Snow, said of Elliot Scott, "Elliot, in my opinion, was one of the best production designers in the business. He was a very clever man, and designed very effectively. He could also do the most amazing things on very little money."

David Wynn-Jones, who worked later at MGM British said, "We named our son, Elliot, after Elliot Scott."

The MGM British Studios logo. Courtesy of Stephen Scott.

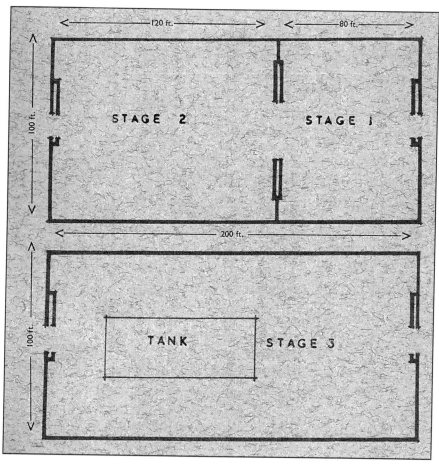

MGM British sound stages 1, 2 and 3. Courtesy of Stephen Scott.

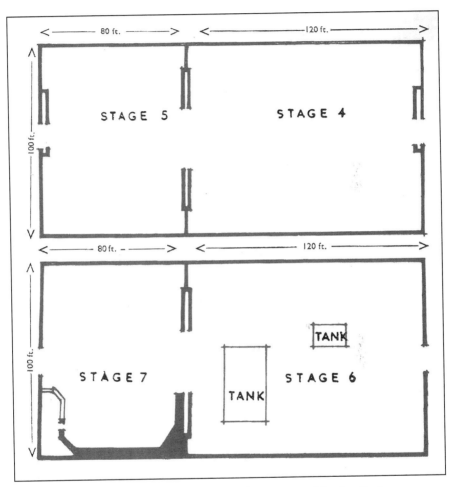

MGM British sound stages 4, 5, 6 and 7. Courtesy of Stephen Scott.

Sound stage 2 at MGM British Studios in the late 1940s. Courtesy of Stephen Scott.

Sound stage 3 at MGM British Studios in the late 1940s. Courtesy of Stephen Scott.

Edward My Son (1949). MGM Studio publicity photograph of Spencer Tracy and Deborah Kerr. Courtesy of James Sharkey.

Conspirator (1949). MGM Studio publicity photograph of Robert Taylor.
Courtesy of James Sharkey.

Conspirator (1949). MGM Studio publicity photograph of Elizabeth Taylor.
Courtesy of James Sharkey.

James Sharkey working in the 'stills department' at MGM British Studios (1948).
Courtesy of James Sharkey.

A young Peggy Spirito standing with Richard Attenborough's Rolls-Royce in the
grounds of MGM British Studios (1948). Courtesy of Peggy Spirito.

Alfred Hitchcock's favourite pub while working at Borehamwood – 'The Plough' in Elstree village (now 'The East' oriental restaurant). Courtesy of Derek Pykett.

Under Capricorn (1949). MGM Studio publicity photograph of Ingrid
Bergman and Michael Wilding. Courtesy of Peggy Spirito.

Under Capricorn (1949). Michael Wilding (far left) chats with Alfred Hitchcock
(far right) between takes at MGM British. Courtesy of Jack Cardiff.

Under Capricorn (1949). MGM Studio publicity photograph of Ingrid Bergman.
Courtesy of Peggy Spirito.

Under Capricorn (1949). Ingrid Bergman having fun between takes at MGM British. Courtesy of Jack Cardiff.

Under Capricorn (1949). Alfred Hitchcock sits at the camera. Courtesy of Jack Cardiff.

Under Capricorn (1949). Jack Cardiff (far right) and Alfred Hitchcock (far left) on set at MGM British. Courtesy of Jack Cardiff.

Under Capricorn (1949). Alfred Hitchcock and Ingrid Bergman taking a look at the sets on the back-lot at MGM British. Courtesy of Jack Cardiff.

An aerial photograph of MGM British Studios in the 1950s. Courtesy of Stephen Scott.

The Miniver Story (1950). Alfred Junge 'production design'. Courtesy of Stephen Scott.

Calling Bulldog Drummond (1951). Alfred Junge 'production design'.
Courtesy of Stephen Scott.

The staff of MGM British Studios in 1952. Studio Manager, George Catt (centre), and
new employee, Kelvin Pike (behind Catt). Courtesy of Kelvin Pike.

Ivanhoe (1952). Alfred Junge 'production design' of Torquilstone Castle.
Courtesy of Stephen Scott.

Ivanhoe (1952). Alfred Junge 'production design'. Courtesy of Stephen Scott.

Ivanhoe (1952). Robert Taylor and Elizabeth Taylor enjoying a cup of tea between takes at MGM British Studios. Courtesy of Stephen Scott.

Ivanhoe (1952). Alfred Junge 'production design'. Courtesy of Stephen Scott.

The *Ivanhoe* (1952) castle, which still stood on the back-lot at MGM British in the late 1950s. Courtesy of Stephen Scott.

Mogambo (1953). Cast and crew production still. John Ford (fourth from right, front row), Grace Kelly (second from right, second row), Clark Gable (third from right, second row), Ava Gardner (fourth from right, second row), Kelvin Pike (beneath camera, left of Ava Gardner), Donald Sinden (behind Grace Kelly), George Catt (third row, second left of camera). Courtesy of Kelvin Pike.

Never Let Me Go (1953). Alfred Junge 'production design'. Courtesy of Stephen Scott.

Never Let Me Go (1953). Alfred Junge 'production design'. Courtesy of Stephen Scott.

Knights Of The Round Table (1953). The crew on location, including cinematographer, Freddie Young (holding tripod) and Nicolas Roeg (standing, far left). Courtesy of Nicolas Roeg.

Beau Brummell (1954). Elliot Scott design for 'production designer' Alfred Junge. Note the figure of Stewart Granger on the right. Courtesy of Stephen Scott.

Seagulls Over Sorrento (1954). Gene Kelly relaxing on the set at MGM British.
Courtesy of Kelvin Pike.

Seagulls Over Sorrento (1954). Cast and crew production still. Gene Kelly (Sixth from right, second row), Roy Boulting (seventh from right, second row), John Boulting (eighth from right, second row), Bernard Lee (fourth from right, second row), George Catt (fifth from right, second row), Elaine Schreyeck (fifth from right, front row), Paul Wilson (seventh from right, front row), Kelvin Pike (behind George Catt). Courtesy of Kelvin Pike.

Betrayed (1954). Lana Turner and co-star Niall MacGinnis filming a scene on location. Courtesy of Kelvin Pike.

That Lady (1955). Olivia de Havilland greets Peter II of Yugoslavia (King of Yugoslavia 1934-45) on set at MGM British. John Harris (camera operator) sits behind the camera. Courtesy of John Harris.

The Dark Avenger (1955). Errol Flynn relaxes between takes on the back-lot at MGM British. Courtesy of Rory Flynn.

Bhowani Junction (1956). Ava Garner and Francis Matthews being directed by George Cukor. Courtesy of Francis Matthews.

Bhowani Junction(1956). Ava Gardner and Francis Matthews relaxing between takes at MGM British. Courtesy of Francis Matthews.

Invitation To The Dance (1956). Rare production still with Gene Kelly (centre).
Courtesy of Peter Mullins.

Photo of Gene Kelly
taken in the 'still
department' at MGM
British for the film
Invitation To The Dance
(1956). Courtesy of
Kelvin Pike.

Invitation To The Dance (1956). Rare production still of Gene Kelly on set at MGM British Studios. Courtesy of Peter Mullins.

Invitation To The Dance (1956). Rare behind the scenes production still with Gene Kelly (left) and Kelvin Pike (clapper/loader) leaving the set. Courtesy of Kelvin Pike.

Anastasia (1956). Yul Brynner relaxes on set at MGM British Studios. Courtesy of Gerry Fisher.

The Little Hut (1957). Elliot Scott's set constructed on a sound stage at MGM British.
Courtesy of Stephen Scott.

Corridors Of Blood (1958). MGM Studio publicity still of
Boris Karloff. Courtesy of Richard Gordon.

Corridors Of Blood (1958). Boris Karloff and Francis Matthews publicity still taken at MGM British. Courtesy of Richard Gordon.

Tom Thumb (1958). Russ Tamblyn poses on an enlarged set designed by 'production designer' Elliot Scott. Courtesy of Stephen Scott.

Tom Thumb (1958). Terry-Thomas and Peter Sellers take a break between filming at MGM British. Courtesy of Stephen Scott.

Woodland set designed and constructed by Elliot Scott for *Tom Thumb* (1958).
Note MGM on the lamp. Courtesy of Stephen Scott.

Tom Thumb (1958). Production still of Peter Sellers and Terry-Thomas. Note Elliot Scott's marvellous woodland set constructed on a sound stage at MGM British. Courtesy of Stephen Scott.

Tom Thumb (1958). Preparing to shoot a scene on the woodland set constructed on a sound stage at MGM British by 'production designer' Elliot Scott. Note a member of the MGM staff wearing a coat with the logo MGM. Courtesy of Stephen Scott.

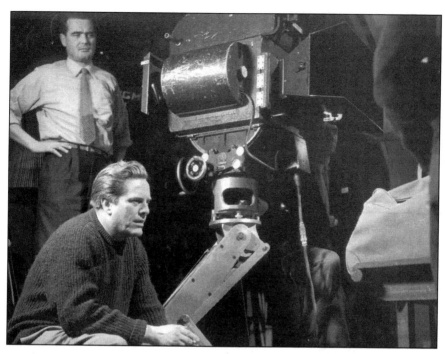

Nowhere To Go (1958). Seth Holt (sitting) preparing to direct a scene. Herbert Smith (focus puller) is behind camera. Courtesy of Herbert Smith.

Ice Cold In Alex (1958). Sylvia Syms and Harry Andrews filming a scene on location. Courtesy of Kelvin Pike.

The Angry Hills (1958). Rare behind the scenes still. Geoff Glover (left) is holding clapper. Courtesy of Geoff Glover.

Look Back In Anger (1959). Mary Ure prepares to shoot a scene on location. Denys Coop (camera operator) sits behind camera and Kelvin Pike (focus puller) helps out. Courtesy of Kelvin Pike.

Look Back In Anger (1959). Mary Ure relaxes on the back-lot at ABPC Studios, Borehamwood. Kelvin Pike (focus puller) stands to the right of the camera, arms folded. Courtesy of Kelvin Pike.

Look Back In Anger (1959). Richard Burton and Gary Raymond chat between takes at ABPC Studios, Borehamwood. June Randall (continuity) can be seen in the far left corner, holding script. Courtesy of Kelvin Pike.

Libel (1959). MGM Studio publicity photograph of Olivia de Havilland and Dirk Bogarde.
Courtesy of Olivia de Havilland.

The Wreck Of The Mary Deare (1959). MGM Studio publicity photograph of Virginia McKenna. Courtesy of Virginia McKenna.

The Scapegoat (1959). Robert Hamer (right) prepares to direct a scene at MGM British. Herbert Smith (camera operator) is looking through camera. Courtesy of Herbert Smith.

The Scapegoat (1959). Bette Davis and Alec Guinness on a magnificent set designed and constructed by 'production designer' Elliot Scott. Courtesy of Stephen Scott.

The Scapegoat (1959). Production still of Bette Davis and Alec Guinness.
Courtesy of Herbert Smith.

MGM British 'make-up department' in the late 1950s. Courtesy of Stephen Scott.

MGM British 'production designer' Elliot Scott. Courtesy of Stephen Scott.

A 'star' dressing room at MGM British Studios in the late 1950s.
Courtesy of Stephen Scott.

The MGM British restaurant in the late 1950s. Courtesy of Stephen Scott.

The MGM British administration building (by night) in the late 1950s.
Courtesy of Stephen Scott.

An aerial photograph of the MGM British Studios sound stages in the late 1950s.
Courtesy of Stephen Scott.

Danziger Brothers

Prolific independent producers of over 140 second features and six television series, Edward J. Danziger (1909-1999) and Harry Lee Danziger (1913-2005), were perhaps the most industrious British low-budget production outfit of the 1950s and early 1960s.

Throughout this period, their second features and television series seemed to be on screens everywhere, their pervasive presence forming part of virtually every British filmgoer's and television viewer's experience during those years.

Before arriving in Britain in 1952, American Jewish brothers, Harry and Edward, had operated a sound studio in New York that specialised in the dubbing of foreign films for US release.

In 1949, they had turned to feature production and produced the race hate drama, *Jigsaw*, starring Franchot Tone and Jean Wallace. They followed this with *So Young So Bad* (1950), a study of female juvenile delinquency. These early movies also included a color parody of the Arabian Nights, *Babes of Bagdad* (1952), filmed on location in Spain and starring Paulette Goddard.

After arriving in England in 1952, they rented space at London's Riverside Studios to produce 13 episodes of a crime anthology series called *Calling Scotland Yard* (employing recently blacklisted Hollywood director, Joseph Losey, as script editor).

While this series was not shown on British television, two compilation features were released to UK cinemas (using footage from the series) as *Gilbert Harding Speaking of Murder* (1953) and *A Tale of Three Women* (1954), both directed by Paul Dickson and introduced and linked by broadcaster Gilbert Harding.

Calling Scotland Yard was also released by Paramount in 1954-1955 to cinemas in both the UK and US as a series of supporting features, lasting 27 minutes each. The series itself was eventually transmitted in the US in 1956 by NBC television under the title *Adventure Theatre*.

101

For the production of their early cinema films and the anthology television series *The Vise* (filmed 1954-55, and shown via various ITV companies from 1955), the Danzigers began leasing space at MGM British Studios.

Here, they filmed what is now regarded as one of their cult movies, *Devil Girl From Mars* (1954) featuring Adrienne Corri and Hazel Court.

Scriptwriter Ken Taylor worked for the Danzigers at MGM British. He recalled, "I first met the Danziger brothers, Harry and Edward, at their flat in 1955. The invitation resulted from an advertisement in *The Daily Telegraph* asking anyone interested in writing for television to reply to a box number with the sole requirement of having work previously published or performed.

"As someone who had a handful of radio plays broadcast by the BBC, the first when I was eighteen, I felt qualified to respond, which led to a screening in a Soho preview theatre where one of the brothers—I believe it was Harry—introduced a half-hour TV drama under the series title *The Vise (or Vice)* with the strap line, 'This is the story of a man who was caught in a vice—a dilemma of his own making.'

"At the end of the screening, I was asked to submit a sample script of a TV film, which might fulfil the series requirements, which I duly did, and thus now found myself in a comfortable chair in the brothers Park Lane apartment considering what appeared to be a very agreeable offer.

"The invitation was to begin work on a trial basis writing similar scripts for the series for an initial payment of £10 a week—a sum which was then regarded as a decent living wage—on the understanding that a fee would be negotiated for any work judged suitable for production. It was explained that writers in America normally produced about one play a week on this basis, though the brothers accepted that the output here might be substantially lower.

"At the time, I was unemployed, having recently abandoned several years of exhausting stage management in weekly rep, so this was clearly an offer I could not refuse.

"All went well for a month or so with occasional reassuring calls from Harry to advise me that I was doing well, so well, in fact, that very soon I found myself in one of the stages at MGM British Studios, Borehamwood, watching a starry cast filming a scene from the first of my scripts to be produced.

"It struck me that the time had come to talk to the brothers about ne-gotiating a fee for my screenplay, to which Eddie made an immediate response. He explained that under English law the copyright in everything I wrote as a salaried employee belonged to my employers with the sole exception of my private correspondence. No payment would therefore be made for anything I had written under my existing contract. I replied that this was certainly not my understanding of the terms under which I had been engaged, to which Eddie responded that I was clearly misinformed and, having accepted a weekly salary, was demonstrably a paid employee. I then advised him that I believed I had been deceived and was immediately terminating my engagement.

"This response was obviously reckless. Eddie was clearly much better informed than I was on English copyright law, and I was again unemployed with a young wife expecting our first child, who now began to receive calls from Eddie warning of the dangers of the stance I had taken up.

"I decided I needed to join a union—the only one available being what was then called the Screenwriters Guild. Having paid my first sub, I was advised to consult the Guild's solicitor by the name of Arnold (later the celebrated Lord) Goodman. At our meeting in his rather Dickensian office off Fleet Street, Mr. Goodman was understandably unoptimistic about my stance with the Danzigers, but agreed to have a go—undaunted by the calls his office now began to receive using language which caused him to introduce monitors to protect his female staff.

"Several months passed before Mr. Goodman rang to advise me that he had no progress to report. Eddie had refused even to come to the office to discuss the issue.

"At this point, I suddenly remembered that on one of my visits to the studio their Production Manager had mentioned to me his regular visits to the American Embassy in order to sign copyright releases for the American networks. Mr. Goodman was immediately enthused. 'That's it!' he cried. 'We'll advise Mr. Danziger we're writing to all the networks warning we shall sue if any of your material is screened without our consent. We won't do it, of course, but the threat might just do the trick.'

"As indeed it did. Within a few days, Eddie had agreed to come and meet me at Mr. Goodman's office. The encounter was decidedly unpleasant, but Eddie finally agreed to make a payment in respect of the copyright in all my scripts in his possession. I think this was for sixty guineas—or about £20 for every script I had written—a small sum even then but a huge moral victory for me.

"Eddie's parting shot was to advise Mr. Goodman he would ensure that I never wrote for anyone in the industry again—an objective he failed to achieve since I went on to win awards from the Writers Guild, the Guild of Television Producers and Directors, the Royal Television Society, and, in 1984, receiving an Emmy nomination for my screenplay for *The Jewel In The Crown.*

"I never saw the Danzigers again, but it's only fair to add that in 1955, Harry and Eddie were smart enough to realise that there was a huge fund of creative and technical television talent in Britain, which the BBC had totally failed to exploit. This prepared the ground for the massive explosion of original television drama, which the coming of commercial television now released, reminding me that the first time I ever saw the caption 'commercial break' was in a Soho viewing theatre at the invitation of the Danziger Brothers."

Brian Clemens, future producer of *The Avengers* at ABPC Studios, would become the Danzigers regular screen-writer from the mid 1950s. "It was a wonderful training ground for me as a writer and I always delivered—in fourteen days. That's what they allowed me for a 60- to 80-minute 'B' movie, of which I wrote over thirty, plus innumerable episodes for their many television series (they gave me a week to write those).

"They would find sets standing at MGM British from more expensive productions that had just vacated, and come to me and say: we want a thriller—and it must take place in a French chateau—The Old Bailey—a coal mine—and a submarine!

"I was under contract to them as an in house writer for about five years, for which they paid me a weekly wage (quite generous it seemed to me then).

"My actual in studio experience was limited because if they ever caught me there, they would demand, 'Why aren't you at home writing?!'

"If they sound horrendous, they weren't; just parsimonious, but, like so many Jews, sometimes very generous. I recall they paid the deposit on my first home in Richmond, Surrey, the first place I ever owned.

"They were not the mafia, as some first suspected. But they were close. They lived in a plush apartment in Park Lane—a very prestige's address—and I recall there my first encounter with Eddie, who had several cans of film and said, 'Come with me. Help carry them down. I'm taking them to the studios.' I'd seen a Rolls parked by the curb, and expected to get into that. Instead, Eddie led me to the bus stop! Very canny with money, they were."

In 1955, they made their final second feature at the MGM British facility. It starred Christopher Lee, appearing in his first major part, playing the title role in *Alias John Preston*. "I played a mad businessman who goes off his chump, beginning at the top of a table and finishing over a tombstone. It's packed with unspeakable dialogue, and when I think what a terrible actor I was in those days, it's a wonder I've ever lasted."

On August 25, 1955, the *Borhamwood & Elstree Post* reported:
"ELSTREE TO HAVE OWN FILM STUDIOS SOON
Danziger Bros Move In"
Elstree village was to have its own film studios, as work was being carried out to convert four small buildings. The studios when ready would also mean work for about fifty local technicians.

The buildings were erected originally by the Ministry of Supply in 1941 and were used by an aircraft firm as engine test beds. For some years after the war, they were lying derelict and overgrown with grass.

Danziger Brothers had decided that when they could not continue to rent space at other studios to make their films, that they would take over the buildings in Elstree as their headquarters. However, when the company moved in, the buildings and surrounding land looked like a bomb site. The tough job of straightening things out was handed over to the company's present Art Director, Erik Blakemore.

Erik designed the buildings and land they stood on to look like modern Hollywood studios. Eventually, after several months of work, the seven and a half-acre site, which would at one time employ some 200 craftsmen and technicians, would open its gates in 1956 as the New Elstree Studios.

The first Danziger movie to be filmed at the facility would be a color film shot in Cinemascope, *Satellite in the Sky* (1956), starring Kieron Moore, Donald Wolfit, and Bryan Forbes.

Brian Clemens remembered the movie for a certain reason. "It was a big film for the Danzigers, and cost them quite a lot of money, but the money should have been spent on the special effects. Sadly, in several shots of the satellite, you can see the wire quite clearly, and the ship bobbles up and down."

Bryan Forbes, who played Jimmy Wheeler in the production, gave his thoughts of the Danzigers. "I only worked once as an actor at the Danziger Studios, which I remember as a shambles, built and operated on the cheap, like everything the brothers touched. They represented to me all that was bad about our industry—people who moved in and exploited all who worked for them and had no real interest in films – films were just another commodity."

To make up for the cost of the studio renovation, the Danzigers hired New Elstree out to other film companies. *The Traitor* (1957) made by E. J. Fancey Productions, and featuring Donald Wolfit and Christopher Lee was one of the films shot at the site.

Christopher Lee recalls New Elstree Studios. "There was water pouring down the cement walls and the duckboards between the stages, traversing a sea of mud. There was an absence of windows in the dressing rooms, and the lights didn't work. That was just a few of the Spartan delights."

Hammer Films also rented the facility to make *Quatermass 2* (1957) starring Brian Donlevy and directed by Val Guest.

Actress, Vera Day, who played Sheila in the latter, recalled, "The Danziger Brothers were famous for their 'B' movies, and you knew that when you was asked to work for them, the money would not be great, but at least you were working and happy to do so!"

From 1957, the Danzigers began a relentless assembly line of television episodes, featuring Donald Gray's one-armed private investigator, Mark Saber, a character that had previously appeared in *The Vise*, and would continue his exploits in the very popular series, *Saber of London*.

Donald Gray, (who had lost his arm during the Second World War), would play Saber in 156 episodes for the Danzigers, finally bowing out in 1961.

June Randall was continuity on many episodes of the series. "We did a television episode every three days. They were done fast and furious. But it was fun. However, you were expected to work very hard. I did a lot of television at this time though. I was known as the 'television Queen'.

"The Danzigers were very nice boys, and they were always very pleasant to me, and they did make some quality films in a very short time.

"I remember that if we were running over schedule, the Danzigers would rip pages out of the script, and say, 'We're on schedule now'. And amazingly the plot still seemed to make sense. It was a very brave thing to do, though."

Peter Newbrook took over from James Wilson as director of photography on a few episodes. He recalled, "One of the most hair-raising experiences was riding with Donald Gray in his car, as not only was he a seriously dangerous driver, but he also only had one arm."

Renee Glynne also remembered Donald Gray. "I did a few episodes as 'continuity' and remember quite vividly that Donald Gray used to put his false arm on the table when we had lunch.

"The studio was a bit like a mini purpose-built factory, and the Danzigers were more like businessmen than film producers. They ran the studio very frugally."

Prolific character actor, Michael Ripper, appeared in four episodes of *Saber Of London*, and remembered an unforgettable incident. "We were filming in the studios, and the set we were on caught fire and was completely destroyed. The next day, though, it had been rebuilt again, looking nothing like the previous set we had filmed on, but we just carried on were we had left off."

Geoffrey Bayldon also appeared in the series. "I knew that the Danzigers were people for getting actors work. You had to be disgustingly bad though, not to work for the Danzigers. They had a very simple studio, and it all seemed a bit casual. So whether you could actually call them film producers is another thing.

It was always enjoyable working at their studios. The productions themselves couldn't be of the best quality, because they didn't spend the time on it. They did have good directors, though. Floundering a little, but then again so were we. There was much flounder."

The studio had no sooner opened when the following report appeared in the *Borehamwood & Elstree Post* on April 11, 1957:

"FILM MEN STRIKE WHEN STUDIO

Jumps The Gun"

Eight film workers went on strike at the studio when told they would be given a weeks notice because of a possible standstill if actors refused to work.

The British Actors' Equity Association had advised members not to accept any new film parts unless there was a clause in their contracts allowing for a ten-hour day, including meal breaks and make-up time. The contract at that time was a twelve-hour day.

Danzigers foresaw possible trouble and, in an attempt to cut their losses, gave a warning to their technicians of notice to become effective on April 12.

Filming of *Teddy Boy* was due to be completed on April 19, but was interrupted by a technicians walk-out. A new film, *The Betrayal,* should have started the following Monday, but the strike continued. The dispute was eventually settled shortly after, and filming resumed.

Apart from their large turnout of television series, they also produced many second features on the quick.

One 'B' picture made at New Elstree in 1957 was one of those quicker than quickies, as character actor Norman Mitchell remembered. "I made a film for the Danzigers called *Three Sundays To Live*. The star was Kieron Moore. It was a serious film, and during one particularly serious scene, someone in the studio farted rather loudly during a take—so loud, in fact, I have no doubt that it could be heard on the soundtrack. So, I thought I'd mention it to the director, Ernest Morris, who responded by saying that they couldn't do re-takes because of someone farting. They didn't have money, nor time. So we carried on. Meaning that somewhere in the history of British celluloid there is this film, *Three Sundays To Live*, with someone enjoying a good old fart during a serious scene."

Joining the repertory of Danziger actors in 1958 was Francis Matthews. His first appearance for the Brothers was in their movie, *A Woman Possessed*. "It is high time I confessed to my Danziger period. Harry and Eddie were entrepreneurial American brothers who are really the subject for a book all to themselves.

"The New Elstree Studios was Hollywood in microcosm, and galaxies of British actors, both well-known and unknown, passed through their gates.

"Their output was mainly black and white 'B' pictures and 'programme fillers' and a few filmed television series.

"They had a unique approach to casting their leads, based on cleverly catching an actor off guard, preferably unemployed and, therefore, easily swayed.

"For them, the casting director, or for that matter the agent, did not exist, and a direct telephone offer would come from Harry D. himself, usually on a Friday morning.

"Hi Francis! How're you doin?"

"I'm fine, Harry."

"Great. Listen, you busy right now?"

"Well, er, not right now."

"OK! I have a script for you."

"Ah, right. Er, is it—?"

"I'll have it biked over right away."

"Well… it's just that… ."

"Great part. You'll love it."

"But when—?"

"Shoot Monday. Two weeks. Lead billing. Usual money."

"Who else is on board?"

"I'm on that right now. Read it. Give me a call tonight."

"But Harry, I may be—"

"It's perfect for you. Talk to you later."

"That was how it was done. 'Usual money' meant £15 a day, and 'two weeks' was ten working days for a seventy-minute picture.

"The first time I was disarmed into accepting Harry's less than tempting offer was to play Margaretta Scott's son in *A Woman Possessed*, a turgid, sub-Bette Davis piece about an over-mothered young man, and on my first morning I was quickly initiated into the methods and economic imperatives that informed a Danziger movie.

"Our director, Max Varnel, came into make-up to tell us that last week's shoot had one brief scene to complete before we could start on ours. This, he told me, was unprecedented and Harry and Eddie were not best pleased. It had cost them £30 to recall their two 'stars' for one brief shot.

"Margaretta and I, who had just met for the first time, worked on our lines, and then went down to the set to stand by.

"Godfrey Grayson, another of their regular directors, was overseeing a conversation at a restaurant table. One take was all he was allowed before calling 'Cut', followed very rapidly by, 'That's a wrap everybody. Thank you all.'

"After a flurry of farewells and 'air-kisses', Max jumped in with, 'Right, leave everything where it is. Margaretta and Francis just sit down at the table where the others were,' then to the camera operator (the soon to be very famous Nicolas Roeg) 'No stand-ins, Nick. Let's go.'

"We filmed that opening master-shot in one take, seated in the chairs that had just been vacated, on the same set, with the same lighting set-ups, the same plates, cutlery, napkins, and table decoration (all supplied from the Mayfair Hotel, London, which the Danzigers owned at that time), and, most wonderful of all, the same old actor playing the waiter again. So Harry and Eddie recouped 10 of those lost pounds!

"The one thing that did make our scene different was that we were served with two dozen fresh oysters, from the Mayfair, of course. So, wastage was not allowed but luxury was.

"The studios were beautifully equipped, the dressing rooms starry, and the time honored, ego-boosting elements in evidence. Personal stand-in, name on your chair, top-table in their restaurant, and food to die for, to say nothing of the coffee breaks."

Nicolas Roeg worked on several of the Danziger films as camera operator, including *Great Van Robbery* (1959) and *The Child And The Killer* (1959). He recently shared his memories of Harry and Edward Danziger.

"The Danzigers gave a lot of work to up and coming people. They gave some their break in the industry. From a business point of view, though, they did only pay half the salary of other studios. They did however put a lot of energy into their productions, and were always enjoyable to work for."

Geoff Glover, also worked briefly in the camera department. "I did a couple of 'Bs' for the Danzigers. Can't remember what they were. I also went uncredited. I don't think I was ever on their payroll, though. But knowing the Danzigers, you probably ended up paying them."

In 1959, Brian Taylor, was employed at the studio as production supervisor, alongside new employees Geoffrey Helman (first assistant director) and Phyllis Townshend (continuity).

Brian Taylor remembers, "I was put in charge of a factory for mass producing movies, with the creative talents of a regiment of writers, actors, designers, and technical staff at my disposal to make it happen.

"One great advantage of working with the Danzigers was their simple philosophy about filmmaking. Keep to the delivery dates and the artistic control is entirely yours to balance any overspend on one project with an underspend on another. Their concept of a continuous flow of movies, geared to an agreed script, copied to the Hollywood formula. It was dependent on 'up front' cash, to commission writers well ahead of the time their stories were in front of the cameras.

"In Britain, this was where the bottlenecks had constantly occurred and why films at the major studios of Pinewood, Shepperton, and MGM British seemed destined to be on a stop-start basis. It was essential to iron out the snags before the cameras rolled, instead of later in the middle of production with all the complications of extra expenditure. This was the theory and the aim.

"Although the New Elstree Studios product did not pretend to win any Oscars, neither did we owe a penny to the banks nor fail to pay its staff. The discipline the Danzigers brought meant survival in a jungle fraught with pseudo-artistic consciences and bloated personal egos. Should you value to future of the industry, then beware the false Messiahs, who proclaim their own integrity above all else. Limiting factors of budgets and schedules require as great a creative principle to fulfil, as the licensing of artistic freedom. This must apply to everything, whether it be the actor employed to play the leading role, or the cameraman to frame the picture. Professionalism is the sole criterion and the prime requirement to a proper and fair reward.

"Too often during my working life in film, television, and theatre I have witnessed the irresponsibility that tries to recruit artistic integrity as an ally, grounds that are generally nothing more than a petty whim.

"On one occasion during a overnight shoot not connected to the Danzigers, I bore witness to a costly production fiasco. Overtime payments and extra facilities were creating chaos with the budget, and then the internationally famous film director demanded that red roses, part of the background decoration on the set, be changed to yellow ones. 'I can't possibly work with that color rose. They must be replaced before I shoot a frame,' he demanded. Some unfortunate assistant was then despatched to Covent Garden flower market to rectify the remiss, although it meant a three-hour delay. It was scarcely important in the black and white movie he was making and barely warrants a mention except as an attitude of mind I totally condemn.

"Yet, however much the critics carped about the Danzigers, some calling their films rubbish, the movies they made were only ever intended as entertainment. That some were lowly in content does not detract from the achievement. For nearly a decade, they provided uninterrupted production runs and continuous employment.

"Many of the stars of today started their careers in a one-line assignment at New Elstree Studios. On one occasion, we nursed a fledgling eleven-year-old Dennis Waterman through his first major part in *Night Train To Inverness* (1960) with Norman Wooland. In that same production, the late Anton Rodgers made one of his first screen appearances.

"In a week, we might have a turn over of 250 artistes, 1,000 crowd personnel, and a platoon of stunt men, doubles, stand-ins, and back-ups."

On April 9, 1959, the *Borehamwood & Elstree Post* reported:

"STAR FALLS FROM MOTOR-CYCLE"

Actor Richard Wyler, who was appearing in the Danziger's *High Jump*, spent a spell in a hospital with a damaged leg. He had tumbled off his motorcycle outside the studios gates.

Wyler would be the star of the Danzigers next television series, *Man From Interpol*, playing a special agent of Scotland Yard's Interpol Division. It gave cause for some to comment, "The uneasy attempt to graft a youthful hero (Wyler's boyish projection) on to a rugged crime-buster framework, usually associated with more mature leading characters—Charles Korvin's Inspector Duval in the 1959-1960 series *Interpol Calling*, for instance—gave *Man From Interpol* little more than an air of tired hysteria."

The series, which ran for 39 episodes, and was created by Brian Clemens. "They wanted me to write the pilot episode for them, to be constructed so that it could be shown at 90 minutes and also as 60 minutes (with 30 minutes cut out), depending on which market they were selling to! The cut had to be just one big chunk. Difficult? I did it, though. But it taught me a lot. But best of all, and I still quote this now (when facing writers' block) is their maxim, 'Writing isn't art; all it needs is arse to chair and pen to paper.' The Danzigers certainly taught me never to be fazed by a writing problem, and in doing so set me impossible tasks. This has certainly stood me in good stead down the years."

Francis Matthews appeared in two episodes of *Man From Interpol*, and remembered its star, Richard Wyler. "He used to drive a great pink Cadillac to the studios. 'Everyone gets out of my way, when they see me in this car!' he used to joke."

Brian Cobby, who was appearing at New Elstree in small supporting roles, also remembered the star of the series. "He'd appeared in a few Hollywood films, like *Little Women* (1949) with Elizabeth Taylor, under his real name of Richard Stapley. Unbelievably, he was actually a descendant of Sir Richard Stapley, noted in history for signing the death warrant of King Charles I.

"All I remember about Wyler, though, was he couldn't remember his lines, as they were doing two episodes at the same time on different sets, so he had to read his lines on cards over my shoulder."

Phyllis Townshend, who had joined Danzigers with Brian Taylor in 1959 was continuity on *Man From Interpol*. "I enjoyed working at New Elstree very much, although there was a very quick turnaround from picture to picture. We were lucky, though, to have an excellent crew and reliable actors. They gave a lot of work to many technicians, and first assistant Geoffrey Helman really kept it all running along nicely.

"The studio itself was very bare. It was custom-made. Certainly nothing elaborate."

Geoffrey Helman had also recently joined the studio as first assistant director. He recalled, "It was really like a conveyor belt there, as far as producing movies was concerned, and we did sometimes get behind schedule. There was also a joke thing about the studio, which the whole industry laughed at, and that was that Harry and Eddie would sometimes tell us to tear a page or two out of the script, and we did do that from time to time.

"The Danzigers also didn't like actors to wear bow ties because they would be known as 'God Damn Fags' in America. And American channels would not want to show any footage or material with actors who were 'God Damn Fags'.

"Harry and Eddie themselves, though, were very low-profile, and when they came on the set there wasn't a big fuss and they didn't demand a big fuss. They never seemed to complain, and they were very easy to work for."

Though the film output at New Elstree was mostly forgettable, several of the films have stood the test of time. *An Honourable Murder* (1960), a modern-dress adaptation of Shakespeare's *Julius Caesar* is certainly an interesting 'B' film of its time. Norman Wooland played Brutus, with Margaretta Scott as Caesar, and Douglas Wilmer as Cassius.

However, Wilmer did not have a high opinion of the Danzigers or their movie. "The Danzigers were a byword at the time for extreme meanness, and of the 'pile em high' and 'sell em cheap' variety, and the film I did for them was a very poor re-hash of *Julius Caesar* in plot.

"They are certainly not high on my list of favourite producers, and the studios, in my mind, were dingy and depressing."

Arguably the best second feature to come out of the studios was an adaptation by Brian Clemens of Edgar Allan Poe's classic horror story, *The Tell-Tale Heart* (1960). It starred Laurence Payne, Adrienne Corri, and Danziger regular Dermot Walsh.

Brian Clemens recalled, "The cheapness and creakiness of the movie made it look like a genuine old horror film. I think it's great."

Brian Taylor shared the same opinion. "Irresistibly, we took a stroll down the Rue Morgue, into the rebuilt streets of nineteenth century Paris, with horrific special effects and flickering gaslights, which brought a chilling quality to our version of the Poe classic.

"It was a strong piece of cinema entertainment, and we even created a pre-film trailer, a throwback to the days when audiences wallowed in nervous thrills from their double seats in the dark of the auditorium. It went something like, 'Beware, when you hear this sound... should you be weak of heart, close your eyes and don't open them again until it stops.' And as the severed heart of Poe's story pulsed its bloody way across the floor of the house in Rue Morgue, the music bleated out a howling screech, of such a piteous nature, only the strongest could refrain from screwing their eyes up tight and clinging to their neighbour... or so we liked to think."

The voiceover on the pre-film trailer was recorded by Brian Cobby. He remarked, "I think it was the best thing about the film."

The star of the film Laurence Payne, who also appeared in another noted Danziger 'B' picture, *The Court Martial Of Major Keller,* (1961), shared his memories of working at New Elstree just prior to his passing in 2009. "I loathed making films. I found the process terribly boring. But with Danzigers it was different, as you were never given time to get bored, as everything was done in one take, certainly no more than two. There was no sitting around, so to speak. It was all done on the rush, and hopefully it didn't show. So, working for them wasn't so bad. You basically turned up, played your part, and went home, all in a few days, and at that you were playing the main part."

Agatha Christie got the makeover in 1960, when her thriller, *The Spider's Web,* was adapted to be produced in color by Harry and Edward.

Brian Taylor recalls the filming. "Agatha Christie spent a lot of time at the studios, helping us to shoot it. A sweet old lady she was, and quite intriguing. Sadly, the film made no great shakes."

Vincent Ball, who had appeared in several B features during the 1950s, played the leading role in both *Feet of Clay* (1960) and *The Middle Course* (1961) for the Danzigers. "Does anyone remember the Danziger Brothers these days? They used to do four-minute takes, which was very demanding on the actors. Half the time you didn't have time to learn the dialogue. To be honest, doing a Danziger was really the end of the line, but I had a wife and a kid and a mortgage to pay. You also got your money in cash, which was most unusual.

"I remember finishing a film for Montgomery Tully at New Elstree, and he pulled out another script, saying, 'Now, what about this one?' And before I'd even had chance to read it, some new wallpaper was slapped up on the set and the furniture was moved around a bit, and we started off again.

"At least they knew they had assured outlet for their films, because it was the time when cinemas showed double features."

The Cheaters, an insurance claims investigator drama series that ran from 1960-1962 starred John Ireland and Robert Ayres. It was later written, 'In missing a perfect opportunity to exploit the tough-cynical characteristics of the leading player (Ireland), the 39 episodes moved with a painful lethargy towards their predictable conclusions, with the most notable feature of this largely static series being John Ireland's carefully sustained somnambulistic performance.'

John Ireland was a Canadian, raised in New York, who appeared in many B movie Westerns, and occasionally in supporting roles in major pictures, including *Spartacus* (1960), *55 Day's At Peking* (1963), and *The Fall Of The Roman Empire* (1964).

Peter Mullins was production designer on *The Cheaters*. "In one episode, we had to have an American Embassy set. So, you immediately think of very grand tables and chairs. So, I sent a buyer down to London to hire furniture, and Harry Danziger found out about this, and said to me, 'You don't need to spend money hiring furniture. We've got plenty of stuff in the studios.' I said, 'Yes, but that stuff isn't suitable. It's supposed to be rich-looking.' But we had to go with it anyway. Anything for cheapness.

"The Danzigers were real kind of wheeler dealer characters, and their studio was a ramshackle kind of place."

Some of the later Danzigers movies had strong stories and themes, which were quite controversial for 1960's cinema.

So Evil, So Young (1961) was set in a British borstal, where there were suicides, bullying, riots, and a strong suggestion of lesbianism. Jill Ireland (future wife of Charles Bronson) played a framed innocent girl, and Ellen Pollock played an evil prison guard.

The script for *The Pursuers* (1961) had particular interest for production supervisor Brian Taylor. "It was inevitable that some projects were more memorable than others and personal experiences, from the past, often represented part of the appeal. One story that came my way, written by Brian Clemens, was almost a repeat of my wartime encounters in Germany. Featuring Cyril Shaps and Francis Matthews, *The Pursuers* showed the conflicts arising between survivors from the concentration camps and the ex-Nazi guards they sought to kill in revenge. This was strong stuff in those days, and I still feel was one of our better, if not best, films."

During the early part of the 1960s, Francis Matthews appeared in four movies for Harry and Edward Danziger. He recalls a funny incident. "They used to steal shots in the street, and not tell the public or the police. Well, on one of the films I was shooting one of these stealing shots. It was actually of me walking down the street, and they were filming from the top of a building. My cue was a waved handkerchief. But as I strolled along on take, who should be walking towards me but my dear friend, William Franklyn, totally unaware that I was filming. So, he smothered me in a huge embrace. I said, 'Bill, I'm filming' to which there was a shout of 'cut' and an 'Oh shit' from Bill."

Matthews also recalls his last visit to the Danziger studios. "The last picture I did for them in 1961 was an oddball comedy about an elderly couple who kill people. It was called *The Lamp on Assassin Mews*. I saw it again recently, and it's really quite a good little film, and quite jolly.

"Mainly, though, their movies were pot boilers, programme fillers, nothing more."

This was though the era of the second feature, as Brian Clemens remembers. "You went to the cinema in those days, and you'd see a major feature, a newsreel, a cartoon, coming attractions, and a second feature. This would also run continuous throughout the day."

In 1960, the Danziger Brothers had a unique film idea. They would set there next film in a naturist camp, and make a color film about nudism. It would be titled *For Members Only* in the UK, and *The Nudist Story* in the US.

Brian Taylor was production supervisor. "We attempted a nudist movie. In fact, it was the first ever British film about naturists, made in the days when the slightest departure from the code of strict purity might saddle you with a picture no one could show.

"But our story of a nudist camp, shot partly in the open air at Five Acres Naturist Club in Bricket Wood, Hertfordshire, was very innocent, with a few songs and a dance.

"It was a bit of a cultural shock for our film crew, though, who had to watch a horde of naked bodies dive into a swimming pool, and if you're the cameraman you have to get on with your job, you can't gaze at the girls.

"Our marvellous first assistant, Geoffrey Helman, also made an unfortunate remark when we were ready to shoot the introductory sequence on a large grassed area (with a group of real naturists) in front of the clubhouse and Tennis court. 'Alright everybody, the cameras turning. Play with your balls.'"

Geoffrey Helman recalls making the film. "There was nothing offensive about the film, and it certainly wasn't a porn picture. Every shot was designed not to embarrass anyone.

"I do also remember that the casting lady and several of the crew decided to join in and strip off."

Bob Jordan had recently joined the Danzigers as a very young clapper/loader, and one of his first jobs was working on *The Nudist Story*. "It was the first time that I'd ever seen naked women *en mass*, and as a young lad, it was quite exciting."

The star of the film was Brian Cobby. "The part was offered to me by the casting lady, and I said, 'No, I couldn't. I'm a serious Shakespearian actor. I'd never work again. Dreadful.' But somehow I was talked into doing it.

"We filmed part of it at a real nudist camp. So, it was a bit of a shock. But very un-sexy. I'd advise any peeping tom to join a nudist camp. Save them peeping through keyholes. They wouldn't bother.

"The crew on the film were mainly all married family men, and I think felt quite embarrassed shooting me nude, as they'd previously all seen me playing a detective with a gun in my hand, and there I was, the next minute, starkers.

"Actually though, my bum was the only thing seen in the finished film, and strangely enough I was recognised in a Turkish Bath in Jermyn Street, London. I was going in to the steam room, when an old man said, 'Now I know where I've seen you. You're in *The Nudist Story*. I've just seen you in the cinema down the round.' He'd recognised me by my bottom.

"Diana Dors, my friend, told me that the Danzigers had once shown her an uncensored version of the film, and congratulated me on my performance.

"I did notice, though, when we were filming that the cameramen put tape across the bottom of the lens, and then another time they would remove it. So there is probably somewhere a version with everything swinging."

The film, even though quite successful on its original UK release, disappeared for many years and became something of a lost movie. It has only recently resurfaced on DVD.

It did, though, continue to haunt its star, Brian Cobby. "When I got the 'speaking clock' in 1984, one Sunday newspapers headline was, 'Who would believe it. The speaking clock once did a nude movie.'

"This article also included a photograph of someone who wasn't me at all. Not such a good body either."

Bob Jordan recently recalled working for the Danzigers. "I was clapper boy for them for two years. They were loyal to their workers, and they didn't interfere an awful lot in the studio. They let you get on with it."

The Danzigers final television series, *Richard the Lionheart,* started filming in 1961. It was, reputedly, their most expensive and ambitious production.

The 39 episodes starred Dermot Walsh as the legendary King Richard I, who took part in the Third Crusade against the Sultan Saladin.

It was an enjoyable swashbuckler, presenting an atmosphere of knightly conduct versus villainous skulduggery, featuring the unforgettable presence of recurring players, Trader Faulkner, a sneering Prince John (amongst others), and Francis de Wolfe as the delightfully monstrous Leopold of Austria.

Brian Taylor produced the series. "We had jousting knights, courtly love, and Infidel Saracens, which made it a much more difficult production to make, as usually our films had modern-day settings, and the actors could wear their own clothes or wardrobe clothes. But with *Richard the Lionheart*, we needed to have costumes made and large sets built in the studio and on the back lot. We also had to use Aldenham reservoir across the road from New Elstree for filming our sea and water sequences. Many horses were used, which can cost time and money, especially if the horse decides to do something on the set during a take. It was a much bigger production than our usual stuff."

The star of the series was Dermot Walsh, a distinguished actor, recognisable on the screen for a grey streak through his hair.

Born in Dublin, Ireland, in 1924, he built up his reputation at The Gate Theatre. His first film role in 1946 was a bit part in *Bedelia*, and after signing a contract with Rank, he was immediately groomed for major roles. In fact, he became a strong fixture for Rank, appearing in plush costume melodramas for Gainsborough Pictures, such as *Hungry Hill* (1946) with Dennis Price, and *Jassy* (1947) with Margaret Lockwood.

In 1949, after parting company with Rank, he would go on to appear as the leading actor in many second features, eventually gaining a reputation as a 'B' movie actor, which he was never able to shake off.

In 1991, Dermot Walsh, shared his memories of the Danziger Brothers. "I did a number of films for them at their studios in Elstree. It paid my bills for a few years, if nothing else. They could film a feature in about eight days. Some were quite good, some were passable, and some were just plain awful. But they had connections with Hollywood, so they managed to get away with it. The best thing I did for them was their series *Richard the Lionheart*. It was a huge success. I did 39 episodes playing Richard. It was filmed over 26 weeks. They'd film a whole episode in about three to four days. I was in every set-up except reverses; and I thoroughly enjoyed it. We could shoot six or seven minutes in a day and on one take. If it went to two takes, with the Danzigers ,there was a real problem.

"I remember one day Ed Danziger coming up to me and saying, 'Dermot, we've got to cut five pages from the script.' I said, 'But those pages are important to the plot.' Ed's response was, 'Well you'd better hope no one notices. We're over budget and out of time.'

"Everything they touched was done on very little money, in very little time, and sadly, on many of the productions, it showed. Not all of the time. Some were actually quite good, like *The Tell-Tale Heart* that I did with Laurence Payne and Adrienne Corri. That one was quite atmospheric.

"One film I did for them was called *Crash Drive* (1959), about a racing driver who has an accident in which his mind is more affected than his body. His mind is affected so that he is unable to walk, and he's convinced that he has lost the use of his legs. In one scene, a doctor is explaining this to the driver's wife and he's supposed to say, 'I have some bad news. Your husband has no legs—I don't mean literally, I mean metaphorically.' Instead of that, though, the actor playing the doctor said, 'Your husband has no legs—I don't mean metaphorically, I mean literally'—and they printed it. Even though at the end of the film I get out of my wheelchair and walk. That proves to you the speed at which we worked."

Trader Faulkner gave excellent support to Walsh's Richard the Lionheart. "My special memory of *Richard the Lionheart* was trying to work out with the make-up man, Gene Beck, how to create facially nine characters, all looking totally different. Gene Beck was a modest little fellow to whom I owed so much. Once I looked in the mirror Gene's work gave me the identity from which to create.

"The Danzigers themselves were nice men, but I hardly knew them. I felt that they were shrewd, but not necessarily mean businessmen. Things were done, and sometimes looked on the cheap, very much makeshift. But as a functional enterprise it seemed to work quite well. The impression I had was of a low-cost outfit ideal for modest television and film production, but I did sometimes feel that corners were cut. The New Elstree Studios were modestly functional and definitely humble in comparison, to say, MGM British, but they seemed to adequately serve their purpose. I worked there for several months, the schedules were tight, but the place had a homely atmosphere.

"During the shoot of *Lionheart*, I was suffering abdominal problems, and while filming a tender, gentle scene, I let out a fart, and it was like a gun going off. Ernest Morris, the director said, 'I don't think there were fire arms in those days Trader.' Everyone laughed, even though I'd disgraced myself.

"The only other thing I remember is that we were an extremely happy unit, thanks to the director of the series, Ernest Morris."

Actress, Sheila Whittingham, appeared throughout the series as Queen Berengaria. "I was working as a waitress at the Mayfair Hotel, which the Danzigers owned, and one day I was serving coffee to this gentleman, and he said, 'You're not a waitress really, are you… .'"

"I said, 'No, I'm an actress. I trained at Bristol Old Vic, but I'm out of work at the moment.'"

"The gentleman happened to be Harry Danziger. I didn't know. I'd never seen him before. So he said, 'They're making a film at Elstree, and I think there might be something in it for you.'"

"Anyway, a couple of days later he came into the hotel and said, 'I've got an appointment for you at the film studio. I'm going down there myself, and I'll give you a lift.'"

"So he drove me to Elstree in his very posh car, and introduced me to a director, Godfrey Grayson, who I don't think was interested in me, but because Harry was palming me off on him, he employed me. It was on a film called *So Evil, So Young* with Jill Ireland. I played Mary, a blind girl, who tragically hangs herself. That was my first film role.

"Funny thing is, I never really saw Harry Danziger again, but I did go on to appear in two other movies for them, which then led to the part in *Richard the Lionheart.*

"So I'm very grateful to Harry Danziger for giving me that opportunity, even though I did at first wonder what he was after when he drove me to the studios and got me the job. But he wasn't after anything; he was just a very nice man.

"Dermot Walsh, the star of *Richard the Lionheart,* was very caring and helpful to me. He gave me quite a lot of advice. He was very experienced, though. I had just appeared in the Danziger film, *Tarnished Heroes* (1961), with him. He said to me one day, 'The only thing that matters, Sheila, is what happens between action and cut. That's all that matters really.' It was a great help, because filming was all new to me. I was actually quite frightened of acting.

"It was certainly a serious problem at Danzigers if we had to do more than one take, which didn't help my nerves. But I do remember us once doing about ten takes on *Lionheart.* An actor who had been employed for the day, who had two lines, kept fluffing them all the time.

"I also remember me and Dermot having fits of laughter during a fight sequence. We were sat on thrones and two actors had to sword fight. They couldn't seem to get it right, and for some reason we got the giggles. Terribly unprofessional really.

"It was also my first time riding a horse, and I'm sure they gave me some really old nag, because it was quiet and couldn't easily be manipulated.

"The lighting cameraman on *Richard the Lionheart* was Jimmy Harvey. He was such a delightful man. I got on very well with him. But that was really thanks to Dermot. He told me to get to know the lighting cameraman, because he said it was important that you get lit properly. So I made a point of getting on the right side of Jimmy."

1960s singer Ian Gregory appeared in the series as Blondel. "The Danzigers were looking for someone who could both sing and act to play Blondel. So I was offered the part.

"I remember us doing this scene on this huge set with Demot sitting on his throne and lots of actors, extras, and I had to rush in and deliver the line, 'I've just found the Kings ring.' Well the whole place collapsed in laughter. We had to do about seven takes. I was very naïve. Only eighteen at the time. I didn't know what they were laughing at.

"Nosher Powell was one of the stuntmen on the series. He did so many dreadful things to me. Jokes. I remember he put a kipper under the bonnet of my car, without my knowing, and for weeks it stank of rancid fish, until I eventually found the fish rotting away. Another time he jacked my car up so that the wheels were just off the ground, so much so that you couldn't notice, and so when I got in it, it wouldn't go anywhere. He played so many tricks on me. But he was great fun. He taught me to fence, to ride, to joust. Such a lovely guy.

"Dermot Walsh was also a supportive man. I remember, though, that he was always chauffeured into the studios. I arrived in my clapped out old banger and he was chauffer driven in a big car. He was though the lynch pin of the series.

"Francis de Wolfe was another of the actors who appeared. I must admit that I was quite scared of him. He was such a big man. Quite intimidating. But actually he was very benign.

"I also recall that we had a real lion in one episode. It was called Bruce, and came from Chipperfield Circus. It was very passive and wandered amongst us with its trainer. However, I'm sure if the trainer had lost control of it we would have been in serious trouble. You can see the headlines now, 'Dermot Walsh (tv's Richard the Lionheart) chomped by man eating lion.' It did actually claw me by mistake, and I do still have the marks.

"The Danzigers themselves were very supportive. There was never any, 'We're going to write you out, because you didn't do what we wanted you to do.' I'm not talking about the casting couch, but in general terms. If you did your job, they were terrific. But if you'd tried to stamp your foot and ask for an extra £5, they'd show you the door.

"The studio they ran was a bit rambling, and if half the set fell down, you'd all join in and glue it back together."

Brian Taylor remembered the star of *Lionheart*. "Dermot Walsh was a very competent actor. He was always very reliable, and you knew when he turned up at the studios in the morning, he knew his part."

Jill Hyem, who would later go on to write many television series, including *Tenko*, played a small acting role in *Lionheart*. "When I was younger, Dermot Walsh, was a pinup of mine. So, it was great to be acting with him, even though the scene was short. But I remember that he was highly professional."

By the time the production of *Richard the Lionheart* had started filming in April 1961, the Danzigers New Elstree Studios was beginning to wind down. The last episode of *Lionheart* was completed in December 1961, as was the last of their second features, the swashbuckler. *The Spanish Sword*; the latter utilising sets, props, and costumes, as well as cast members, from the *Lionheart* series. These included Trader Faulkner and Sheila Whittingham.

Derrick Sherwin, who would later go on to produce episodes of the television series, *Doctor Who*, would appear in supporting roles in both *Lionheart* and *The Spanish Sword*. "The Danzigers was the repertory of 'B' movies and TV filmed series at that time. I was, happily, one of the selected repertory of actors appearing either with or without a moustache, as an English peasant, an Arab named Ali, or whatever.

"I remember one particular incident on *The Spanish Sword* (in which I played a handsome local blacksmith/hero), was when I was appearing with Nigel Green—a particularly robust and sizable character. I was involved in a fight sequence and he was supposed to chin me and send me flying over the battlements. It was a normal stunt, and in those days, I insisted on doing all my own. Nigel, however, didn't 'pull' his punch and did indeed chin me quite forcefully and sent me flying spectacularly over the battlements to land on a pile of cardboard boxes to break the fall. Unfortunately, the budget didn't allow for sufficient cardboard boxes, and the fall knocked the wind out of me, not to mention the saw jaw from Nigel's punch.

"In another incident during the making of *The Spanish Sword*, I had to run and leap upon a giant-sized horse, bearing a length of sturdy rope slung around my shoulders and a 14-pound sledge hammer! I made the leap on the horses broad back, but I swear to this day it is why I could not father any children—all mine are adopted.

"*The Spanish Sword* was quite successful and got me a flood of fan mail, owing, I'm sure, to my oiled bare-chested appearance. One in particular from a gentleman, who offered to take me to the Mr. Universe contest. I'm not sure to this day whether his motives were simply those of a fan or perhaps more suspect!

"There were many more interesting and memorable moments, as those were happy days when work of any sort was welcomed and one had to put up with all sorts of difficulties and humiliating circumstances. I remember them, though, with affection."

Trader Faulkner recalled his co-stars in *The Spanish Sword*. "Nigel Green was a very virile man, but a great actor to work with. The female lead was June Thorburn, who was tragically killed in an air crash in 1967. She was a genuine, gentle, sensitive, beautiful, but now, sadly, a forgotten young actress.

"The star of the picture was Ronald Howard, a very nice man, who sadly lived in the shadow of his father, Leslie Howard."

Brian Clemens also recalled actor, Nigel Green. "He had that wonderful booming voice. So he could tell a dirty joke better than most. He also liked a drop of the sauce."

Directing both *Lionheart* and *The Spanish Sword*, as well as dozens of other Danziger productions was, Ernest Morris.

Trader Faulkner took time to remember him. "Ernie was an old timer. He knew exactly what he was doing. He knew his camera angles. I don't think he was a David Lean, but I'm sure he didn't wish to be. He was a good, working director."

Ian Gregory also remembered working with Morris. "Ernest was a softly spoken man. A gentle man. Not a bully."

While *Richard the Lionheart* was shooting, the Danzigers were already in negotiation over their next series, *Ali Baba and the Forty Thieves*. However, Associated Redifussion (the commissioning company) was uncertain about their commitment to the UK rights. They had just transmitted a musical extravaganza, which had proved an expensive flop, so they were unhappy to sign a contract. Eventually they withdrew, and the *Ali Baba* project got delayed.

There was also another worrying factor for the Danzigers. Color television was taking over fast: they planned to shoot in black and white, but seriously needed to consider color, but the extra costs of color negatives would be high.

At that time, too, distributors were blaming television for the loss of their audiences in the cinemas, and this forced a gap in the production line.

By the end of 1961, shooting ended at Danziger Studios, and New Elstree came to a complete standstill.

Harry and Edward Danziger sold New Elstree Studios in October 1965 to RTZ Metals, for £300,000, as warehouse storage. It was eventually demolished.

Geoffrey Helman recently remembered the Danzigers. "I look back with respect. These two guys put together a studio, a real, purpose built studio and movie company that actually worked. There were never any big egos. Perhaps mine, but that was about it."

Bob Jordan also praised Harry and Eddie. "I learned so much from them and their film studio. Danzigers was my film school."

Jill Hyem said of them. "Danzigers was a marvellous training ground for young actors. Working for them was like working in Rep. Everyone supported each other.

"It would be so easy now though, all these years later, to dismiss their films, their production company, and to laugh at them. But when you think of the time they were made, some are actually pretty good."

The Danziger Brothers never again returned to film and television production, even though during the late 1950s early 1960s, they were the most financially successful independent television production company in the United Kingdom, and their B' features had sold worldwide.

Danziger regular, Francis Matthews, has the final word. "Sadly, Harry and Eddie, and the pictures they made, are now, over fifty years later, a forgotten world of films."

Borehamwood: Britain's Hollywood

During the last few months of the 1950s, well-endowed Jayne Mansfield visited MGM British to star in the Terence Young-directed film, *Too Hot To Handle*.

The shooting of the picture did not come without its problems, as reported in the *Borehamwood & Elstree Post* on October 1, 1959:

"TROUBLE AT LOCAL STUDIOS HALTS JAYNE MANSFIELD FILM

Hold-Ups Over Pay Dispute"

According to the report, everyone from the clapper boy to the director were like a cat on a hot tin roof at MGM, when the Jayne Mansfield movie, *Too Hot To Handle* came to a sizzling halt following a pay dispute.

Supporting actors complained to Equity that their salary checks had been returned from the bank, so Union men demanded immediate payment of some £1,000 in wages.

The rumpus had begun when it was learned that the film's main backer, producer Sydney Box, was seriously ill at his home in Mill Hill.

Director Terence Young said of the disaster at the time, "I want to make it clear that I do not blame our backer. He is a one-man empire, and now he is too sick to do what he was asked to do."

Equity immediately put a ban on any of the actors taking part until the dispute had been cleared. So the £250,000 film came to a standstill.

Mr. Young had to discuss finance with a number of prospective backers, and within a few days, he had managed to raise enough money to complete the movie. However, no one would name the backer, other than saying it was a private individual.

Was it therefore Miss Mansfield? She had no money worries herself, because she was paid under her contract with 20th Century Fox.

When the honey blonde Hollywood actress walked into the studios, wearing a skin tight sweater and trousers to match, she would neither confirm nor deny her involvement. Her only response to reporters was, "Terence Young is a genius. I'm sure everything will be all right."

Ninety minutes later, the cameras had started rolling, with no one any the wiser about who was the backer. Even with the money in place, the film still had problems, and production was stopped seven times, putting the movie ten days behind schedule.

Considered notorious in its day because of its star's risqué see-through clothing and racy musical numbers, *Too Hot To Handle* did not get a release in the United States until 1961 because of its controversy.

The movie, though sadly, marked the beginning of Jayne Mansfield's descent into low-budget productions, as by the late 1950s, her box-office popularity had faded. One reviewer called the film, "A rotten, hilarious British gangster picture."

Mansfield was tragically killed on June 29, 1967, after suffering severe head trauma in a car accident.

On the set of the film *Jazz Boat* made at MGM Borehamwood at the end of the 1950s, Anthony Newley thought he would play a practical joke on his leading lady, Anne Aubrey, but to his dismay, it backfired.

Aubrey, during one scene, had to climb on top of Newley, but during the first take had jumped up and ran off the set complaining to the producer, Cubby Broccoli, that Newley was being disgusting and had a large erection. Newley then had to admit that he had committed a prank and had deliberately put a Coca Cola bottle down his pants, which Aubrey had leant on.

The films cinematographer was Nicolas Roeg. "What happened to *Jazz Boat*? It had some interesting people in it, but seems to have disappeared off the planet."

1960 and the new decade started well for MGM British, beginning with production of *Village Of The Damned* starring George Sanders and Barbara Shelley.

Shelley enjoyed making the film, and found Sanders marvellous to work with, admitting that he was full of humor, the perfect gentleman.

The director, Wolf Rilla, had a different recollection of Sanders, and remembered him as looking bored throughout filming.

The film, which was originally made as a low budget 'B' picture that was produced to keep the studio busy, is highly regarded today amongst Science Fiction and Fantasy film fans as a classic of its time. Only recently, a *Village Of The Damned* reunion was held in the movies location—Letchmore Heath in Hertfordshire.

Another film that has gained something of a cult status in recent years is *Gorgo*, which was also filmed at the studio in 1960.

Gorgo is a British giant monster movie that stands up better than most from the period, mainly due to first-class direction from Eugene Lourie, superb production design from Elliot Scott, excellent photography from Freddie Young, and a strong acting cast headed by Bill Travers and William Sylvester.

The special effects in *Gorgo* were achieved by an actor, Mick Dillon, in a monster suit and several miniature sets in the studio, a technique that was first pioneered in the *Godzilla* films.

The result was, with a help of 150 technicians, pretty impressive, and the scenes of the monster attacking various London landmarks, including Tower Bridge (a beautifully constructed and realistic miniature set on the stage at MGM), look highly effective on screen. To also create this sense of scale, the actor in the creature suit was shot with a then pricey slow motion camera.

These effects were complex in their day (as it was years before the now grossly overused CGI), but are well respected by special effects artists and fans.

The man behind the special photographic effects on the movie was Douglas Adamson. "One of the producers on *Gorgo* was Frank King. He used to chew on cigars and spit them out all over the studio. They looked like dogs droppings.

I remember most of all the work of Elliot Scott. His production design was first class. He was also an extremely nice gent, and charming with it."

Peter O'Toole was at the studio next to appear in one of his first movie roles, opposite Aldo Ray, in the John Guillermin-directed *The Day They Robbed The Bank Of England* (1960).

Geoffrey Bayldon played an uncredited role as a bartender. "I had a nothing of a part in that film. A very uncomfortable part, too, as directly in front of me was a large tank full of dying trout, that kept dying as we filmed. I was suffering from piles that day, and I connected the death of these trout with my own discomfort. Eventually I said to the director, John Guillermin, 'Can you do something about these trout, because if they don't stop dying I think I will.'

"Peter O'Toole was a sweet man. He had brilliant bright blue eyes, as sharp as could be. He was lovely."

The Millionairess (1960) was the first in several movies Peter Sellers would make at MGM Borehamwood in the 1960s. In this film, Sellers was teamed with Sophia Loren and an excellent supporting cast, including Alastair Sim and Dennis Price.

Gerry Fisher was camera operator on the film. He recalled, "MGM British was always regarded in awe as the ultimate studio. Even the area around the admin block was an immaculate garden, thanks no doubt to George Catt, one-time gardener at MGM but now studio manager.

"Everything there was of the highest standard. Hollywood-style layout and stages; first-rate camera and sound equipment, and a construction department capable of building sets of fabulous quality.

"MGM, though, stood for quality. It was a privilege to work there and be recognised by the gate keepers when passing through the security gates.

"*The Millionairess* was my first movie there in the studio as a camera operator. It was a happy time, and I remember on my birthday the cast and crew got together and we drank champagne."

Actor Gary Raymond also shared his memories of working on the film. "I don't remember much, but I do remember Alastair Sim throwing his arms around Sophia Loren because he thought her such a delightful person, and the camera and sound guys also being besotted by her because she was so thoughtful and caring about the atmosphere on the set."

Sophia Loren and Peter Sellers recorded a song to promote the movie entitled "Goodness Gracious Me!" This became an instant worldwide hit, and the success of the film followed.

During filming, the two stars had developed a close friendship, so much so that Sellers declared his love for Loren in front of his first wife, Anne. This led to continuous rows at the Sellers' home (The Manor House, Chipperfield, Hertfordshire), with their young son, Michael, growing an instant dislike to Loren. Eventually, Anne walked out, and a divorce was settled in 1963.

The Sellers/Loren friendship, however, did not develop any further, as Sellers had wished, due to Loren's then happy marriage to Carlo Ponti.

Loren's own vivid memories of the *The Millionairess* were of being robbed of a fortune in jewels while staying locally at The Chantry on Barnet Lane, Elstree. Each piece had held some memory of her life with Carlo. The thief and jewels were never found.

The early 1960s proved to be busy years for MGM England, with American money continuing to pour into the British film studio, so production remained high.

Steady work was also provided to many in the industry by a hit television series, *Danger Man*. This series proved so popular that it ran for eight years between 1960-1968. The star was Patrick McGoohan.

Brian Clemens wrote several episodes, including the pilot. "I was also script editor, and was at the studio every working day during the black and white, half-hour series.

"I liked MGM where it was shot, as we would be cheek by jowl with some big studio productions, so you would often bump into big stars.

"I remember I was taught a valuable lesson there by *Danger Man* producer Ralph Smart, who had persuaded renowned writer, Jack Davies, to write an episode. We discussed payment to be offered. Ralph reckoned 'the usual £500.' Just then, we heard a roar outside, and looked out the window to where Davies was arriving in a snarling, and very expensive sports car. 'Oh, God', said Ralph, 'we'll have to make it a £1,000!'

"I never forgot that, and as soon as I could afford them, I ran a series of Ferraris just to keep my fees up!"

According to Clemens, the second unit director on the pilot had shot some location and background stuff and sent the dailies back to the editing room at MGM, where Ralph Smart looked at them, hated them, and phoned up the second unit director and said, 'Look, these dailies are terrible! You'll never make a film director!' And then he fired him. The name of that second unit director—John Schlesinger.

During the summer months of 1960, most of the MGM studio was devoted to construction work of massive sets for the 20th Century Fox film, *Cleopatra*, which was shot in Italy, Spain, and at Pinewood Studios.

Maurice Evans brought his production of *Macbeth* to the studios late in 1960, directed by George Schaefer, and with an excellent cast, including Evans (as Macbeth), Judith Anderson, Ian Bannen, Michael Hordern, Felix Aylmer, Jeremy Brett, Megs Jenkins, and Michael Ripper.

The movie also boasts some stunning location photography by Freddie Young, and breathtaking battle sequences, which were copied many years later in Mel Gibson's *Braveheart*.

For all its brilliance as a film production in every department (both technical and acting), it is rarely seen today.

Playing the role of Seyton, henchman to Macbeth, was Trader Faulkner. "The MGM Studios in Borehamwood, as I remember them, were very well-equipped to do the work that MGM required in Britain. They were certainly more lavish than the other studios in Borehamwood at that time, and quite large by English standards. The canteen was excellent, as was the bar. We had good well-equipped dressing rooms. The wardrobe and make-up facilities were what you would expect of MGM Hollywood.

"The director of *Macbeth*, George Schaefer, seemed to work very well with the technicalities at his disposal.

"I remember I became good friends with fellow Australian, Judith Anderson, who I remember seemed very happy to be working in the well-run Borehamwood studios, as was Maurice Evans.

"The brief impression I have now of filming *Macbeth* is of a very happy production, and this, of course, was partly due to an efficiently-run studios.

"So, to sum up MGM Borehamwood: an ideal studios for the purpose it served."

Appearing as Second Murderer in the film was Douglas Wilmer. He recalled, "I had the somewhat undemanding role as one of the 'murderers' and my chief memory is my extreme embarrassment from my almost total amnesia of the lines. I attributed this, at the time, more to the commonly held jinx associated with the play, than to premature softening of the brain. But who knows? Anyway, we had several goes at it, involving poor Maurice Evans in a longish lead-in each time. He was charming and understanding about it. So was the director.

"The MGM Studio was very large and, as far as I remember, without much character."

Even though production remained continuous in the last months of 1960, it didn't stop the following report appearing in the *Borehamwood & Elstree Post* on November 17, 1960:

"STUDIO WORKERS FEAR A JOBLESS CHRISTMAS
Redundancy Threat as Men are Laid Off
'Sinister Signs'"

MGM British 'put off' 87 employees. This move was made by the studio because there was not enough work.

"The signs are sinister," said one worker, "and it looks as though plenty of people will be touring the area looking for work over the Christmas period. It is a risk we take though, because everyone knows that the film industry has its slack times."

The New Year got off to a good start, though, as far as film production was concerned, with the movies *Invasion Quartet* with Bill Travers; *Light In The Piazza* with Olivia de Havilland, and *A Matter Of Who* with Terry-Thomas, all being shot on sound stages at MGM British.

In 1961, Peter Sellers made his directorial debut at MGM Borehamwood with *Mr. Topaze*, in which he also played the title role. Sellers portrayed an ex-schoolmaster in a small French town, who turns to a life of crime to obtain wealth.

You would have thought that with such heavy support from Herbert Lom, Leo McKern, Martita Hunt, Michael Gough, Billie Whitelaw, and John Neville, that nothing could go wrong, but the critics of the time slated it, and Sellers rarely mentioned it again.

It is believed, in fact, that Peter Sellers took all copies of the film and had them destroyed, with the only print known to still exist being in the hands of the British Film Institute.

Geoff Glover was clapper/loader on the film. "I remember Peter Sellers directed the film (with a lot of help). However he showed his appreciation and was very generous to the crew. I received a Sony Radio from him. Sony was unheard of in those days."

Murder She Said (1961) was the first of four Agatha Christie films shot at MGM British. All four were successful (especially in Europe), and established Margaret Rutherford once and for all as an international star as Miss Marple.

As a note of interest, the character of Miss Marple's friend, Mr. Stringer, was not in any of the original stories, but was written into the films, with Stringer Davis, Rutherford's real life husband, playing the role.

Davis married Rutherford in 1945, and remained by her side until she died in 1972. He was private secretary and general dogsbody, lugging bags, tea pots, hot water bottles, teddy bears, and nursing Rutherford through serious periods of depression. These illnesses, often involving stays in mental hospitals, a fact that did not become known until after her death.

Regardless, though, of her own private demons, she was loved by all in the profession. Actor, Geoffrey Bayldon, remarked, "In rehearsal, she never gave anything at all, which could be quite worrying, but on an opening night, or on a first take, she was pure magic. She drew you to her with absolute magnetism, and was beautifully funny."

It is true that Rutherford's Miss Marple stands as a finely tuned comedy performance, but it did not meet with Agatha Christie's full approval. Shortly before her death, she said, "Margaret Rutherford, a splendid character actress though she is, was not and would never have been my first choice as Miss Marple."

Christie was also unhappy with the finished movies, as she did not consider them faithful to her original plots.

Despite this, though, she did dedicate her book, *The Mirror Crack'd From Side To Side*, to Margaret Rutherford, "in admiration."

Camera operator, Paul Wilson, worked with Rutherford on the second Miss Marple film, *Murder At The Gallop* (1963). He took time to remember this quintessential English actress. "Margaret was a sweet old lady. Very gentle. She used to invite the crew to her house in Gerrards Cross, Buckinghamshire. I also remember at the end of the shoot she bought every member of the production (cast and crew) a little gift."

On the final Miss Marple instalment, *Murder Most Foul* (1964), actor Ron Moody appeared opposite Rutherford. He recalled, "First of all, MGM British, where that movie was mostly shot, was, for an actor working there, no different from any other studios. I remember it with much affection, however, because I had such a happy time on that film.

" It was fun to play a ham actor (some would say type casting!). The director, George Pollock, was a warm, friendly man, great to work with. The cast were all excellent actors and we all got on well.

"But most of all, the grande dame, Margaret Rutherford, was a dear, kindly woman, who treated us all as friends and made everybody, cast and crew, feel special. The peak of my day was to be invited into Margaret's dressing room at MGM for afternoon tea, with—would you believe it—cucumber sandwiches!. The British Raj lived on in Borehamwood."

In the series of films, the home of Miss Marple, "Milchester Cottage," was actually Misbourne Cottage on Village Road in Denham Village, Buckinghamshire. This same charming cottage was the home of John Mills and his family between 1942-1945.

The William Holden movie, *Satan Never Sleeps*, caused a stir at MGM Borehamwood on July 6, 1961. The *Borehamwood & Elstree Post* reported:

"MEN STOP WORK ON FILM SET

Claim for 'Dust' Money"

A group of twenty-five electricians walked off the set while filming the 20th Century Fox production. They claimed they were working under dirty and dusty surroundings, which entitled them to "abnormal conditions money."

The company announced, however, that conditions on Stage 3 at MGM did not warrant extra money.

The men eventually returned to work, after an examination headed by Management and Union members considered it to be safe.

The movie, starring Clifton Webb giving his final film performance, was shot on the same sets that had been built for *The Inn Of The Sixth*

Happiness in 1958.

Director Leo McCarey disliked working on the picture so much that he walked out of the studios five days before it was supposed to wrap. His assistant, David W. Orton, was left to finish the shooting.

Nine Hours to Rama, shot at the studios during the summer of 1961, would later cause controversy in India.

The movie depicts the life of Nathuram Godse, the assassin of Mahatma Ghandi. It shows how Godse planned the assassination and how he became a Hindu activist, who (unfairly) blamed Ghandi for the killings of thousands of Hindus by Muslims. This is revealed in the film by a series of flashbacks.

Because of this, the movie was banned outright in India upon its release, due to what they called the negative portrayal of Ghandi.

While the Indian Government at the time may not have liked the portrayal, Ghandi does not appear very much in the film at all, and when he does have some screen time, he is presented and played in a respectful way by J. S. Casshyap.

The film gives equal time to his assassins and portrays them somewhat sympathetically, which may have been the true cause of the Indian controversy.

A lorry load of Triffids arrived at MGM British from Shepperton Studios during the late summer of 1961. They were needed to shoot additional scenes for the troubled *The Day Of The Triffids*.

Actress, Janette Scott, takes up the story. "Earlier in 1961, I had made a film for director Freddie Francis called *Paranoiac* with myself and Oliver Reed. My mother, Thora Hird, was appearing at the Grand Theatre, Blackpool, for the summer season, and it was while visiting her and my father that I received a call from Freddie telling me that the producer of *Triffids*, Philip Yordan, had sent the rough cut of the film to studio bosses in Hollywood, who had watched it and said, 'Well it was meant to be a horror film and that's what it is—horrible! Fix it!' So, the writers had gone away and come up with the idea of interjecting a brand new story to run on parallel lines (so to speak) with the original film.

"The original story starring Howard Keel and Nicole Maurey would be cut down, and new characters—in a lighthouse and never to meet up with the originals—would have their own scary storyline.

"Freddie Francis had been asked to direct this new story, and he asked me and Kieron Moore to come to MGM for five weeks and see if *Triffids* could be saved. It was a bestselling book by John Wyndham and was worth a go!

"I adored Freddie, and packed my things and left for Borehamwood the next day. What followed was a month or so full of fun and laughter, and the Triffids themselves were much loved on the set. My favourite we named 'Blodwin.' She was radio controlled and the prop men would have her follow me, try to creep up behind me.

"I recall that green smoke filled the set and our noses. Green slime filled our shoes. But Kieron Moore was a joy to work with, and this film turned out to be the first of three following films we made together.

"Having worked with Oliver Reed earlier in the year, Freddie Francis and I were not totally surprised when he turned up on our set one day for a visit. However when he arrived on the set the next day and the next, little alarm bells went off in our heads, and when he proclaimed his love for me and how he couldn't live without me, it became necessary to ask him to leave the set.

"I like Oliver and had enjoyed working with him, but didn't realise that my friendship and perhaps small kindnesses had been misunderstood. Oliver's drinking at this time was beginning to get out of control, and I think, because he wasn't working, his drinking became dangerous. His driving certainly was. He nearly caused me to crash my car while following me home from Borehamwood. The gate men at MGM had to be told not to allow him to enter the studios, and gradually, after a few days hanging around outside, he gave up. I never saw him again.

"The movie, *The Day Of The Triffids*, got put together, and years later when I was living in Coldwater Canyon, Beverly Hills, my next door neighbor came to my front door one day and introduced himself by saying, 'We starred in a film together.' It was Howard Keel."

Freddie Francis also took time to remember *The Day Of The Triffids*. "The whole idea was to make the film cheaply and quickly. Allied Artists had put some money into it in America. It just didn't work. So, the original director, Steve Sekely (whom I never met), who shot all the stuff at Shepperton, decided to walk. I couldn't blame him, to be honest. The original footage, before we added material, was terrible—awful. I had seen some low-budget films and worked on some, but I was appalled by this.

"Anyway, I was asked if I would direct a new storyline to be edited in. I agreed, but I don't remember being asked if I wanted a credit. I know I never got one, but to be honest I didn't want one either, as the finished film, even after we tried to salvage it, was by no means a classic."

It was Janette Scott's final film at MGM British. She said, "As a studio, MGM Borehamwood was very factory-like. Maybe because of its size, or maybe because it lacked the warmth (for me) of Pinewood and ABPC, or the other smaller studios, such as Bray, that had big film stages built in the grounds of what had been country estates and therefore retained some older buildings, MGM and Denham were large and cold, although both held happy memories for me."

During filming of *I Thank A fool* starring Peter Finch and Susan Hayward, a twenty-four-hour strike was staged by 170 MGM maintenance men. It was reported in the *Borehamwood & Elstree Post* on October 5, 1961:

"TOKEN STRIKE HITS MGM FILM

No Compensation – No Overtime"

The protest was against what the strikers alleged to be "bad organization and bad planning, which led to redundancy." They continued to state "that unless compensation was paid to redundant members for loss of office, a complete bar on all overtime will operate."

The strike had been said to be caused by the sacking of three stagehands, who were fooling around at the studios the previous week, but this was immediately dispelled as just a rumor.

It was said that the redundancies had been caused by the completion of two films at MGM, and that this could occur at any film studio. After an agreement had been met, the 170 strikers returned to work.

1962 saw the release of *The Dock Brief* with Peter Sellers and Richard Attenborough, *The Password Is Courage* with Dirk Bogarde, *Private Potter* with Tom Courtenay, and *Tarzan Goes To India*, all shot on sound stages at MGM British.

At the ABPC Studios, Borehamwood, during the early part of the 1960s, a number of classic comedy movies were shot, two of which starred the now legendary comic actor, Tony Hancock.

Kelvin Pike was focus puller on *The Rebel* (1961). "Tony Hancock was a very serious man, like all comedians, really. He was very concerned about his performance. Sadly, he was very screwed up with depression, too.

"I remember us rehearsing one of his scenes with Irene Handl. We rehearsed it the night before so we could work out where to place the cameras. Well, they both got carried away with their scene, and it was absolutely riotous, and we all had handkerchiefs stuffed in our mouths. It was so funny, but all we could think was that they couldn't repeat it, and sadly, they didn't. They just couldn't top that performance, and it's a shame that no one other than the few of us present at that rehearsal got to see it.

"The script is the Bible to comic actors like Hancock. They never ad lib. The audience think they do, but they don't.

"Ray Galton and Alan Simpson, the scriptwriters on that film, were very clever men. They used to stand around the set picking up dialogue from conversations crew members were having."

June Randall was continuity on the Hancock movie, *The Punch And Judy Man* (1962). "Hancock's health was going downhill on that film. He could be difficult because he was an alcoholic at that point. He wasn't sure of himself either. Don't get me wrong, he was a nice man sometimes, but he was drinking too much. But there was nothing we could do about it. We also had to have music playing between takes for him, as he was a manic depressive."

The comedy *The Cracksman,* filmed at ABPC in 1962 and starring Charlie Drake and George Sanders, also saw June Randall credited as continuity. "I actually did three films at ABPC with Charlie Drake. *The Cracksman* was one, and to my surprise, it had that wonderful actor, George Sanders, in it. Now when I saw this great actor working on a load of crap like this with Charlie Drake, I thought his career must have taken a dive. I was in absolute awe, though, when that man walked on the set. He was aloof, but charming."

ABPC, Borehamwood also turned out some of British pop cinema's most famous movies during the early 1960s, including *The Young Ones* (1961) and *Summer Holiday* (1963), both starring Cliff Richard, and the highly entertaining *What A Crazy World* (1963) featuring Joe Brown, Marty Wilde, Harry H. Corbett, and Michael Ripper, who played numerous memorable roles.

The same studio also saw Vivien Leigh give her final on-screen performance in *The Roman Spring Of Mrs. Stone* (1961) featuring a young Warren Beatty.

Leigh suffered from recurrent bouts of chronic tuberculosis, first diagnosed in the mid 1940s, and which ultimately claimed her life when she was found dead at home in London, aged just 53, in 1967.

For Hollywood tough guy, Robert Mitchum, a visit to ABPC Studios to film *Man In The Middle* (1963) meant several hard drinking sessions with his co-star, Trevor Howard.

Howard lived local to Borehamwood on Rowley Lane, Arkley, and drank frequently at The Gate, Barnet Lane in Arkley, either with or without acting chums.

Mitchum joined Howard for several sessions at The Gate, and it was after one of these that Howard hit newspaper headlines.

On July 19, 1962, the *Borehamwood & Elstree Post* reported:

"BANNED FOR EIGHT YEARS FROM DRIVING
Trevor Howard Faces Trial"

Howard was alleged to have crashed into roadworks along The Ridgeway, in Mill Hill, early on June 5, 1961. He was charged with driving his red Morris Minor while under the influence of drink.

A Police motorcyclist claimed, "I was drawn to the sound and speed of Howard's car. I then saw the car swerve to the offside of the roadway to avoid some roadworks. It appeared to me that he couldn't control the car and it struck a trestle pole and some hurricane lamps!"

Howard was said to be unsteady on his feet, his speech slurred, and his breath smelling strongly of drink. He was, therefore, arrested and taken to Edgware Police Station.

Inspector Sidney Windmill stated that when Howard reached Edgware Station, he smelt of drink, his cheeks were flushed, and his eyes shone. His demeanor was impatient and intolerant. He was given a £50 bail.

Although having a reputation as a heavy-drinking hellraiser, Trevor Howard, was always professional in his work and was much respected by his fellow actors.

He was, in fact, one of British cinemas finest movie actors, and was often seen on screen giving powerful, highly convincing performances.

Robert Mitchum later said of him, "Trevor was one of those actors who was enormous fun to work with, but if you were not careful he would steal every scene."

One of the most successful television productions to be shot at the ABPC Studios was *The Avengers*. Running for six seasons between 1961-1969, and with 161 episodes made, it is still widely shown today and has a large worldwide cult following.

The series originally starred Patrick Macnee (as John Steed) and Ian Hendry. Then, after Hendry left the series, it was restyled to center on Steed and several female sidekicks.

The first was Cathy Gale (played by Honor Blackman), replaced by the iconic Miss Emma Peel (played by the beautiful Diana Rigg), both appearing for two seasons each, and finally Linda Thorson played Tara King.

Each episode mingled established actors, such as Peter Cushing and Christopher Lee, with up and coming talent, such as Charlotte Rampling and Donald Sutherland.

The star was most definitely Patrick Macnee, who became a familiar figure around Elstree/Borehamwood with his trademark bowler hat and umbrella.

Macnee took time to share his memories. "The first series of *The Avengers* was not filmed at Borehamwood; it was recorded live at Teddington Studios, down by the Thames. It was live! Can you imagine? It was the most frightening thing in the whole world, because if you forgot your lines, you can't go back, or if you say a naughty word, which I'm not inclined to do of course, or if you have any other problems, you can't solve them. Whereas, when we went down to ABPC in Borehamwood, we started filming episodes, and we had probably the best team in the whole of Great Britain at that time.

"Going onto that stage to do film was very exciting. It meant we could do all sorts of things. We also shot all around the countryside there in Hertfordshire, and it was beautiful country. I remember us going out into the back roads, going into little tiny villages, seeing people doing their ordinary work, and they used to see us sp-e-e-e-e-e-ding along in our motor cars, and they probably thought, 'What the devil are they all doing?'

"I started the series on £150 a week, and that eventually rose to the huge sum of £300. I remember it all, though, very affectionately."

Brian Clemens worked as both producer and writer on *The Avengers*. "Patrick Macnee once had his whole wardrobe stolen from his car in Chelsea. It was in continuity, and we were hard-pressed to get more of the custom-made stuff overnight. Desperately, we turned to the stunt boys, who, it was suspected, some dabbled in various illegal activities. Through them, the word went out, and mysteriously the whole wardrobe of clothing turned up again!

"Incredibly, a few weeks later, the same thing occurred. Again, Pat's clothes were stolen. Again, we turned to the stunt boys for help, but to no avail. After many inquiries, they had to admit defeat and explain, 'This must have been the work of an amateur!'

"At one time, we had working on the series a dangerous armed robber, the finest jewel thief/cat burglar in Europe, and a 'collector' who, to stimulate return of a bad debt, would razor their face and promise more if the cash wasn't paid soon! Crooks, yes, but wonderful, funny company, and an ordinary member of the public had little to fear from them.

"I do recall that Stage 5 at ABPC, where we filmed a lot of *The Avengers*, was everyone's bête noir. I think it might have been built during the war. Whatever, it was painfully inadequate as far as sound proofing was concerned as we always had to stop shooting when a plane went by. No one wanted to occupy it, but, as it was cheaper and available for long periods, series, like ours, tended to be shuttled into it a lot. I grew to have some affection for it. It also had birds nesting in its rafters (up amongst the gantry electricians), and they, too, gave us sound problems. Somehow it added to the charm of the place!

"I also remember the back lot, which I often would wander when stuck on a script point and seeking inspiration. Back there, I would climb fairy tale stairs leading nowhere, walk through tunnel sections, climb around and through submarine conning towers, and always find the answer to whatever script blockage I had been facing.

"We also used the huge tank from *Moby Dick* several times. *The Avengers,* in particular, lent itself to the weird and wonderful that could be found in profusion amongst the scattered remnants of sets on that back lot.

"It also occurs to me that *The Avengers* 'Epic" episode was shot in and around the ABPC Studios and back lot, since the episode was all about the making of a movie. It unashamedly showed it as it was. I had written the episode for economy reasons. We had reached a hiatus where we did not have a great deal of time (or money) to do much building, nor did we have much budget for cast. I solved it with a more or less six-part cast and full use of the existing studios back lot and existing set pieces. I think it worked rather well indeed!"

June Randall worked as continuity on episodes of *The Avengers.* "A film is never shot in continuity, which can make my job very hard. Actors also seldom remember what they've done in previous takes.

"I did two years on the filmed series of *The Avengers.* It was actually the first series that featured Diana Rigg. Now she was very good as regards continuity, but dear old Patrick Macnee could never remember where his umbrella was in previous shots. To be honest, that umbrella was a continuity nightmare, and at the end of the two years, I could have set fire to it."

Peggy Spirito would also work on the series as continuity. "*The Avengers* was fantastic to work on. They used to film the episodes back to back. It was a family affair really. Patrick Macnee was delightful to work with, and so was Diana Rigg. They were very professional, and so easy to work with.

"You had to work your bum off on those television series, though. It was very hard work, but good practice. Good training."

On August 23, 1962, journalist, Des Wilson, wrote the following article in the *Borehamwood & Elstree Post*:

"Tucked away in a disused workshop at Associated British Picture Studios is a treasure chest—a room that harbours the memories of our film industry.

"Here I found one of Moby Dick's teeth and Captain Hornblower's flintlock lying side by side on a shelf.

"This is a film museum as entertaining as the studio's finest screen products. Each article is superbly made—each article is a reminder of our filmland's greatest moments.

"Pride of place here are some amazing replicas of actors and boats from the 1956 production of *Moby Dick*. There is also the huge whale's tooth, fashioned out of steel. Rubber figures of Gregory Peck and James Robertson Justice glare down from a shelf. They are only a foot high, yet easily recognisable.

"The models of the longboat used in the film are so perfect that the cameras could get within a few feet of them. The figures in them are all copies of actors in the film, and a different model had to be made for each movement—each stroke of the oar.

"There is a flintlock pistol used by Gregory Peck playing the title role in *Captain Horatio Hornblower* (1951). This is skilfully made from an old American rifle cut down. The date on the butt is 1878.

"Gordon Scott, who played Tarzan at MGM British, left his knife behind, and there is a resplendent banner once carried by the late Errol Flynn as The Black Prince in *The Dark Avenger* (1955).

"One of the biggest Associated British successes was *The Dam Busters* (1955) starring Richard Todd. There is a model here of the Mohne Dam used in the film. On the walls are continuity sketches of the bombing scenes. This part of filming was so complicated that a complete sequence of camera shots had to be drawn. It is no wonder that it took two years to prepare for this film.

Various scripts lie side by side on a table used in Tony Hancock's film *The Rebel* (1961). Everywhere there are memories of our favourite films, articles – many of them made by Borehamwood and Elstree men."

When Richard Burton was offered $500,000 to appear in *The VIPs*, Elizabeth Taylor said she'd take part for $1,000,000.

They both arrived at MGM Borehamwood in early 1963, and while looking around the huge Heathrow Airport sets, Elizabeth asked sarcastically, "Will I never be finished with MGM?"

Their co-stars in the movie were Rod Taylor, Maggie Smith, Orson Welles, and Margaret Rutherford.

Taylor and Burton were being hounded by journalists at this time, as they had just embarked on an off-screen romantic affair while filming *Cleopatra*.

This affair broke up both their marriages and would cause them enormous problems when they dared to venture out in public.

One such incident took place while trying to relax at the Kings Arms (now a Harvester restaurant) on Stirling Corner, Borehamwood.

Actor Brook Williams, who was playing a small (uncredited) role in the film as a reporter, happened to be with them at the Kings Arms. "I was with them that evening, as I'd known Richard for years, and would later become his closest confidant; personal assistant, and friend.

"On this occasion, however, I was just invited by Richard and Elizabeth to join them for a drink or two, but sadly, it turned ugly, and not because of their drinking, I have to say.

"Richard spotted photographers outside, and for the first time, I saw him in a complete rage, yelling and shouting and swearing at them, and it wasn't really like Richard to be like this. Elizabeth was more the fiery one, as I found later.

"But because of their love affair while filming *Cleopatra*, they were now both being followed everywhere, and Richard got to the point were he thought he couldn't go to the loo without thinking a photographer wouldn't be waiting there.

"We did manage to eventually calm him down this particular night, but not before he'd finished his tirade of language, some of which was hurled at a poor autograph hunter, but sadly Richard hadn't realised. I was actually worried that he might lash out, as this was not unknown with him, but it certainly wouldn't have helped his and Elizabeth's relations with the newspapers. Not that he cared at that particular moment I don't think."

Jimmy Dawes who was a grip on the movie, also remembered the famous couple. "Burton could be a bit of a shit sometimes. I used to walk down into Borehamwood to put bets on for him. He couldn't do it himself, as he and Elizabeth were getting a lot of attention from the press. This, I think, upset Orson Welles, as he liked attention, and they were getting more than him. Elizabeth was lovely, though. I'd known her for years."

Gerry Fisher was camera operator on the movie, and shared his memories of the films other star, Orson Welles. "Welles was a difficult man. He would turn up at the studios late, keeping the crew and actors waiting around. He also hadn't bothered to learn his lines, so they had to put them on boards around the set."

Playing a supporting role in the film as a B.O.A.C. (now British Airways) Desk Attendant was, Lance Percival. "I had a scene with Margaret Rutherford, in which she had to empty her purse on to the counter between us. We did seven or eight takes and the items in the purse fell out in exactly the same order every single time.

"This was not luck, it was rehearsed by her many times elsewhere and proved to me the value of rehearsing 'business' with props—a remarkable lady.

"I also had a short scene at the same counter with Orson Welles, filmed late in the afternoon. Orson kept making little mistakes and even walking behind the counter to my side.

"At 5.20 p.m. (wrap time), we had just finished Take 35, and Orson said how sorry he was, but he'd be back tomorrow to finish it, thus getting an extra day's salary.

"The director, Anthony Asquith, smiled and said, 'No thank you Orson, I'm using Take 14, I just wanted to see how far you would go to get an extra day!'

"All I can say about the studios—MGM—is that it was basically quite a few big sound stages, along with a lot of offices, and not much else. There was nothing exceptional about it."

The VIP's turned out to be a box office winner, and won Margaret Rutherford the Best Supporting Actress Oscar for her role as the Duchess of Brighton.

Cornel Wilde and his wife, Jean Wallace, visited the studio next to shoot part of *Lancelot and Guinevere*.

The film, also directed by Wilde, featured strong support from Hollywood actor Brian Aherne and English actress Adrienne Corri.

1960s singer/actor Ian Gregory played the role of Sir Tors. He recalled, "My part in that film came about from the role I had played in the Danziger television series, *Richard the Lionheart*, and I remember being asked to do a test for Cornel Wilde at MGM Borehamwood.

"MGM was much much bigger than the Danziger studios in Elstree. It was a huge complex with great big stages. Probably three or four times bigger than Danzigers. It had much more facility, as well.

"While shooting *Lancelot and Guinevere*, Cornel asked me if I would double up and play a Barbarian, just to fill out a scene. Anyway, when they edited the film together, there was me as the character, Sir Tors, pointing at this Barbarian, and I draw this long bow and shoot him through the chest and he falls down dead. It was actually me though shooting me, only in a different costume.

"Cornel was playing Sir Lancelot in the movie, as well as directing. As a person, he was a mixture of things. He could be an absolute charmer, or a complete pig.

"I had a bit of a problem with Jean Wallace (Cornel's wife), who played Guinevere. She, unfortunately, took a shine to me, and kept leaving me little notes. Cornel got wind of it, and there was a dodgy moment.

"He also one day during the shoot came at me with a broad sword because I was laughing on set. He went totally ape shit. I thought he was going to kill me. He was a sabre champion, though, and an incredibly athletic man. He certainly put me in my place.

"Brian Aherne played King Arthur. Now, he was a big personality, but a very charming man. A Hollywood actor and star, who came to surprise me when he said that he was born in England."

MGM British became home to a number of horror movies next, starting with a sequel of sorts to *Village Of The Damned*.

Children Of The Damned starred Ian Hendry and Alan Badel, but was not as successful as its predecessor, even though it had good production values and nice performances from its two lead actors.

Hammer Films had first arrived at the studios of Elstree/Borehamwood in the 1950s, on lease from Bray Studios, their main base.

Maniac (1963) would be the first of their movies to shoot on the stages of MGM. Directed by Michael Carreras, the film was to have originally starred Peter Cushing and George Sanders, but instead Kerwin Mathews and Donald Houston were cast.

This was followed in 1965 by *Hysteria*. As with *Maniac*, it was written by Jimmy Sangster, but this time the director was Freddie Francis. He recalled, "The star of this particular Hammer Film was Robert Webber. I think I enjoyed working with him as little as I've ever enjoyed working with anybody. He was impossible, and he decided to make life as difficult as possible for everyone involved, but most especially the actress we had in the picture, Lelia Goldoni. He was just generally nasty towards her. So it was a very unhappy film."

Michael Carreras chose the stages of MGM British to shoot the opening sandstorm sequence in Hammer's *Curse Of The Mummy's Tomb*

(1964), as the stages at ABPC (where most of the film was shot) were not large enough to create a vast Egyptian desert.

Another horror that was only shot in part at MGM was *The Masque Of The Red Death* (1964), starring "master of terror" Vincent Price. It was also the first time director Roger Corman had shot one of his Poe pictures in England.

Over two miles of corridors were constructed in sections spread over three soundstages at MGM for actress Jane Asher to run through while she was being held captive.

Jane Asher shared a special memory of working on the movie. "The filming coincided with John F. Kennedy's assassination, and I can remember all of us standing in the middle of the studio floor with our heads bowed in a few moments of shocked and quiet thought. Particularly moving and poignant, as both our star, Vincent Price, and director, Roger Corman were, of course, Americans."

Asher asked Corman if her then boyfriend could visit the set and join them for lunch. She explained that her boyfriend was a musician, who was about to do his first gig in London that night. At the end of lunch, Corman, wished the boyfriend good luck with his concert, not realising that this would be the start of a great career for both Paul McCartney and The Beatles.

By far the most powerful horror movie to be filmed at MGM British was *The Haunting* (1963), with all the interiors of Hill House constructed and shot entirely on the sound stages of the studio, while exteriors were filmed on location at Ettington Park Hotel in Warwickshire.

Directed by Robert Wise, with a $1.1 million budget, it is a ghost story stylishly handled, and featuring some of the scariest and most chilling moments in cinema history. It is a movie that proves "it's what you don't see" that is the more frightening.

Julie Harris plays the tragic victim, while Richard Johnson, Claire Bloom, and Russ Tamblyn try to save her from her own doom.

In probably one of the film's most nerve-tingling moments, we see Harris and Johnson climbing a metal spiral staircase, heading for collapse as they dare to take each step.

This rickety staircase effect was the idea of production designer Elliot Scott, who constructed the metal frame (with the help of a metalworker at the Borehamwood Studios) right up to the roof of the studio, giving it a vertigo like depth, which was scary to work on for both the actors and camera crew alike, so scary that Robert Wise had to ascend the staircase while it was shaking to show the cast and crew that it was safe.

Robert Wise credited Scott's design as a "major contributor," with each set designed to be brightly lit, with no dark corners or recesses, making the unseen menace even more forbidding. All rooms also had ceilings, to create a claustrophobic effect on film. Actor Richard Johnson said the sets created a subdued feeling among cast and crew.

This, along with the cinemascope cinematography of Davis Boulton, would only add to the impeding menace.

Wise and Boulton also wanted to make distances in the movie (such as hallways) look much longer than the audience could anticipate. They also planned shots that kept the camera moving, utilizing low-angle shots, and incorporating unusual pans and tracking shots. This was to accentuate that the house was alive.

These elements, along with nerve shattering sound effects of "spooks" you never see, add to the movie's cult appeal over fifty years later.

A film adaptation by Clive Exton of Emlyn Williams' psychological stage thriller, *Night Must Fall*, directed by Karel Reisz was shot in part at MGM Borehamwood. Freddie Francis was the cinematographer. "Karel was great to work with. He always involved me on the making of a movie and understood the job of the lighting cameraman completely.

"We had a shot in *Night Must Fall*, which we filmed on the stage at MGM British, were Mona Washbourne, as an invalid in a wheelchair, travels round the house where she lives in search of the psychotic killer she has employed, played by Albert Finney. Well, we decided to do this shot in one take, and attach the camera to the front of Mona's wheelchair. It was quite tricky to set up because of the lighting, but worked beautifully, and Mona, the old pro that she was, never complained."

Pamela Francis was continuity on the movie, and recalled MGM. "It had more of a feel of a film studio than ABPC (which was nothing special, it was just a studio), and it was well liked by people in the business. You certainly couldn't fault it, as every department worked to a very high standard. Personally, though, I always found Pinewood to be the prettier studios, but as regards to moviemaking and the art of moviemaking, it would have to be MGM."

The Chalk Garden, a film version based on the Broadway play by Enid Bagnold, was directed by Ronald Neame. He shared his memories of filming at MGM England. "I had a lovely cast in that movie. Deborah

Kerr, who was at that point in her career an important Hollywood star with several Oscar nominations; old friend, Johnnie Mills, came along for the ride, as did his daughter Hayley; while Dame Edith Evans and Felix Aylmer gave strong support.

"Occasionally, though, during rehearsals of the longer dialogue scenes, Felix, the eminent old character actor, would fall asleep, only to be reprimanded by Dame Edith. 'Stupid old man,' she would exclaim. 'Quite unforgivable.'

"We shot on location at several picturesque settings, including Beachy Head, but we also had to recreate some of this in the studio.

"The very clever Carmen Dillon designed the film. Her past credits had included Laurence Olivier's *Henry V, Hamlet,* and *Richard III,* so she knew her craft.

"The interior of the English country house, which had to be constructed in the studio, had to be slightly shabby with a lived-in look, giving the impression that Mrs. St. Maughan (played by Evans) had spent many years there. But Ross Hunter, the producer, started to change everything.

"Carmen came to me in tears. 'Ronnie, it's just awful what he wants me to do. He's ruining everything.'

"When I talked to Ross about it, he countered, 'Who cares about authenticity? I can't put that tatty stuff on screen. The home belongs to a well-off lady and it has to be beautiful.'

"I commiserated with Carmen, but there was little we could do. Ross was the boss. She was disappointed, but, like a true professional, she carried on.

"Edith was a joy to direct. She brought as much to a role as Alec Guinness did, but unlike him, she always expected to be the center of attention.

"'I don't know anything about film,' she would complain to me. 'It's all so difficult. I mean I am supposed to stop on this little dot or that one? How can I possibly do so and concentrate on my lines?' In fact, it was a ploy. She knew exactly where to position herself and she never missed her mark.

"She and I would often sit together while waiting for the next set-up at MGM, and we would chat, mostly about her. Out of the blue one day, she said, 'You know, I've never been a beautiful woman.'

"'You are beautiful,' I told her.

"'No, no, no,' she protested, 'I'm not beautiful. But in my long career in the theatre, I've had to play many beautiful women. Do you know what

I do? Five minutes before my entrance, I stand in the wings, and I think beautiful. Then, when I walk on stage, I am beautiful.'

"Not only was Deborah Kerr's performance meticulous, but also her demeanour towards Edith was one of patience and understanding. She stepped back, making Edith feel the star, even though Deborah was by far the most important film actress. I was terribly grateful to her for that gesture. It would have been impossible if my two leading ladies had competed for center stage.

"Working with Johnnie and Hayley was a personal delight. Hayley was so good in her role, and so professional. I'm sure Johnny worked with her at home. We also had a birthday party for Hayley on the set, which was enormous fun.

"So, except for mine and Carmen's disappointment with the clean white sterile décor, the shooting period itself was most enjoyable.

"And as regards to the studio, MGM Borehamwood was a well-run studio, and there was no reason whatsoever to complain.

"I had started work in Borhamwood, age just sixteen, at the BIP Studios. The silent days of films. Now I had come full circle working at MGM. I would never work there again."

Peter Sellers dropped in next to MGM British, this time with director Blake Edwards, to shoot the sequel to their hugely successful *The Pink Panther* (1963).

Sellers once again played the now famous bumbling sleuth, Inspector Clouseau, while Herbert Lom joined him for the first time as the slightly insane Inspector Dreyfus, both giving masterly comic performances.

A Shot In The Dark also featured George Sanders, Elke Sommer, and Douglas Wilmer.

Wilmer shared his memories of Sellers. "Peter had an unfortunate habit of 'corpsing' at his own antics. This would cause several re-takes. Other than that though, he was easy to work with."

Not everyone found Sellers easy to work with. Dennis Fraser worked as grip on the movie. "I hated Peter Sellers. I didn't like him at all. He was a nightmare to work with. Very selfish. Not a very nice man really."

Peter Sellers later admitted that he disliked working on the movie, and considered the finished film as so awful that he wished it had never been released.

Christopher Challis was director of photography on the Sellers film. "It was always a pleasure working at MGM, for the studio was well-equipped and run, particularly the camera department overseen by Les Smart.

"Of course, Freddie Young, one of our greatest cinematographers, was resident there for a number of years, and as a young lighting camera-man I always found a warm welcome and a helping hand.

"I've worked in the film business since the 1930s, and I think, together with Denham Studios, MGM Borehamwood was my favourite venue."

John Ford, a director in poor health, turned up at the gate's of MGM during the final months of 1963. He was there to film *Young Cassidy* with Rod Taylor, Maggie Smith, Flora Robson, and a young Julie Christie, just prior to her shooting to fame in *Doctor Zhivago* (1965).

Shortly after the cameras rolled on *Young Cassidy*, Ford collapsed on one of the stages, and it was decided that he was unfit to direct and must return home to Hollywood immediately.

So, with production at a standstill, another director was sought. Jack Cardiff takes up the story. "I happened to be in Switzerland when I got this cable, asking me to return to England at once and finish the picture.

"I liked the sound of it and thought it might be interesting, so I flew over and read the script, which was wonderful.

"They warned me, though, that I might have creative troubles with Rod Taylor, because like so many actors he was talking like a producer or a director.

"Rod did like to think he was running the whole show, but when we started on *Young Cassidy* (my eighth film as a director), I made it clear that I was running things.

"When the film was released, it got good press, but several critics had decided that the film was mostly the work of John Ford. The credits said that it was a John Ford production, directed by Jack Cardiff, which could have meant anything.

"In the final edit, I did include all the work which had been shot by Ford, and it totalled 4 minutes and 5 seconds out of a 130-minute picture. However, the damage was done, and most of the critics thought that it was largely the work of Ford."

In 1964, the cinema releases of productions made at MGM Borehamwood included, *The Americanization Of Emily* starring James Garner and Julie Andrews; the war epic *633 Squadron*, and the entertaining all-star comedy directed by Anthony Asquith (his final film) entitled *The Yellow Rolls-Royce*.

The latter was a big-budget movie with an international cast, including Ingrid Bergman, Rex Harrison, Omar Sharif, Shirley MacLaine, and George C. Scott, and it took nearly six months to complete.

Dennis Fraser, a highly respected MGM film grip shared both his memories of working on the film, and of the studio. "When we were filming on location for the movie, *The Yellow Rolls-Royce*, I actually saved the star of the movie, which of course was the Rolls-Royce, from the scrap yard, as it accidentally drove off of the road and nearly over a cliff. Anthony Asquith, the director, couldn't thank me enough, as building a second Rolls-Royce wouldn't have met the already oversized budget.

"I actually started work at MGM British in 1953, when I was just seventeen. Before that, I had worked at the British National Studios, Borehamwood.

"MGM British, though, was by far the best studios in Europe, and I think I'm right in saying, it was the biggest. All the best people came out of there. Everybody was taught properly. It was like a big family.

"It was operated like the American MGM studios, and it was all self-contained. They also got all the top American films in there. They had a different Hollywood star every week. It was overwhelming. We even built some of the sets for *Ben Hur* in that studio.

"It was a truly fantastic place. I even met my wife there, and you could order a bunch of flowers for her, and they'd be delivered to the stage, straight from the MGM gardens."

It was during this period that Sally Jones started work at the studios as a secretary. She recalled, "It was my first year in the film industry. I was a Teenager, and got a job as junior secretary in Studio Operating, which was run then by a lady called Judith Coxhead (prior to which she was assistant to Mr. Catt, who ran the studio).

"This office was the heart of the studio and did all the necessary call sheets, schedules, and script re-writes, etc. for all the renting films that came in.

"*633 Squadron* was being filmed at the time, I recall. My job was a goffa, really. Any department that needed assistance of any kind, I was farmed out. I was farmed out quite a lot, really. Maybe they wanted rid of me. I did drop and break the coffee percolator on my first day!

"I helped out in the prop department, the accounts, ran errands for Margaret Rutherford. In those days, actors didn't have assistants like they do now.

"I really enjoyed a few days in the Special Effects department when the secretary Vicky Manning needed a few days off. George Chakiris (who was starring in *633 Squadron*) came in to see Tommy Howard, the Special Effects Supervisor. George decided to wait for Tommy, who had popped out, so we had a coffee and a little chat. The name, George Chakiris, meant nothing to me until Vicky returned and saw his name written on the notepad. She almost swooned. He was her heartthrob! I was very green about movie stars and life, really.

"As I was returning from an errand to the office, I was fascinated to see a film unit in operation. They were shooting *The Americanization Of Emily*. I watched while James Garner came out through a doorway and got into a car. He smiled at me, so I figured it was okay to be there while they shot the same scene several times. While watching, an assistant director came to me and pressed a piece of paper into my hand. 'James says see you in ten minutes.' I looked at the paper, confused. Holy Cow! It had his dressing room number written on it! I panicked and fled back to the office."

Sally would go on to work as script supervisor on many big movies, including *Braveheart* (1995) and *Mamma Mia!* (2008).

The Alphabet Murders, shot at MGM Borehamwood during late 1964, starred Tony Randall playing Agatha Christe's famous detective, Hercule Poirot.

The completed movie also featured, in a guest appearance, Margaret Rutherford, returning to the role of Miss Marple.

Next on the scene was a British television crime series, filmed at both ABPC and MGM British. *Gideon's Way* starred John Gregson and ran for twenty-six episodes.

It was while this was being shot at MGM that Sean Connery was making the brutal Sidney Lumet-directed and Kenneth Hyman-produced *The Hill*.

The movie, set in a British Army "glasshouse" (military detention camp) in the Libyan Desert during World War II, sees five prisoners subjected to a repetitive drill in the blazing desert heat. This includes running *The Hill*, a cruel method of breaking down soldiers.

The exterior of the camp was constructed on location in Almeria, Spain, while the inside of the prison was built on a sound stage at MGM, the work of art director, Herbert Smith.

Under the direction of Lumet, Connery gives one of his very best screen performances, in scenes so brutally realistic that the movie cannot be faulted.

It is a tour-de-force in acting, and Connery is given fine support from Ian Hendry, Michael Redgrave, and Ian Bannen, who all pack a powerful, violent, punch.

Oswald Morris was cinematographer, and working as his camera operator was Brian West. "First of all, MGM was the best studio in the United Kingdom. It was a truly marvellous place to work. Everything you wanted was there, as far as the camera department was concerned. It was also a very clean studio, with a fabulous canteen.

"Sidney Lumet was a nice man, but very demanding on set, and I suppose that's how he got the performances he did from his actors. He was a one take director though, and things moved very quickly.

"I remember us filming a scene in which actor Harry Andrews had to walk up and down a line of soldiers, and after the first take, Sidney turned to me and said, 'How was that Brian?'

"'Fine,' I said.

"'OK,' said Sidney. 'Print it, and let's move on.'

"Harry Andrews looked at me and said, 'Sudden death, eh Brian?' It was how the film would proceed, with speed, and very rarely a second take, which can sometimes be alarming to the crew, and the actors."

Angela Allen, who worked as continuity with Lumet on a later film, *The Offence* (1972), also gave an idea of the director's technique. "Lumet was an incredible director. Very disciplined. In fact, the most disciplined director I have ever worked for. He rehearsed the whole film beforehand, and all the actors had to be word perfect. No arguments. Word perfect. He also used to mark up every shot in the film beforehand, and would always beat his own schedule. If it was six weeks, he'd do it in five and a half. He was a master film director. Very economical. Definitely not seventy five takes if he can do it in one or two. But preferably one."

The Offence, made at Twickenham Film Studios, also featured Sean Connery and Ian Bannen, and arguably gives Connery his finest screen moment, as the scenes between himself and Bannen (who gets viciously beaten by Connery) are award worthy.

Connery even admitted later that his work with Lumet was among his best, and it isn't hard to see why.

Actor John Cairney was appearing in an episode of *Gideon's Way* at MGM, the same time as *The Hill* was being filmed, and remembered meeting Connery in the canteen at the studio. "Sean had decided to set up a Scottish table in the restaurant for all Scots working there at the time. So, Ian Bannen, John Fraser, Ian Hendry, and myself turned up for lunch each day with a Scottish accent. One day, we were joined by Sophia Loren. 'She's not Scottish, Tam,' we all cried out. We called Sean 'Big Tam.'

"'She's Sophia Loren' said Sean.

"And that settled the matter."

Sophia Loren was at the studios shooting *Lady L* (1965), directed by Peter Ustinov, and featuring Paul Newman and David Niven.

On December 10, 1964, the *Borehamwood & Elstree Post* reported:

"FIREMAN BATTLE 100,000 POUNDS STUDIO INFERNO"

Fire crews from Borehamwood and nearby Barnet and Radlett battled with a storeroom blaze at MGM Studios.

The studios own firefighters fought the blaze until the local fire brigades arrived. The store, a steel framed and asbestos building was completely gutted by the fire.

Most of its contents, furnishings, and other studio property were destroyed, with damage estimated at £100,000.

The Liquidator (1965) saw Rod Taylor return to the studios, once again under the direction of Jack Cardiff. "We got on well together, Rod and I. He seamed to like me very much and treated me well. I never had any trouble with him and I don't recall us ever having an argument on set.

"He wasn't the sort of man to take anything lightly though, and he would pick a fight with anybody. I remember one of the electricians had said something jokingly to him and Rod just quietly handed me his glass, which I knew meant that he was going to go for this chap. I had to calm him down; he was that sort.

"Trevor Howard I remember was extremely good, as was Wilfrid Hyde-White. Now he was an interesting character.

"I remember us having slight problems with the censor as regards to a line of dialogue. The line was, 'This thing stinks more than a Turkish wrestler's jock-strap.' That line, sadly, had to go, but I thought it was wonderful.

"Well, the film had a producer called Jon Penington, and I had come onto the film quite late as a director. When I was in the MGM office doing the preparations, I noticed this young man with red hair and glasses and asked who he was, and they told me not to worry about him; he was just some young chap learning the business. But in fact, he owned the rights to the story, so he had some sort of say in the making of the film.

"Anyway, after we started shooting, this boy suddenly came out of the shadows and started saying that he didn't like the way things were being done, and so he had Jon Penington, the producer, fired. So, we had no producer.

"So, I lumbered on without a producer, continuing the film alone, wandering if I was next for the chop. However, I completed the picture only to be told that they hadn't secured the rights to the story from this boy, a story that basically aped the James Bond films. So, because he had refused us the rights, the film couldn't be released, and it had to be put away in a vault.

"If it had come out when we finished the picture, I think it would have been a big success, because it was just the right moment for it. But because they put it away, when they did come to release it, the flavor had gone, and in the meantime someone else had made a film that was playing on Bond. So it was a disaster."

On Thursday April 22, 1965, the following report appeared in the *Borehamwood & Elstree Post*:

"*DANGER MAN* SERIES TRANSFER"

Actor Patrick McGoohan held a party at the Borehamwood Football Club to mark the end of his filming at MGM British Studios. His *Danger Man* series was now being transferred to Shepperton.

On the same day, the local press reported that film legend, Bette Davis, was in Borehamwood, filming *The Nanny* for Hammer Films at the ABPC Studios.

The Hollywood actress had also been seen at London Airport collecting her son, Michael, age thirteen, who had flown in from New York to join his mother, who was staying while filming *The Nanny* at The Chantry on Barnet Lane, Elstree.

Kelvin Pike was camera operator on the Hammer Film, and recalled its famous star. " She was always Miss Davis, except to the director, Seth Holt, who was a lovely man, lovely director, but, sadly, died quite young. But she had to be Miss Davis for the entire shoot to the crew. I got along extremely well with her, though. Very well indeed.

"The young boy on the film, William Dix, was incredible. He knew every line of the script. Every Que. Someone would say, 'Good morning' to Bette, and she would hesitate, a sort of dramatic hesitation, and he would tell her, under his breath of course, who was talking to her.

"She stayed very aloof all the way through shooting, and then at the end she would give you a big cuddle, and say, 'I think you're fantastic.' which was superb.

"In fact, the next film she did for Hammer, *The Anniversary*, she asked where I was, and when she discovered I wasn't on the picture, she wanted them to employ me, even though they already had a camera operator. I got a call, but I couldn't do it, as I was doing another film. I actually felt sorry for the operator they'd employed. I'm sure he was very competent. But Bette was like that.

"I recall saying to her once, because I couldn't get her in shot properly, and the atmosphere was tense, 'Miss Davis, do you think you could do it side saddle?'

"She responded, 'Gee honey, I think I've tried it everywhere in my life, but I've never tried it side saddle.'

"That, of course, broke the atmosphere completely.

"If she didn't like someone, though, that was it. She had the publicity man on the film fired within five minutes. She could be a tough old cookie."

Renee Glynne was continuity on *The Nanny*. "Bette Davis gave an after party speech at The Thatched Barn in Borehamwood (now a Holiday Inn). She said, 'This is the only film were I have not wanted to fire the director, or get rid of some members of the crew. It is one of the happiest films I've ever done.' I liked her."

However, when she returned to Borehamwood again two years later to film *The Anniversary* at ABPC, the story would be quite different.

While Davis was shooting *The Nanny* on one stage at ABPC, Herbert Lom, had arrived to film the second series of his drama, *The Human Jungle*.

Lom's portrayal of a psychiatrist—a role that resulted in him receiving up to 2,000 letters a week from viewers who thought he was the real thing—was very successful, though some of the storylines were controversial at the time. Sadly though, Lom did not reprise his role after series two, and returned to making movies. *The Human Jungle* then disappeared for over forty years, only recently resurfacing on DVD.

On August 26, 1965, the *Borehamwood & Elstree Post* reported:

"MGM BUILD LARGEST SET FOR *OPERATION CROSSBOW*"

The scenes in which Espionage Agents sabotage the rocket in its underground launching nest were filmed at the Borehamwood studios, on the largest sets ever built there.

It also had a large all-star cast to go with it: Sophia Loren, George Peppard, Trevor Howard, John Mills, Richard Johnson, Tom Courtney, Jeremy Kemp, Anthony Quayle, Richard Todd, and Sylvia Syms.

Despite having top billing, Loren only appears in an extended cameo role. Producer, Carlo Ponti (Loren's husband), believed his wife's popularity in the United States would boost the films chances at the box-office and had her billed accordingly.

Sadly, neither the magnificent sets, nor the cast (including the top-billed Loren), did anything for the film, as it only did modest business, and wasn't as well-received as MGM would have liked.

On December 2, 1965, the following report appeared in the *Borehamwood & Elstree Post*:

"AMBITIOUS SCIENCE FICTION FILM TO COST 6 MILLION POUNDS"

It was reported that one of the most ambitious productions was about to go under the camera at MGM British, with filming of the gigantic epic expected to go way into 1967.

Technicians and carpenters were working hard to create some of the most elaborate sets the film world has ever seen, sets so fantastic and new that it would take a fully qualified James Bond to get in and see them without official permission.

The movie–Stanley Kubrick's *2001*—would mean the beginning of the end for MGM Borehamwood.

Kubrick's *2001*

Afters the release of *2001: A Space Odyssey* on April 2, 1968, Stanley Kubrick would become known as one of the world's master filmmakers.

Love him or hate him, his work as a director, and the movies he captured for all time on celluloid, will forever be acknowledged by some as the work of a genius.

Most of his movies were made in the film studios of Borehamwood, in the county that he grew to love—Hertfordshire.

Here is the story of the man and his movies, as told by the people who worked with him.

Born in New York City on July 26, 1928, Stanley Kubrick grew up in the Bronx. A precociously intellectual child, he inherited an interest in still photography from his father, and would become a staff photographer on *Look* magazine at the age of seventeen.

Turning his love to motion pictures, in the space of five years, Kubrick directed three short documentaries and three low-budget independent features: *Fear and Desire* (1953), *Killer's Kiss* (1955), and *The Killing* (1955), which he also wrote and photographed.

These early films gained sufficient notice for him to attract the attention of Kirk Douglas, who would star in Kubrick's first Hollywood picture, *Paths of Glory* (1957).

Douglas was so taken with Kubrick as both a director and filmmaker that he hired him, at a weekend's notice, to take over his massive production of *Spartacus* (1960), after he'd fired its original director, Anthony Mann.

Spartacus was the only movie in Kubrick's repertoire of which he did not have full control. However, Kubrick's creative independence on the epic production did not go unnoticed by Hollywood executives, and because of this he made a decision in the early 1960s to work and reside in Britain, which lent a certain distance from the seats of executive power in Hollywood.

From then on, once a project had been approved Kubrick was generally left alone to complete his motion pictures to his own satisfaction, at his own pace, and under his own guidance.

This was a rare privileged position in the movie business, shared by few others (among them, Charlie Chaplin), and it is this that would give him his titanic international reputation, especially among his fellow filmmakers.

Kubrick first arrived in Borehamwood in 1960. He was to shoot an adaptation of Vladimir Nabokov's scandalous novel, *Lolita,* at both ABPC and MGM Studios.

From the controversial book about a fourteen-year-old nymphet (Lolita), Kubrick fashioned a brilliant black comedy of manners, avoiding elements of physical eroticism.

James Mason plays the middle-aged college professor, who becomes infatuated for the young girl. Mason's is a superb performance, matched also by his co-stars Shelley Winters, Sue Lyon (as Lolita), and, as the chameleon-like Clare Quilty, Peter Sellers.

Playing Vivian Darkbloom opposite Sellers was Marianne Stone. "I have happy memories of both ABPC and MGM Studios in Borehamwood, and *Lolita* was shot at both.

"I remember Stanley Kubrick inviting me to see the rushes at MGM during lunchtime, a great privilege. We all sat in the viewing theatre and he provided delicious sandwiches so we wouldn't go without lunch.

"He was a brilliant man, and he encouraged his actors to suggest and invent things for their characters. Not all directors are so secure.

"MGM British, where it was partly shot, was a very modern and pretty studio with very nice gardens, I seem to remember."

Kubrick became fascinated by the complex Peter Sellers. They also became friends, and would often rehearse scenes for the movie in the garden of Sellers home in Chipperfield, Hertfordshire.

During production of *Lolita,* local press printed two stories with connections to the movie. The first of which appeared in the *Borehamwood & Elstree Post* on January 19, 1961.

"JAMES MASON IN TWO CAR CRASH
Woman Thrown Through Windscreen"

A chauffeur-driven Rolls-Royce, with passenger James Mason, was involved in a crash with another car at the junction between Furzehill Road and Barnet Lane. A local woman was seriously injured.

Mr. Mason, who was starring in *Lolita* at ABPC Studios, escaped unhurt, and kept an appointment at a children's party in London after the smash.

The other car was driven by Mr. Arthur Ernest Lewis of Borehamwood. His passenger, Mrs. Eileen Greenwood, is reported to have been "thrown through the windscreen." Both cars were badly damaged. Mr. Mason was said to be naturally shaken.

On March 2, 1961, another report appeared.

"LOST RING HALTS *LOLITA*"

Work on the film at ABPC Studios was delayed because a heavy gold signet ring worn by star James Mason during some of the scenes was reported missing.

A spokesman for the film company said, "Mr. Mason usually took the signet ring home with him each night, but had left it at the studios. The following morning, it was missing. Filming was, therefore, held up while a replica was found."

For his next film shot at Shepperton Studios, Kubrick turned another controversial subject matter into the stuff of high comedy.

Peter George's novel *Red Alert*, a straight thriller about an accidental American nuclear attack on the USSR, became a cold war satire with Peter Sellers performing three different roles, including the title role in *Dr. Strangelove* (1963).

Sellers was paid $1 million for portraying three characters, which was 55% of the films budget. Kubrick famously quipped, "I got three for the price of six."

The Dr. Strangelove character was mostly improvised by Sellers, with Kubrick using three cameras to capture Sellers at his best.

It was during the shooting of these sequences that the usually stone-faced Kubrick found himself laughing out loud on set, so loud that it brought him to tears.

One such moment is when the wheelchair-bound Strangelove finds his right arm taking control of itself, and forcing on him a Hitler-style salute.

Kelvin Pike who was camera operator on the film, recalls how he came to work for Kubrick. "I was working on a film called *Two Weeks In Another Town* (1962) which Vincente Minnelli was directing, and which had Kirk Douglas and Edward G. Robinson in the cast.

"We filmed most of it in Rome, and the first scene I had with Kirk Douglas he tried to catch me out mechanically, as I had this complicated shot. He kept deliberately missing his mark, and Vincente would say, 'Kirk, you are not on your mark.' This, of course, let me off the hook.

"Anyway, when I came back to England, I got a call to go and meet Stanley Kubrick at Shepperton. The first thing he said to me was, 'How did you get on with Kirk?' because he'd worked with him and had some problems with him. But Kirk could be difficult.

"As regards to Stanley, though, we got on extremely well. We worked very closely together. He was super, and was open to ideas all the time. The delightful thing was that your contribution was acknowledged and it was there on the screen.

"A lot of people looked on him as a hard man, but when you actually got to know him he was a big softie, with a sense of humor behind him. I wouldn't have done three movies for him otherwise."

The critical and commercial success of *Dr. Strangelove* helped persuade MGM to shell out $10.5 million for a science fiction epic.

2001: A Space Odyssey (released in 1968), is unquestionably the most abstract, *avant garde* blockbuster ever made. It is also justly regarded as Kubrick's masterpiece.

Based on a short story by Arthur C. Clarke, the movie took four years of planning and production, with the final edit being Kubrick's vision (in 1968) of what life might be like at the start of the twenty-first century.

Principal photography began on December 29, 1965, at Shepperton Studios, before moving to MGM British in January 1966.

Kubrick was told that MGM was the most technically advanced studio outside of Hollywood, but the studio was soon to discover that, for his film, it needed to be.

2001 would have 205 special effects shots, and Kubrick ordered the technicians at MGM to use the painstaking process of creating all visual effects seen in the film "in camera" to avoid degraded picture quality from the use of blue screen and travelling matte techniques that were so often used in Science Fiction and Fantasy movies.

The film would shoot for over two years at MGM Borehamwood on some of the most impressive futuristic movie sets ever constructed, the most breathtaking of these being a massive vertical revolving wheel that formed a space station, with different compartments to represent different rooms. This was 38 feet in diameter, 10 feet wide, 30 tons, and travelled around at 14 mph. It was known as the "centrifuge" and cost £750,000 pounds to build.

Because of this, the many other set pieces needed to make the movie, and Kubrick's meticulous detail, MGM had little sound stage availability for a long period of time, resulting in what some would later say was the "downfall of the studio."

Kelvin Pike once again joined Kubrick as his camera operator. "I remember we had a scene inside the brain of the spaceship, a very complicated set, and to achieve our shot we had to turn the whole thing over and around, and turn the cameras around the other way. This we needed to do overnight, which took hours.

"Anyway, when it came to shoot the shot we needed, I looked up inside this assembled set and said to Stanley, 'It's been assembled the wrong way round. I'm quite certain.'

"Stanley took a look and said, 'Well we'd better change it.'

"I said, 'Stanley, it'll take two or three hours.'

"He said, 'Are you certain it's been done wrong?'

"I said, 'Yes.' He said, 'Well put it right then.'

"That was something that was fantastic about him as a director, that he accepted your word.

"It turned out to be a tough film technically, with lots of complicated camera shots and special effects, but I think we achieved what Stanley wanted in the end."

David Wynn-Jones worked on the movie as clapper/loader. "It was more or less my first job in the film business, and you have to remember I was working with some incredible people, at England's most superior film studio, MGM.

"Stanley liked me, I think, because I was keen to get things right, and hopefully very efficient with it."

For, Trevor Coop, *2001* was his debut in the film business. "The movie had already been shooting for over two years when the second assistant camera fell ill, and I was called in by Les Smart (Head of Camera Department) to take over.

"Geoffrey Unsworth (cinematographer on the film) had long since left, and his focus puller, John Alcott, had taken over as cameraman.

"We were to shoot the sequence with the rectangular obilisque tumbling through space.

"Wally Veevers had set up a dolly and geared head operated through stepper motors and worm drives to match the mechanical movement of the block. At four seconds per frame, the shot took seventeen hours to traverse the set built.

"We would load a magazine in the morning, test that everything was working okay, then set it in motion. We would then lock up the stage, go and shoot various pick up shots and inserts elsewhere, then after seventeen hours, return to the closed stage, unload the shot, and send it off to the labs.

"Every day, minute changes were made to the shot, and this went on six days a week for a month until Stanley was finally happy with the result."

Pamela Carlton worked for Kubrick as continuity. "Stanley was fine to work with, as long as you knew your job. He expected the best from you because he was a perfectionist.

"The MGM Studios were we shot *2001* were certainly the best studios in Borehamwood, if not the country. It had good personnel in all departments. I enjoyed working there."

Brian Johnson was also on the set of *2001*, helping in the special effects department. "It was funny working with Stanley, as he only allowed the crew to wear specially designed carpet slippers on the set."

Playing the lead role of Dr. Bowman in the film was Keir Dullea. "I recall the sound stages at MGM as being truly vast. After all, it had to house a three-story-tall centrifuge, plus many other fantasmagorical sets.

"I had a large and very pleasant dressing room in which I spent many, many happy hours between set-ups. Sometimes, Stanley would only do two set-ups in a day."

Stanley Kubrick's daughter, Katharina, has her own special memory of MGM Borhamwood. "The back lot of that studio was practically my playground when Dad was filming there. It was a very exciting place.

"I also think that the unique smell of a sound stage should be bottled. There is no other smell that can quite conjure up the promise of romance, magic, mystery, torment, and boredom, and the eagerly anticipated arrival of the tea trolley!"

Kubrick had so enjoyed working at the Hertfordshire studio and its surrounding countryside, that the family moved to live at Abbots Mead on Barnet Lane, Elstree in 1968.

By March 1968, *2001* was ready for showing to MGM executives. There reactions however were mixed, as were those at a special press showing, and so Kubrick made several cuts before the film's general release.

When it finally opened in April 1968, showing as Kubrick intended in 70mm Cinerama, audience reactions were either of ecstatic praise or vehement derision. Some calling it pure magic, while others found it confusing and therefore annoying.

2001 is nonetheless a breathtakingly immersive cinematic experience, as well as a compelling cerebral puzzle.

It is also, in parts, surprisingly moving, with the demise of HAL-2000, and the birth of the Star Child.

It went on to receive thirteen Oscar nominations yet gained just one win for Special Visual Effects, which was awarded to Stanley Kubrick, and while he himself did indeed design much of the look of the film and its effects, many of the technicians involved thought it was wrong for him to receive the sole credit.

Like all movies, after completion, the sets and props are either destroyed or disregarded. If lucky, some survive.

A few years after the release of *2001*, the seven-foot model of Space Station 5 was discovered in a poor state, covered in weeds, on a farmer's field some twenty miles from Borehamwood. It was later destroyed by vandals, a sad end, you might say, for a prop that became a piece of cinema history, from a film that has gone on to receive $190 million worldwide in box-office takings.

Kubrick's next project, a biopic of Napoleon, was cancelled by MGM due to a recession in the film industry. So, he turned instead to adapting Anthony Burgess's satirical fantasy *A Clockwork Orange* (1971). The resultant movie turned out to be Kubrick's most controversial, including scenes of extreme violence and rape.

Shot mainly on location in and around Borehamwood and Elstree, the film stars Malcolm McDowell as the leader of a gang known as the "droogs," who engage in an evening of ultra-violence that includes beating a man to the point of crippling him, and raping another man's wife while singing "Singin in the Rain."

Adrienne Corri played the wife, and at her audition for the movie was asked to strip by Kubrick and have nude Polaroid pictures taken. Corri subsequently told Kubrick where he could shove them, resulting in her getting the role.

The rape scene was shot many times, with Corri complaining that it was uncomfortable to keep having a ball pushed in her mouth and tape wrapped around her head (trapping the ball), thus also resulting in the tape being difficult to tear from her hair when preparing for the next take. Kubrick's response was, "If Miss Corri doesn't stop complaining and get on with the job, she'll have two balls shoved in her mouth."

June Randall was continuity on the film. I stumbled by mistake on to the set of *A Clockwork Orange*. Stanley said, 'Can you type?'

"And I said, 'Yes.'

"And he said, 'You've got the job.'

It was as easy as that. I was then given a few pages of the script. I wasn't allowed to look at the full thing. Later on, I found out why. The original script looked nothing like the one I was working with.

"I was also to discover that working with Stanley Kubrick was extremely hard work, as he never knew when to stop. The working hours were long and difficult. But he was a difficult man, a perfectionist.

"If there were three cameras running, he was behind every one, running from one to another.

"Let's face it, he was the best director I ever worked for. A genius, but a tough one.

"I remember he advertised for a girl to be raped by fifty men. We had a hundred replies.

"We had to paint this poor girls pubic hairs purple, like a heart, and all these guys have to rape her. Stanley said to me, 'If any man's penis is shown, I want you to... .'

"I said, 'I'm not going anywhere near them.'

"He said, 'I can't have a penis in shot.'

I didn't care. I was a real prude then."

June Randall offered a few days of work on the movie to her friend, Peggy Spirito. "I was scared to death. I thought Stanley would kill me. So I wouldn't work with him. No way. He would have made mince meat out of me."

Despite a good general reception from critics upon its release, the British authorities considered the sexual violence in *A Clockwork Orange* to be too extreme. The movie also became connected to copycat violence, and the Kubrick family themselves also received anonymous threats. This resulted in Kubrick withdrawing the movie from British distribution in 1973, disliking the allegations that it could in any way be connected to real life violence.

Quoting Kubrick from an article that was printed in the *Borehamwood & Elstree Post*: "To try and fasten any responsibility on art as the cause of life seems to put the case the wrong way round. Art consists of reshaping life, but it does not create life, nor cause it. Furthermore, to attribute powerful suggestive qualities to a film is at odds with the scientifically accepted view that, even after deep hypnosis in a posthypnotic state, people cannot be made to do things which are at odds with their natures."

Kubrick's next motion picture enterprise would be a lavish adaptation of William Thackeray's period novel, *Barry Lyndon* (1975).

Regarded by some as his most beautiful-looking film, with each scene looking like an exquisite eighteenth century painting, the movie was shot entirely on location, mainly in Ireland.

Cinematography was overseen by John Alcott, who created images on screen, during the filming of interiors, using just natural light and candlelight. This, in turn, gave the film Kubrick's desired look of an era in time devoid of electric light but elegant in both costume and colours, therefore capturing on film, using the above lighting methods, the painting style of the day. William Hogarth was a particular inspiration.

Exteriors were also filmed using a similar technique, by shooting landscapes in the same way that Watteau and Gainsborough had painted them.

A breathtaking movie to look at, it is not difficult to see why it won Oscars for Costumes, Cinematography, and Production Design.

Playing the Recruiting Sergeant in *Barry Lyndon* was Norman Mitchell. "Stanley Kubrick was a cinema great. By training, he was a photographer. He's started out taking stills and this had a lasting effect on his work.

"At the beginning of the movie, you see a beautiful picture of the Irish countryside, and then suddenly before your eyes it comes to life and starts to move.

"Kubrick's films were the product of oceans of work and time. He would spend hours lining up a shot and then he would do umpteen number of takes. No expense was too great to get the right shot.

"For one scene, he got 600 real-life Irish soldiers to dress up as British soldiers in the eighteenth century redcoat uniform. He took a look at the shot and shouted, 'Paddy!'

"600 Irish soldiers shouted back, 'What?'

"He then turned to his first assistant and said, 'There's a sparrow on the haystack, get rid of it.' So, the first assistant went running across the field clapping his hands.

"Ryan O' Neal, the star of the film, was exasperated by Kubrick's methods. He said, 'For Christ's sake, when are we going to shoot something? I'm getting cold.'

"Kubrick, without taking his eye from the camera said, 'Coat for Mr. O' Neal.'

"Kubrick did so many takes because he didn't know what he wanted until he saw it. You'd get to the end of a take and he'd just say, 'That's no good, do something else.' But when you did the right thing, he knew. That was his genius.

"The filming schedule was worked out while the shoot was in progress, as was much of the dialogue. This makes for a long and very expensive shoot.

"During filming in Ireland we all stayed at the same hotel in Waterford. One night, at about 1 a.m., there was a light knock at my door and a call sheet was slipped underneath. I got out of bed and took a look at it. 5 a.m., Scene 235. I was in 235 and so I looked it up in the script. It said, 'To Be Written.' Nevertheless, there was nothing for it but to get up at 4 a.m., stand under a cold shower, and then get a cup of black coffee from the hotel restaurant.

"I was sat there sipping when Kubrick walked in. 'What scene are you called for, Norman?'

"'235', I replied.

"Kubrick turned and shouted to Ryan O' Neal, who was lying down on a sofa in the lounge, 'Ryan, 235's not written yet, is it?'

"'Too damn right' said O' Neal. 'Let's just make it up as we go along.'

"You won't be surprised to learn that I was originally contracted to do two weeks on the film and ended up staying for three months.

"Often we shot until 10:30 p.m., with many re-takes. One scene, we got up to Take 72. An actor, who simply had to say one word and then exit through a door, was a nervous wreck by Take 60, terrified he was going to do something wrong and shaking violently.

"We eventually progressed to doing some shots in a castle. It was late in the evening, and all of a sudden all of the lights in the castle went out. Pitch black.

"Kubrick shouted, 'What the f**k is going on?'

"'Must be a power cut,' returns the first assistant.

"'Then get candles. Hundreds of them.'

"So the props people did. There were candles and candelabras everywhere, dripping wax on everyone. The costume lady was livid. She had to spend hours with brown paper and hot irons, removing the stains to keep continuity.

"This is how I believe the filming with candles was introduced to the movie. It worked beautiful, and the scenes have a lovely, gentle light. Religious you might say."

Barry Lyndon was not the commercial success Kubrick had been hoping for, and its disappointing reception would set the pattern for his future work.

Actor/director Stuart Cooper remembers meeting Kubrick in the mid 1970s. "Stanley's photographer, Johnny Alcott did a film for me— *Overlord*—which I directed in 1975. Alcott was a world-class photographer. Definitely one of Britain's best. He was also a terrific person.

"I remember him inviting me to Borehamwood. He had just finished *Barry Lyndon* with Stanley, and we met at The Red Lion public house.

It was actually a set-up, as he took me to meet Stanley. But the reason for this was that Stanley had just seen a print of my film, *Overlord*, and wanted to meet me. So, off we go to his office at EMI Elstree Film Studios.

"Stanley was a real film buff. An absolute charming man. Anyway, at the end of my meeting with him, he said, 'I've got one problem with your film *Overlord*, just one problem.'

"I took a deep breath.

"He said, 'You know, Stuart, *Overlord* is one and a half hours too short.'

"It was the nicest compliment one could possibly get.

"Stanley was an interesting character, and I got to know him quite well afterwards. And, as reclusive as he was, he was very interested in what else was going on, and what else was being made. And if he saw something which inspired him, he made the effort to reach out to you."

The air of disappointment that loomed over *Barry Lyndon* factored into Kubrick's decision to next film Stephen King's best-selling horror novel, *The Shining*, a project that would not only please him artistically, but also be more likely to succeed financially.

The film is best remembered for Jack Nicholson's axe wielding, leering performance, but it is also a genuinely frightening ghost story and one of the screen's most intensely evocative portraits of madness.

Before embarking on this cinematic journey however, Kubrick and his family moved home in 1978. No longer would Abbots Mead on Barnet Lane, Elstree, remain his fortress. He moved to a bigger property but remained within the county he loved—Hertfordshire. Childwickbury Manor was the Kubrick's new home, lying between the towns of St. Albans and Harpenden.

Principal photography on *The Shining* began in May 1978 at EMI Elstree Film Studios (formerly ABPC).

The set for the interior of the Overlook Hotel was one of the biggest built on sound stages at the studio, while the exterior of the hotel constructed on the back lot was a full recreation of Timberline Lodge on Mount Hood in Oregon, USA.

Kelvin Pike was back with Kubrick as camera operator. "One day on *The Shining*, he was pushing Jack Nicholson hard, and he knew Jack would usually peak in his performance on the fifth or sixth take. When we got to Take 10, Jack looked straight into the camera and said, 'Make up your f**king mind, Stanley' and left the floor. Stanley walked off the set after him, obviously upset, even though he wouldn't show it, to sort things out. It was sorted, eventually.

"Jack Nicholson was a fun actor to work with. You could have a laugh with him. He was one of the boys. At the same time, he was dubbing his film *Goin South* (1978) at Elstree, and I remember that he had a showing of it and invited all of the crew of *The Shining*.

"I felt sorry for Shelley Duvall, who was playing opposite Jack. She couldn't really be expected to churn out the same physical and emotional performance after Take 10. It was very hard on her, I thought. She often walked into a scene ready to go, emotionally, but Stanley expected her to keep dragging it out. It's amazing how she managed to get through it really. But she was a method actor, and she often had to wind herself up in to a scene. Stanley, though, was not a method actor type, and he did have communication problems with her. He actually treated actors depending on the strength of them, and particularly liked actors who could stand up to him. He respected them more.

"I remember the most takes I ever did with Stanley was on a scene with Scatman Crothers. 142 Takes. Poor old Scatman, Stanley drove him into the ground. Wore him down completely. He ended up in tears.

"About one day a month, Stanley would be on your back and give you problems. And I remember we were doing a scene with Jack Nicholson at the typewriter, and Stanley was giving me a hard time. Well I turned to the cinematographer, John Alcott, and said, 'I've had enough. I'm not putting up with this anymore. I want to get it sorted out. I'm definitely going to corner Stanley, and tell him to cut it out.'

"Anyway, all of a sudden, Jack Nicholson, said, 'Stan, leave the guy alone. He knows a hell of a lot more about operating a camera than you do.'

"So that was the end of that."

Danny Shelmerdine had joined the crew of *The Shining* as assistant camera. "Sadly, I walked out of the filming after sixteen weeks. I could never see eye to eye with Stanley, and his attitude and working conditions just didn't work for me. When you shoot one shot over 100 times, its time to call it a day, I think."

James Devis, who worked on the film as second camera operator, had a different opinion of Kubrick. "Stanley was very knowledgeable about everything. He was also a hard task master, but I found him nice to work with, and if you were good at what you did, he would be very appreciative."

Working with Kubrick again as continuity was June Randall. "Jack Nicholson was a dream to work with, but he found the long hours tough. I loved him, though. He was so funny, and so rude. He never fluffed his lines. He could do day and night and never fluff a line. A marvellous actor.

The best ever. A laugh a minute and a lovely man. The men on set liked him, as did the women. If the crew like an actor, they must be very special. Jack likes, as an actor, to go over the top. He enjoys himself. It's very funny, because I'd trim Jack's beard, I'd mop his brow, I'd stand in for him. In fact, I did just about everything on set.

"Stanley didn't like too many people on the set, though. He said he'd like to make a film with five people.

"When Scatman Crothers first came on the set, Stanley said to me, 'See if he knows his lines.'

"So I said to Mr. Crothers, 'Can I go through your lines with you?'

And he said, 'Who are you?'

"And I said, 'I'm the script girl.'

"And he said, 'I'll only go through them with Mr. Kubrick.'

"So, I told Stanley, and in the next breath I was going through Mr. Crothers' lines with him. In fact, from then on, I couldn't get rid of Mr. Crothers. He was following me all over the set going through his lines. We must have done over 100 takes on one scene with him, because he couldn't remember his lines. He was a lovely man, though.

"I remember I had to type, 'All work and no play makes Jack a dull boy' hundreds—probably thousands—of times, in all languages. Stanley had also stressed that it should be typed like a maniac, and sometimes late at night I would type this with my toes on the guide keys.

"Stanley checked the rushes one day, and said to me, 'Do I not employ you to notice things?'

"I said, 'Yes. What?'

"He said, 'There was a door knob missing off of one of the hotel room doors when Danny rode past on his bicycle.'

"I said, 'Who's looking at the doors? He's moving so quick.'

"He said, 'I'm looking at the doors, so put the knob on.'

"Stanley could be very stubborn. Everything, and I mean everything had to be perfect. He didn't con the public. I did admire him."

Roy Walker was the film's production designer. "I worked on *The Shining* at EMI Elstree Film Studios for the period of about a year.

"Stanley was quite a nervous guy, and always worried about the safety of himself and his family.

"As a director he was very demanding. He didn't suffer fools kindly. You had to be very patient with him."

During the latter part of shooting *The Shining*, disaster happened on set. June Randall tells the story. "We were on the huge hotel set, with all these beautiful props in it, and we had all this fake snow outside, as it was supposed to be snowing. Anyway, a member of the crew ran in and said something was on fire outside, but it was a big fire. Then, all the lights went out. Complete darkness. No lights. And we were on a set built wall to wall, which would never happen now. So everyone was running around, and the big doors wouldn't open, as they'd locked because of this fire. I can recall the thick black smoke. We just done the scene with Scatman Crothers were he gets the hatchet in his chest. So, when he ran off the set, covered in blood, the fire brigade put him in an ambulance. They didn't realise it was make-up. Just as I left the set, I realised that the script was left behind, with all the important notes, and so I ran back to save it. I couldn't by this time find the desk with it on, because of all the smoke, which was choking me. I did manage to find it, though. But it was a mad thing to do. I'd never do it now. However, it's what you do at the spare of the moment. I couldn't have continued on the movie without that script, because it had all the important continuity notes in it.

"Anyway, the set and sound stage was destroyed. It had even buckled the sound stage doors. That's how bad the fire was. It was lucky that it happened near the end of the shoot, and we'd really finished with that set. It was a brilliant set, too."

Katharina Kubrick remembers her father's reaction to the fire. "He was mortified, as you might well imagine, but took a bizarrely morbid delight in the fact that the set (of the Overlook Hotel) was so realistic that the hapless fire fighters mistook the service corridors of the hotel set for the real corridors of the sound stage and were perplexed and frustrated that nothing worked!"

The fire caused extensive damage, resulting in the rebuilding of one of the sound stages, pushing back the next film due to be shot there, *The Empire Strikes Back* (1980), by several months.

It is also sad to note that where the exterior of the Overlook Hotel once stood, now stands a Tesco supermarket.

The Shining had a slow start at the box-office, but gained momentum, eventually doing well commercially and making Warner Bros. a profit.

Stephen King, though, was not pleased with Kubrick's adaptation of his novel, as he felt that it strayed too far from what he had written.

For his next movie, *Full Metal Jacket* (1987), Kubrick left the confines of the Borehamwood film studios and went on location to shoot his film set during the Vietnam War.

He did plan a return visit to Borehamwood to shoot his last movie,

Eyes Wide Shut (1999), but decided in the end to film at Pinewood.

The stars of the movie, Tom Cruise and Nicole Kidman, actually stayed at High Canons in Well End during filming, a mansion house that lies a short distance from Borehamwood.

Taking 400 days to complete, *Eyes Wide Shut* turned out to be one of Kubrick's most successful movies at the box-office.

However, he wasn't to know this, because after showing a final cut to Cruise, Kidman, and Warner Bros. executives on March 2, 1999, Kubrick died in his sleep of natural causes five days later. He was seventy.

Among those who attended the quiet family funeral on the grounds of the Kubrick estate were Tom Cruise, Nicole Kidman, and Steven Spielberg, who had been collaborating with Kubrick on a project, which would become *A.I. – Artificial Intelligence* (2001), which, in the end, displayed more of Spielberg's authorship than Kubrick's.

Stanley Kubrick would be buried next to his favorite tree at Childwickbury Manor, and in Christiane Kubrick's book that was dedicated to him, she included one of his favorite quotes by Oscar Wilde: "The tragedy of old age is not that one is old, but that one is young."

June Randall recalls her memories of the famous director. "In all the time I worked with him, I never really got to know Stanley well. What I can tell you is that he loved animals. I also remember that a butterfly flew on to the set of *The Shining*, and Stanley shouted, 'Kill all the lights! It might get burnt!'—and he meant it.

"I remember he bought me a bracelet, which I've never had off my wrist, and with it was a little note, which read in his scratchy writing, 'You're wonderful.'

"And when my husband, Morris, died, whom Stanley knew well, he sent me a note which read, 'You must be very very unhappy.'

"He was certainly one of the best directors in the world. A great man. I was very lucky to work with him."

The last word on Stanley Kubrick goes to his camera operator, Kelvin Pike. "It's a funny thing, shortly after he died me and my wife were driving local to Borehamwood, and this car drove towards us very slowly from the opposite direction, and it looked like Stanley was driving. I thought I wouldn't put it past that bastard not to have died at all.

"I do miss him though."

Harry Lee Danziger (left) and wife Angela, with Edward J. Danziger (right) and wife Gigi.
Courtesy of Nick Danziger.

The Tell-Tale Heart (1960). Publicity still of Laurence Payne. Courtesy of Phyllis Townshend.

The Tell-Tale Heart (1960). Publicity still of Adrienne Corri, Dermot Walsh (centre) and Laurence Payne (left). Courtesy of Phyllis Townshend.

The Tell-Tale Heart (1960). Adrienne Corri and Laurence Payne prepare to shoot a scene. Phyllis Townshend (continuity) is seated, Bob Jordan (clapper) is standing behind camera, wearing dark glasses, and Ernest Morris (director) is behind camera, wearing dark coloured sweater. Courtesy of Phyllis Townshend.

The Tell-Tale Heart (1960). Dermot Walsh (seated) and Laurence Payne prepare to shoot a scene. Note the boom microphone. Courtesy of Phyllis Townshend.

The Spider's Web (1960). Brian Taylor chats with Agatha Christie on set.
Courtesy of Brian Taylor.

The Spider's Web (1960). Glynis
Johns relaxes between filming.
Courtesy of Phyllis Townshend.

Tarnished Heroes (1961). Publicity still of Dermot Walsh and Sheila Whittingham. Courtesy of Sheila Whittingham.

Fate Takes A Hand (1961). Assistant director, Geoffrey Helman holding clapperboard. Courtesy of Geoffrey Helman.

Richard the Lionheart (1961-63). Publicity still of Dermot Walsh as Richard the Lionheart. Courtesy of Sheila Whittingham.

Richard the Lionheart (1961-63). Trader Faulkner (left), Sheila Whittingham, Francis de Wolf (third left), Dermot Walsh (fourth left), Conrad Phillips (fifth left), Michael Peake (Right, front), Ian Gregory (right, foreground). Courtesy of Trader Faulkner.

Richard The Lionheart (1961-63). Dermot Walsh goes over his lines for the next scene. Geoffrey Helman (assistant director) stands far right, and Ernest Morris (director) stands far left. Courtesy of Geoffrey Helman.

Richard the Lionheart (1961-63). Dermot Walsh prepares to shoot a scene. Bob Jordan (clapper) is seated. Courtesy of Bob Jordan.

Richard the Lionheart (1961-63). Publicity still of Dermot Walsh and Trader Faulkner. Courtesy of Trader Faulkner.

Richard the Lionheart (1961-63). Trader Faulkner (third right), Sheila Whittingham (second right) and Dermot Walsh (first right) filming a scene. Prudence Hyman is seated with script. Courtesy of Trader Faulkner.

Richard the Lionheart (1961-63). Gene Beck does Trader Faulkner's make-up. Francis de Wolf (right) and Michael Peake (left) wait patiently. Courtesy of Trader Faulkner.

Richard the Lionheart (1961-63). Sheila Whittingham prepares to film a scene on horseback. Courtesy of Sheila Whittingham.

Richard the Lionheart (1961-63). Sheila Whittingham sits behind the camera with director Ernest Morris (standing). Courtesy of Sheila Whittingham.

Richard the Lionheart (1961-63). Ernest Morris (left) directs Dermot Walsh and Sheila Whittingham. Bob Jordan (clapper) can be seen through centre. Courtesy of Bob Jordan.

Richard The Lionheart (1961-63). Publicity still of Ian Gregory (left), Dermot Walsh (seated), Ian Fleming (second right) and Alan Haywood (right). Courtesy of Ian Gregory.

Richard the Lionheart (1961-63). Dermot Walsh and Sheila Whittingham film a scene. Jimmy Harvey (cinematographer) is left of camera. Courtesy of Sheila Whittingham.

Richard the Lionheart (1961-63). Bruce the Lion loose on set at New Elstree Studios. Courtesy of Ian Gregory.

Richard the Lionheart (1961-63). Rare behind the scenes photograph of Dermot Walsh and Sheila Whittingham shooting a scene. Jimmy Harvey (cinematographer) is fifth from right, and Bob Jordan (clapper) is behind him. Courtesy of Bob Jordan.

The Spanish Sword (1962). Publicity still of Ronald Howard (left), Derrick Sherwin and Sheila Whittingham. Courtesy of Sheila Whittingham.

The Spanish Sword (1962). Publicity still of Nigel Green (left) and Trader Faulkner on horseback. Courtesy of Trader Faulkner.

The Spanish Sword (1962). Publicity still of Nigel Green (standing) and Trader Faulkner. Courtesy of Trader Faulkner.

The site of the Danziger Brothers New Elstree Studios in 2015. Courtesy of Derek Pykett.

'Blue Plaque' on the site of the Danziger Brothers New Elstree Studios.
Courtesy of Derek Pykett.

Gorgo (1960). Model miniature of Tower Bridge constructed in the studio by 'production designer' Elliot Scott. Courtesy of Stephen Scott.

Gorgo (1960). Model miniature being destroyed by Gorgo. Courtesy of Stephen Scott.

The Millionairess (1960). Camera Operator, Gerry Fisher (right) celebrates his birthday on set at MGM British with Alistair Sim (left), Sophia Loren and Anthony Asquith (director). Courtesy of Gerry Fisher.

The Millionairess (1960). Camera Operator, Gerry Fisher (right) celebrates his birthday on set with Alistair Sim and Sophia Loren. Courtesy of Gerry Fisher.

The Millionairess (1960). Sophia Loren prepares to shoot a scene. Gerry Fisher (camera operator) is to the left of her, and Anthony Asquith (director) is to the right. Courtesy of Gerry Fisher.

The Millionairess (1960). Peter Sellers and Sophia Loren relax in the grounds of MGM British between takes. Courtesy of Michael Sellers.

Mr. Topaze (1961). Rare behind the scenes still of Peter Sellers and Nadia Gray relaxing between takes at MGM British. Geoff Glover (clapper) in sitting on floor, to the right of camera. Note - MGM - on the camera. Courtesy of Geoff Glover.

Nine Hours To Rama (1962). Cast and crew relaxing between takes on the back-lot at MGM British. Jose Ferrer (first left), Horst Buchholz (fourth left), Diane Baker (fifth left), Robert Morley (seventh left), Mark Robson, director (eighth left), Arthur Ibbetson, cinematographer (ninth left) and Paul Wilson, camera operator (behind camera). Courtesy of Paul Wilson.

The Dock Brief (1962). Richard Attenborough (first left), Herbert Smith, camera operator (second left), James Hill, director (third left) and Edward Scaife, cinematographer, clowning around between takes at MGM British. Courtesy of Herbert Smith.

What A Crazy World (1963). Michael Ripper (prolific character actor) playing one of numerous memorable roles. Courtesy of Michael Ripper.

The VIP's (1963). Anthony Asquith (director), and Elizabeth Taylor relaxing in the grounds of MGM British Studios. Courtesy of Gerry Fisher.

The VIP's (1963). Richard Burton and Elizabeth Taylor relaxing between takes at MGM British. Courtesy of Gerry Fisher.

Lancelot And Guinevere (1963). Publicity still of Cornel Wilde (left) and Ian Gregory (right). Courtesy of Ian Gregory.

The Haunting (1963). Corridor set designed and constructed by 'production designer' Elliot Scott. Courtesy of Stephen Scott.

The Haunting (1963). The metal staircase designed and constructed on a sound stage at MGM British Studios by 'production designer' Elliot Scott. Courtesy of Stephen Scott.

The Haunting (1963). Impressive production still featuring Julie Harris and Richard Johnson, showing the height of the metal staircase constructed in the studio by 'production designer' Elliot Scott. Courtesy of Stephen Scott.

Night Must Fall (1964). Shooting a scene. Karel Reisz (far right), Gerry Fisher, camera operator (behind camera), Freddie Francis, cinematographer (behind Fisher), Pamela Francis, continuity (sitting). Courtesy of Pamela Francis.

Night Must Fall (1964). Preparing to shoot a scene. Albert Finney (seated on moped), Freddie Francis, cinematographer (standing by camera, in dark glasses), Gerry Fisher, camera operator (behind camera), Jimmy Dawes, grip (second left, standing). Courtesy of Pamela Francis.

Murder Ahoy (1964). Margaret Rutherford relaxes on set between takes. Note the painted back-drop, and MGM on the lamp. Courtesy of Francis Matthews.

My partner, Ruth, standing outside 'Misbourne Cottage' in Denham Village, Buckinghamshire – once the home of John Mills and his family, but more famous as being the home of Margaret Rutherford in the Miss Marple series of films. Courtesy of Derek Pykett.

The Chalk Garden (1964). Beachy Head set constructed on a sound stage at MGM British. Ronald Neame can be seen directing Hayley Mills and Deborah Kerr in the far left corner. Courtesy of Paul Wilson.

The Chalk Garden (1964). Preparing to shoot a scene in the studio. Hayley Mills (first right), Deborah Kerr (second right), Arthur Ibbetson, cinematographer (third right), Ronald Neame, director (fourth right), Paul Wilson, camera operator (sitting behind camera). Courtesy of Paul Wilson.

A Shot In The Dark (1964). Peter Sellers showing his new Mini to co-star George Sanders in the grounds of MGM British. Courtesy of Michael Sellers.

Young Cassidy (1964). Jack Cardiff, director (in dark glasses) and Edward Scaife, cinematographer (standing to right of Cardiff) on location. Note MGM trucks in foreground. Courtesy of Graeme Scaife.

Young Cassidy (1964). Rod Taylor (right), Edith Evans and Jack Cardiff chatting on the back-lot at MGM British. Courtesy of Rod Taylor.

Young Cassidy (1964). Rod Taylor (centre) relaxing in the grounds of MGM British with Jack Cardiff (right) and Maggie Smith (left). Courtesy of Rod Taylor.

Young Cassidy (1964). Rod Taylor and Maggie Smith relax on set at MGM British Studios. Courtesy of Graeme Scaife.

The Hill (1965). Sean Connery (first right), Sidney Lumet, director (second right), George Catt, studio manager (third right) and Kenneth Hyman, producer (fourth right) relaxing on set at MGM British. Courtesy of Kenneth Hyman.

The Hill (1965). Kenneth Hyman (centre) on location with Sean Connery (right) and Sidney Lumet (left). Courtesy of Kenneth Hyman.

The MGM British reception and administration office in 1965. Courtesy of Stephen Scott.

Aerial photograph of MGM British Studios in 1966. Courtesy of Dennis Fraser.

Eye Of The Devil (1966). Elliot Scott 'production design'. Courtesy of Stephen Scott.

Eye Of The Devil (1966). Elliot Scott 'production design'. Courtesy of Stephen Scott.

Eye Of The Devil (1966). Rare production still of Kim Novak (holding umbrella) on the back-lot of MGM British Studios. Novak was later replaced by Deborah Kerr. Sharon Tate is also pictured, along with Dennis Fraser, grip (second right). Courtesy of Dennis Fraser.

One Million Years B.C. (1966). Ray Harryhausen shows visiting Princess Muna footage of his dinosaurs at ABPC Studios, Borehamwood. Courtesy of Ray Harryhausen.

One Million Years B.C. (1966). Ray Harryhausen shows Princess Muna his dinosaurs from the film. Courtesy of Ray Harryhausen.

The Dirty Dozen (1967). The Dozen preparing to shoot a scene on location. Courtesy of David Wynn-Jones.

The Dirty Dozen (1967). Part of the General Worden's office set designed and constructed by 'production designer' William Hutchinson. Courtesy of Tim Hutchinson.

The Dirty Dozen (1967). Ernest Borgnine (left), Robert Webber (centre), and Lee Marvin playing cards off set at MGM British Studios. Courtesy of David Wynn-Jones.

The Dirty Dozen (1967). Model of the chateau by 'production designer' William Hutchinson. Courtesy of Tim Hutchinson.

The Dirty Dozen (1967). The chateau, as designed by William Hutchinson, being constructed on the back-lot at MGM British Studios. Courtesy of Tim Hutchinson.

The Dirty Dozen (1967). The chateau and bridge, as designed by William Hutchinson, being constructed on the back-lot at MGM British Studios, Borehamwood. Courtesy of Tim Hutchinson.

The Dirty Dozen (1967). Interior chateau set, designed by William Hutchinson, constructed on a sound stage at MGM British. Courtesy of Tim Hutchinson.

The Dirty Dozen (1967). The chateau after filming the final explosion, which caused complaints from local residents in Borehamwood. Courtesy of John Richardson.

The Dirty Dozen (1967). Trini Lopez relaxes on the back-lot at MGM British Studios, Borehamwood. Edward Scaife (cinematographer) is standing right of the camera. David Wynn-Jones (clapper) is far left. Courtesy of David Wynn-Jones.

The Fearless Vampire Killers (1967). Sharon Tate relaxes on the back-lot at MGM British. Courtesy of Dennis Fraser.

The Fearless Vampire Killers (1967). Roman Polanski, director (behind camera) and Douglas Slocombe, cinematographer, preparing to shoot a scene. Courtesy of Robin Vidgeon.

The Prisoner (1968). Patrick McGoohan chats with Dennis Fraser (grip) on set at MGM British Studios. Courtesy of Dennis Fraser.

The Avengers (1961-69). Publicity still of Diana Rigg as Emma Peel.
Courtesy of Brian Clemens.

The Avengers (1961-69). Publicity still of Patrick Macnee as John Steed standing on enlarged set at ABPC Studios, Borehamwood. Courtesy of Brian Clemens.

The Avengers (1961-69). Diana Rigg and Brian Clemens (producer) on set at ABPC Studios, Borehamwood. Courtesy of Brian Clemens.

The Avengers (1961-69). Cast and crew on location. Patrick Macnee (far right) Peggy Spirito, continuity (kneeling). Courtesy of Peggy Spirito.

Downfall of a Legend

Whether *2001* was partly responsible for the closure of MGM British will never be properly verified. Its final years as a studio, though, were still productive, with several major features being made at the site.

Eye Of The Devil (1966) had started filming with a different director and a different star, Kim Novak.

On Thursday December the 2, 1965, the *Borehamwood & Elstree Post* reported:

"DEBORAH TO TAKE OVER KIM'S PART"

Deborah Kerr had been brought in to take over from Kim Novak, who had apparently injured her back falling from a horse.

Her entire part was to be re-shot, also using a different director, and was estimated to cost the film's insurer's over £500,000.

Novak had indeed fallen from a horse, but according to members of the crew, this was not the reason for her being replaced.

She was fired, along with the director, Michael Anderson, for violent outbursts of anger on the set, as the two did not see eye to eye. This came to an abrupt end when Novak, in a towering rage, threw a steaming cup of coffee over Anderson, which saw them both being shown the door by the producers.

Replacements, at high cost to the budget, included Deborah Kerr getting the lead role and J. Lee Thompson taking over the director's chair.

The plot, revolving around the occult, supernatural, and black magic, was certain to be a sure-fire winner, and with a supporting cast including David Niven, Donald Pleasence, Flora Robson, and David Hemmings, everyone involved expected a box-office success. Sadly, it flopped, and only recently has it gained some cult recognition, mainly due to the casting of Texas-born television actress and fashion model, Sharon Tate.

It was actually Tate's first major role of only a handful of film roles, two of which played out at MGM British.

"PRINCESS MUNA VISITS BOREHAMWOOD"
This was the report in the *Borehamwood & Elstree Post* on Thursday
July 28, 1966.

Princess Muna, the then wife of King Hussein of Jordan, visited the
film studios of Borehamwood, where she met top international stars. At
a lunchtime reception, she was introduced to Yul Brynner, Britt Ekland,
Roger Moore, and Charlie Drake. She was also introduced to special effects legend, Ray Harryhausen, who was working on Hammer's *One
Million Years B.C.* (1966) at the ABPC Studios. Harryhausen recalled, "I
showed the Princess my dinosaurs, which I'd made for the picture. She
seemed very interested."

Harryhausen also remembered making the movie. "I felt we could
make *One Million Years B.C.* better than the 1930s version with Victor
Mature, which Hal Roach directed, and which had men in Dinosaur suits.

"At ABPC Studios, they made a special room for me up by the scene
docks. This was also close to the tank, which they used in Huston's *Moby
Dick* film. It's a shame to say this, but I think where that tank was is now
a Tesco supermarket.

"We shot all the earthquake scenes at that studio. In miniature first,
and then through travelling matte we put the people in.

"I got pneumonia during the filming of the volcano scenes. I went
out from a very warm sound stage, and without wearing my heavy coat,
I walked in the cold to my little studio. So, I ended up in bed, and missed
several days of filming.

"All the cave sequences were built and shot on the sound stages at
ABPC. They actually built some quite elaborate rock work.

"Raquel Welch was our star, and I've often said, if cave women looked
like her we've regressed considerably over the years.

"I certainly enjoyed working at those studios in Borehamwood. It's
just sad that most of the studio that was ABPC has now disappeared."

At the same time as Ray Harryhausen was busy animating his dinosaurs, Yul Brynner and Britt Ekland were at ABPC filming *The Double
Man* (1967), a complex espionage thriller, directed by Franklin J Schaffner.

Renee Glynne was continuity. "Schaffner was very tall. He reminded
me of James Stewart. A very gentle man, who spoke very gently.

"Yul Brynner was very interesting as a person. He was also a bit difficult and bad tempered, with his own set of demands. But, he was a Hollywood star, and a very good actor. He could also be caring, too.

"The producer on *The Double Man* was Hal E. Chester. He didn't give in to anything, not even Brynner's demands."

While Yul Brynner was strutting his stuff on one stage, Roger Moore was shooting on another the fifth year of the series, *The Saint*.

The Saint, like *The Avengers*, was a great television success, especially for Moore, and ran for 118 episodes between 1962-1969, all filmed at the ABPC Studios.

The character played by Moore, Simon Templar, was originally intended for Patrick McGoohan, who had turned the role down. Moore was then cast and became a top television name in a part that undoubtedly led to him being cast as movie icon *James Bond* in the early 1970s.

Meanwhile at MGM British, a number of war films were in production. These included *Submarine X-1* (1967), and *Attack on the Iron Coast* (1967) with Lloyd Bridges.

Neil Binney was camera operator on both. "Those films were quite low-budget and shot back to back at MGM Borehamwood.

"It wasn't the first time I'd worked there. Previously, I had been a camera assistant on one of the many cameras shooting *Around The World In 80 Days* (1956), and was amazed at the extravagance and the power of the production.

"Earlier still, I was junior assistant on *Mogambo* (1953) and so thrilled to be touched by the cast of Hollywood greats.

"At the time, I remember being struck by the care of the gardens on the frontage of the studios. There was even a pig farm on the grounds!

"The stages were huge. It was certainly a special place to work."

As far as war movies go, the next one to be filmed at MGM British during 1966 was one of the biggest. Featuring a tough all-star cast, mega-budget, and lots of explosive action, *The Dirty Dozen* would be remembered by residents of Borehamwood for a very long time.

Shot almost entirely on sound stages at MGM, and in the studios back lot, Robert Aldrich took charge of the production as director, while Kenneth Hyman returned to the studio as producer, after his previous success with *The Hill*.

With a $5.4 million budget, John Wayne was cast to play the lead role, but then turned it down after objecting to adultery scenes present in the original script. Hollywood hard man, Lee Marvin, took over the role of Major John Reisman.

Jack Palance also turned down the part of Archer Maggott after expressing his unhappiness with racism in the screenplay. Telly Savalas took his role.

Stuart Cooper played Roscoe Lever (one of the dozen), and tells his story of the production. "We did two week's rehearsal for *The Dirty Dozen* in one of the sound stages at MGM British, which was a premium studio. Definitely the grandpappy.

"Bob Aldrich had a huge oval table made, covered in felt like a billiard table, and every member of the cast sat around it, and we did a full on read through. I remember that each chair around this table had our names on it, and in front of each chair was a red leather-bound screenplay, with our names on the cover and the character we played. It was so impressive, but sadly, I no longer have it.

"I remember that they brought in a technical advisor to start us marching, and do all the military stuff. Anyway, a few days into this, Charles Bronson, said, 'This isn't how you do this stuff,' as he was ex-military. So, he started to argue with the technical advisor.

"Lee Marvin then stepped in, another ex-military, and said, 'Jesus Christ, Charlie, what the man is doing with us is right.'

So, Charlie and Lee then start to argue, and it started to get a bit hot. The rest of the cast, at this time were starting to back off. Ralph Meeker, the loveliest man on earth, I remember seeing disappear into the shadows. I started to think to myself that this isn't good, as these were two big heavy guys. Serious guys. Suddenly, Bob Aldrich, who was quite a heavy-set guy himself, put his face between the two of them, and his jowls were hanging down and shaking, and he said, in not a very polite manner, 'You c**k suckers, you do it the way the man says, or there is going to be a problem here.' Everyone froze. Bob Aldrich took complete control of the situation. I'll never forget it.

"We had a huge cast in *The Dirty Dozen*. Lots of big personalities. Major players. A competitive cast. So many damn stars. There were members of the cast, who were early morning drinkers, and I don't mean tea or coffee, I mean the hard stuff. Ralph Meeker liked the early morning single shot.

"It took twenty-seven weeks to shoot the picture, and that included lots and lots of night filming, and with night filming, you get a bit screwed.

"There was a lot of bad weather, and this would hold up shooting, and of course it becomes costly.

"Continual rain was one of the things putting us behind schedule, and at one point we were told that the movie was being moved to Spain. Bob wanted to complete the picture in Spain. I think there was some tension between him and Ken Hyman. We never moved, of course, but Bob desperately wanted to get the filming out of the bad weather. It never happened, though.

"Bob Aldrich was a fabulous director. The way he handled the cast was superb. He was respected as the boss. I learned more about directing from watching Bob Aldrich than I have learned anywhere else. You have to remember he had all these big personalities in his face every morning, and having to deal with them. He did a great job. I always found him to be polite and nice. He was good fun to be with. We had a lot of jokes. We called him 'fat man.' Bob was terrific. Kenneth Hyman, the producer, was also a very lovely man. Very hands on.

"Lee Marvin was marvellous. Sensational. I got to know him quite well afterwards. He was a cool guy. Funny. I remember seeing him one day during shooting hunched over on the stairs at MGM, and I said, 'Are you OK, Lee?'

"And he said, 'No, my back.'

I helped him to his dressing room. He'd been wounded during his military days, and it kept coming back to haunt him. It was shrapnel, I think, lodged very close to his spine, so close, in fact, it couldn't be operated on. It was probably one of the reasons that he drank so heavy, to help him deal with the pain. His drinking never affected his work, though. He was a consummate professional.

"Charles Bronson, on the other hand, was a miserable man. You never really got to know him. He just seemed miserable most of the time. He was reclusive, though. A bit of a manic depressive as well. He kept to himself. When he opened up and let loose though, he was kind of fun. Quite cute. He was always bleak in the morning. He was prickly a lot of the time. He also didn't invest any time mixing with the younger actors, like myself.

"Ernest Borgnine is a sweetheart of a man. What you see is definitely what you get with him.

"Robert Ryan was also delightful. Accommodating. Helpful. Interesting. Totally not aggressive. As mild as can be. A fabulous man.

"Richard Jaeckel was a lovely man. A very quiet man, but with a great sense of humor.

"Trini Lopez left the picture. He met up with Frank Sinatra in London and said that he wasn't happy with the schedule, and Frank said, 'Well f**k em, come home.' So, Trini went home just as we started the chateau sequence. He left the movie. Bob Aldrich just sailed through it, as if nothing had happened.

"The film had a great unit. We had a fine time. But we were making a big picture, and it turned out to be a huge success, and still is.

"However, it was *The Dirty Dozen* that actually convinced me that I didn't want to go on and become an actor, and I actually turned to directing afterwards, which is what I really wanted to do. Acting is just too frantic. *The Dirty Dozen* definitely pushed me quicker into becoming a director."

Trini Lopez played Pedro Jiminez, and gave his own reasons for leaving the movie. "Frank Sinatra came to England on his honeymoon with Mia Farrow and invited me to dinner on their first night in London. At this time, we had been filming *The Dirty Dozen* for seven months, and it was only scheduled to be a four-month shoot.

"Frank told me that I needed to get back recording my music, because the public was fickle and they would forget me. So, I got my lawyers to work out a deal and I left the picture. In the script, they just killed me off, just prior to the chateau sequence. In the original screenplay I was supposed to blow up the chateau, but never did, of course.

"Working at MGM Borehamwood, though, was very pleasant for me. Everyone was very friendly.

"When we were filming interiors I would sometimes slip away, when I had a chance, and watch other movies being made, including *2001*.

"It brings back some very nice memories. I also recorded an album while I was there, entitled *Trini Lopez in London*."

Ernest Borgnine, who portrayed the role of General Worden, was also happy to share his memories. "I rented a place a short distance from the studio, but most of my scenes, apart from one very frank meeting with Lee Marvin, were shot on location in the lovely countryside just outside London.

It was short and sweet for me at MGM British, but I do recall the fellows of the studio, who were a great bunch of lads."

Set designer on the movie was Tim Hutchinson. "I have a huge recall about filming *The Dirty Dozen* at MGM British, as my father, William Hutchinson, was the art director, and it was also one of my first jobs in the business.

"First of all, the studio had a great quality about it, with superb departments and a marvellous workforce.

"It also had a massive back lot with an artificial lake, which had been dug out for the film *Ivanhoe* many years before.

"We built the bridge that you see in *The Dirty Dozen* over this lake. In fact, we built the whole chateau set around it.

"I remember that we started to build that chateau in January 1966, and it was a fourteen-week build, which was actually quite generous for something as big as that. It cost about £50,000 to build it, with a crew of about sixty for the construction.

"There was a lot of night filming on *The Dirty Dozen*, which was usually from 7 p.m. until 4 a.m.

"I remember all of the actors. Charles Bronson could be a bit of a problem, but Robert Aldrich was a remarkable director and knew how to deal with this. I particularly recall a scene were Lee Marvin had to drive this army vehicle on to the bridge we had constructed on the back lot at MGM, and then pushes it into the lake. Well, the first time we did it, there were problems; it didn't seem to work, and Charles Bronson thought he would tell everyone how it should be done. Anyway, Robert Aldrich, said to the special effects people to be on set early the next evening, and Charles Bronson said, 'Bob, do you want me to come in as well?' thinking he could show these top professionals how to do it.

"Robert Aldrich just turned to Bronson and said, 'Yes, and I'll get Charlie the gardener (the resident MGM gardener) to come in and run your lines.' It was a wonderful put-down.

"Robert Aldrich was a good man. A courteous man. He knew what he wanted. After all, he had to work with some tricky actors."

Angela Allen was continuity on the movie. "We were supposed to do two weeks of night shooting. Seven weeks later, we were still at it. It went on and on. I remember going home in the early hours of one morning after a long shoot, and the paper lad saying to me, 'Just come out the night club miss?'

"I said, 'Bloody funny night club. Look, I've got mud on my boots.'

It was a very hard film to do, and went miles over schedule.

"Lee Marvin was wonderful, though. We all adored Lee. He'd have his moments. Drinking moments. The assistants would often have to go looking for him in the pubs of Borehamwood if he'd not turned up for filming. They knew where to find him, though, usually at The Red Lion, and Lee would always apologize afterwards, after he'd sobered up, of course. He was a very good-natured man, though.

"Charles Bronson, on the other hand, moaned all the time. He was awful, in fact. The crew couldn't stand him.

"John Cassavetes was not very disciplined as regards continuity. He never did the same thing twice. In fact, the whole cast had different acting methods, and unfortunately you often had the whole bloody mob in one scene. They did all stick to the script, though.

"Aldrich, the director, was very good. Very old-fashioned. He used to cover everything. His style of shooting was quite tough, though. But he also knew how to marshal his troops. Very much like a sergeant major. He loved to play poker with Telly Savalas, I remember.

"I recall during shooting that there was a big murder hunt taking place in London, and we had lost a weapon from the props room, which was not funny with this hunt going on. Luckily, it didn't get picked up by the papers."

Joining, Angela Allen, also as continuity was Peggy Spirito. "Angela contacted me and asked if I could help out. She wanted me to be on the second camera as continuity. Well, I had a ball, but it was very difficult. The 'Dozen' themselves were buggers, but quite fantastic. Those boys, I remember, used to play up terribly, and give, Angela, such a hard time. They were wicked, in fact.

"Ernest Borgnine, though, was a fantastic man, and so was John Cassavetes. He was great fun. Trini Lopez, as well. He was a doll."

Jimmy Dawes was 'grip' on *The Dirty Dozen*. "I did the night shoots on that movie, and all I can remember is that they were horrendous."

Cliff Richardson was special effects supervisor on the movie, and his son, John Richardson, was part of the special effects team. "MGM Borehamwood was probably the best studio facility in the country. However, I don't think it was the best-run studio, and it could be a difficult place to work. It did have the best back lot of any studio I have ever worked at. You could turn 360 degrees and not see anything other than trees on the horizon.

"One thing that always amused me was that it had its own fire department."

Brian Johnson was also a member of the special effects team. "MGM British where *The Dirty Dozen* was made was a 1930s brickwork studio, and each soundstage had dividing walls, so you could have either two small stages or one big one. It was an immaculate studio, beautifully laid out. It was the best studio this country ever had. No question about it.

"*The Dirty Dozen* themselves were top guys to work with, but each and every one had a massive ego, and spent most of their time pissed.

"Bob Aldrich was a great director on that one."

Nosher Powell, one of the greatest stuntmen in the British movie business, was part of the large stunt team. "The one great thing about

MGM in Borehamwood was that it had one of the best studio restaurants in the business, and they didn't call me NOSHER for nothing."

Even though running over schedule, *The Dirty Dozen* production ran quite smoothly, without serious problems until the night they blew up the chateau.

On Thursday September 15, 1966, the *Borehamwood & Elstree Post* reported:

"FILM MEN MADE THAT BIG BANG!"

A violent explosion, followed by bursts of machine gun fire, rocked Borehamwood during the early hours of Tuesday, September 14, but there was no cause for alarm, according to the report. It happened at MGM Studios, where they were filming the final scenes of *The Dirty Dozen*, and it was reported that the explosion was the blowing up of a specially constructed French Chateau.

However, it was more than just an explosion. Several weeks of night shoots had disturbed the sleep of many Borehamwood residents, with the sound of small explosions and repeated gun-fire.

The blowing up of the chateau was the final straw, as this "big bang" as it was called could be heard as far as fifteen miles away in central London.

John Richardson was part of the special effects team that set it up. "We used fifty-seven different charges to blow that chateau up. It was very successful."

Stuart Cooper also remembers the blast. "It scared the hell out of me, as I was quite close. You could feel the blast on your face. So, acting at that point wasn't a problem. It was just one huge explosion, and there were complaints all over Borehamwood."

Paul Wilson was third camera operator on the chateau sequence. "I certainly remember the trouble with local residents. But then again, it was a big noise. Parts of the chateau actually ended up in a local school's swimming pool. Luckily, though, it was in the middle of the night, so no one was seriously hurt."

The complaints came thick and fast, starting on Thursday September 22, 1966, when the *Borehamwood & Elstree Post* reported:

"MGM FILM MAKING ANGERS RESIDENTS"

The anger started with one woman, who laid a complaint against the studios under the Herts County Council bylaws to abate the terrible noise within fourteen days, or she would take out a summons. She was Mrs. Helen James of Shenley Road, Borehamwood, who was a mother of two young sons.

In the report she stated, "My patience has run out. As ratepayers, I think we are entitled to a little peace at night. For three weeks now, we've been getting hardly any sleep at all."

Another resident, Mrs. Doris Gravett, also of Shenley Road, said the noise at night from the studios was making her spastic daughter even more nervous. She said, "I think the filmmakers should shoot these scenes during the day, or go to another place, which is not a built-up area. It was bad enough being woken up during the war by falling bombs. We should not have to put up with losing any sleep this way in peace time. Mrs. James complained to the *Post* last week about this infernal noise, but it gradually got too much, and on Tuesday I felt I also had to do something about it."

A spokesman for MGM responded by saying it was impossible for him to say what time or when the explosions and machine gun fire would occur during the night.

As tempers raged among residents, and letters of complaint came flooding in, a bizarre, unexplained incident took place at MGM British. In a strange twist of fate, the remains of the chateau were mysteriously set fire, causing £40,000 worth of damage.

The blaze was discovered by two studio fireman shortly after 6 a.m. during the last days of shooting. One of the firemen, Mr. George Robinson, was burned on the arm while tackling the blaze. Another, Mr. William Gillett, said, 'I heard two loud bangs, and then saw flames leaping from the set.' He alerted the studio fire brigade and then called in the local fire brigade.

Among the burning wreckage was found two Calor gas cylinders, which were responsible for the two explosions, causing severe damage to the chateau.

Tim Hutchinson, whose father had designed the chateau, recalls the incident, "The chateau was more or less completely destroyed. Luckily, we had completed filming it. But no-one ever found out how that fire started."

On Thursday September 29, 1966, the following report appeared in the *Borehamwood & Elstree* Post:

"COUNCIL DEPUTATION OVER THE MGM NOISE"

Elstree Rural Council sent a deputation to MGM to get an assurance that noisy incidents do not occur again.

Councillor Alec Atkinson made a strong complaint against the filmmakers for "kicking up a terrific racket." Mr. Atkinson also said that the people of Well End (close to the studios) had not heard such a noise since a German V2 rocket fell in the village during World War II. He continued that the machine gun fire and explosions from the studio lot were terribly frightening and of a serious concern to people who did not enjoy good health. He declared that the noise from the studio was deplorable and there was no excuse for it "when you think that a kid lets off a firework in the streets and is hauled before the magistrates."

Another Councillor, Christian de Lisle, wondered if the filmmakers could notify police when they were going to set off an explosion so they in turn could tell the public what the bang was. Councillor de Lisle heard a sizable bang himself and rang up the police to find out what it was all about.

A spokesperson for the producers replied by saying that night filming had been completed and the chateau, which had been destroyed by a mysterious fire, would not be rebuilt.

MGM Borehamwood also responded by saying that in the future the public would be notified about any night shooting, which may include loud bangs or explosions.

Despite latter production problems, *The Dirty Dozen* was a massive commercial success. It was the fifth highest-grossing film of 1967 and MGM's highest grossing movie of the year. To date, it has made $45.3 million, and it stands up as one of the cinema's all-time greats.

As one big-budget movie made its exit, another arrived. *Casino Royale* (1967), a James Bond spoof, would turn out to be a production that was both chaotic and troubled. It would also require the services of five directors (Val Guest, Ken Hughes, John Huston, Joseph McGrath, and Robert Parrish). As well as being filmed at MGM Borehamwood, it would also be filmed on sound stages at both Pinewood and Shepperton, due to the production running months over schedule.

The movie had a big cast of screen names in supporting roles and cameos, but the star, Peter Sellers, would be the film's biggest problem.

Sellers had suggested Orson Welles to appear opposite him, but from the moment that Welles arrived on the set, filming spiraled into chaos.

A visit to the set by Princess Margaret, long time friend of Sellers, did nothing to help the situation, as she decided to make a bigger fuss over Welles, causing Sellers to storm off the set.

His return the following day would be the start of major problems for director Joseph McGrath. Sellers told McGrath and associate producer, John Dark, that for the remainder of shooting he would not appear in the same set-up as Welles.

This, said McGrath, was the whole reason for having the two stars on screen together, that they shared the same scene and appeared in the same shots.

Sellers continued his standoff, resulting in a raging argument between director and star, so raging that Sellers threw his fist, and in turn McGrath threw his fist, until they were both parted on set by a stuntman who said, holding the two apart, he didn't know which one to punch first, as he loved them both.

Sellers left the studio immediately and disappeared for several days, leaving McGrath to direct Welles, who constantly asked, "What's happened to our thin friend, Joe?"

McGrath decided that he could not continue to direct a film in which its star made the decisions about when and when not he would turn up on set. So, McGrath left the movie and was replaced by Robert Parrish.

Sellers continued to be absent for days at a time, holding up the schedule and leaving his fellow co-stars unclear about what was happening. In the end, Sellers left the movie before shooting was complete. It is unclear whether he was fired or if he simply walked off.

For the final big sequence, a cardboard cut-out of Sellers had to be used, and some very clever editing.

Geoffrey Bayldon appeared opposite Peter Sellers playing the role of "Q." "I was one of the lucky ones, as Peter Sellers turned up to film his scene with me, as I know that some of my colleagues in the business were hanging around for days, waiting for him to show. But for me he was at the studio on time, and I have to say he was very nice, kind, and I found him easy to work with. I also think that our scene together is one of the best in the picture."

Renee Glynne worked on part of the movie as continuity. "I started work on *Casino Royale* at Shepperton with director Val Guest. He was called in, as he rightly said, to save the picture, to do link sequences, and then do his own sequence.

"I then moved to MGM British to film the segment with Woody Allen. The interior of his palace had been constructed there. Little did I know that this weedy little thing, Woody Allen, would go on to become an international star. In *Casino Royale* he wrote most of his own dialogue, and I was typing every word he uttered. I had a very good close relationship with him. He was always nice to me. A very zany man, who did what he wanted to do. He was being nurtured by the producers to become a big star.

"The finale of the film, shot at MGM, was very exciting. We had just about every wonderful actor in the world in that scene. They arrived by helicopter. I remember David Niven, Jean-Paul Belmondo, George Raft, Orson Welles, Ursula Andress, and many others. It was lovely.

"It's sad, because *Casino Royale* has a reputation for being one of the worst films ever made. I personally love it."

On completion in November 1966, the movie had cost $12 million to make, which was way over its original budget. It was also considered a mish-mash of wasted talent. The critics ravaged it and the public showed little interest, giving it a cold reception at the box-office.

In more recent years, *Casino Royale* gained a somewhat cult reputation because with its big star cast and catchy theme tune, it can't all be bad.

The Fearless Vampire Killers (1967), made partly at MGM Borehamwood during the shooting of both *The Dirty Dozen* and *Casino Royale*, is a comedy based on classic horror movies.

Director Roman Polanski (who also plays a leading role), coming straight from his international success with *Repulsion* (1965), mounted this film on a lavish scale with anamorphic cinematography, huge sets, elaborate costumes, and choreography suitable for a period epic adding to its beautifully gothic style.

The cast, all in superb form, include Jack MacGowran, Ferdy Mayne, Alfie Bass, and Sharon Tate, returning to MGM British for the second and last time.

Dennis Fraser was grip on the film. "Sharon Tate was a lovely person. She used to mix with the crew, which not many actors did. She was very friendly.

Polanski was hard work as a director. He used to do many takes on one scene, which I thought was unnecessary. He was a bit like Kubrick."

The cinematographer was Douglas Slocombe. "*The Fearless Vampire Killers* was just one of many titles it had. None of them, I think, actually suited the picture.

It was a very inventive film, though, and extremely demanding in terms of sets. We actually ran out of studio space at MGM, and so had to film at both ABPC and Pinewood as well.

"Polanski was an extraordinary man, quite marvellous to work with. I had great admiration for him. Like Spielberg, he breathes film and is a very natural director.

"At first he was rather reluctant to cast Sharon Tate, as she wasn't delivering the lines the way he wanted. However, he did cast her in the end because she was under contract to MGM and had just finished a film for them. The rest, of course, is history, as the more he went over her lines with her, the more he fell in love with her, and they married not long after."

Sharon Tate's marriage to Roman Polanski in Chelsea, London, on January 20, 1968, was short-lived.

On August 9, 1969, at the Polanski home in Los Angeles, Sharon Tate was brutally murdered by the Charles Manson "family." She was two weeks from giving birth, and died from stab wounds to the heart, liver, and lungs, causing massive haemorrhage.

On Thursday February 23, 1967, the following report appeared in the *Borehamwood & Elstree Post*:

"OPEN VERDICT ON FILM EXTRA"

Finchley Coroner's Court recorded an open verdict on a film crowd man [extra], who died after being found lying on the ground near the dressing room stairs during the filming of *The Prisoner* television series at MGM.

The thirty-eight-year-old man, William Rutherford Carl Lumley of West Hampstead, was dead on arrival at Barnet hospital, the cause of death being asphyxia due to the inhalation of blood, due to the fracture of the bones of the face. The Coroner's Court added that to sustain injuries of this type the deceased must have either fallen from a height or been running quite fast to give him the impetus to fall so heavily.

The Prisoner, a series of seventeen episodes starring Patrick McGoohan, combined spy fiction with elements of science fiction, allegory, and psychological drama.

An enormous hit, as it is considered today nearly fifty years later, one of the all time great British television series, with a huge cult fan base.

Several members of the crew from *The Prisoner* remember McGoohan as a terrific actor to work with. He was also said to be a very social man, who enjoyed a drink at the King's Arms on Stirling Corner.

Another series shot on sound stages at MGM British during this period was *Journey To The Unknown*. Virtually unseen since its broadcast in 1968/69, it is an anthology series of seventeen episodes featuring stories with a fantasy, science fiction, and supernatural theme.

Produced by Hammer Films and distributed by 20th Century Fox television, it starred both British and American actors, but ,sadly, it did not gain the recognition it probably deserved.

Hammer Films would fare much better with the third in their Quatermass series of films, *Quatermass And The Pit*, shot at MGM during the early part of 1967.

Andrew Kier would take over the role of Professor Quatermass from Brian Donlevy, and Roy Ward Baker would direct, fresh from directing Hammer's *The Anniversary* (1968) with Bette Davis at ABPC.

The Bette Davis picture had been a problem for Hammer, but more so for Jimmy Sangster, the producer. It had started shooting with Alvin Rakoff as director, but this would soon change.

Rakoff, a vastly experienced television director, liked to block his scenes, moving the actors so that they hit their marks for the camera. This style did not work for Hollywood legend, Davis, who remarked, "The camera works for me. I do not work for the camera." She insisted to Jimmy Sangster that Rakoff be replaced, as he had no idea of the star system. Sangster had no choice; it was either Rakoff or Davis, and he did not want to lose his leading player ,who's name would sell the picture, and she knew it.

So, given the task of taking over the director's chair was Roy Ward Baker, an old friend of Davis. The rest of the cast were unimpressed at first, as they had enjoyed working with Rakoff, and many considered Baker an old-fashioned war horse when it came to directing.

The uneasiness on set soon lifted, and Baker, a veteran of directing classic British movies like *A Night To Remember* (1958), would lend the film a wicked style, with Davis on top form as the vicious-tongued mother.

June Randall was continuity on the movie. "It was great to work with Bette Davis. We were not allowed to call her Bette, though. We were only allowed 'Miss Davis.'

"The publicity manager on the film, a wonderful fellow, asked her something and called her 'Bette,' and the next thing we knew, he wasn't on the film anymore.

"Our original director was Alvin Rakoff, who was a lovely man. He started on the film, and two weeks in, Bette had an altercation with him and stormed off the set. Well, that was the end of him. She had him fired.

"They then brought in Roy Ward Baker, an old-fashioned director, but very nice, and extremely good and reliable. Bette liked him. They'd met before.

"Anyway, at the end of filming, Bette gave me a huge signed picture of herself, which read, 'Great working with you.' I'm sure it's worth quite a lot of money now."

The Anniversary turned out to be another hit for Hammer, and still stands as an enjoyable comedy of pure venom.

After the Bette Davis picture, and that is most certainly what it was—especially in her eyes—Roy Ward Baker would direct *Quatermass And The Pit* at MGM Borehamwood with relative ease, even though he admitted later that Andrew Kier (playing Quatermass) and he could never see eye to eye, and he found his Scottish manner at times somewhat arrogant.

The movie is a classic piece of Hammer science fiction, delivering enough chills to keep the viewer happy.

On Thursday March 23, 1967, the *Borehamwood & Elstree Post* reported:

"NOISE WARNING FROM STUDIOS"

MGM Studios were warning local residents of night shooting, and that it would involve a certain amount of noise from an aero engine and muffled explosions.

The film being made was Hammer's *Quatermass and the Pit*, and the warning followed the previous year's controversy when filming of the multi-million-pound *The Dirty Dozen* meant weeks of sleepless nights for residents.

Working as clapper/loader was Trevor Coop. "During the eight weeks we shot at MGM, we picked up our camera barrow each morning from Les Smart, who was in charge of the camera department, and returned it each night. Only once do I remember him saying good morning or goodnight. Years later, when MGM had been closed for some time and Les was now working at Pinewood, he would greet me like a long lost son!

"On *Quatermass And The Pit,* our camera operator was chain-smoking Murray Grant. For the first week of production, three or four times a day, he would say to me, 'Pop over the road and get me 20 Rothmans, there's a good lad.' which I duly did. Over the first weekend, I thought I could save myself some legwork and I purchased two ten-pack cartons. He never asked me to get him cigarettes again!

"During the final week of *Quatermass,* with a view to doing another Hammer picture, I was summoned to ABPC one lunch hour to see Dennis Berterra, a production manager with a voice so deep that it made Paul Robeson sound like a falsetto by comparison. On *Quatermass,* I was paid £22 pounds for forty hours. I was determined, though, to put the rate up, and when the subject of money came up, I risked my career (or so I thought) by asking for £24. Dennis Berterra said, 'I've got £25 in the budget, is that alright?' Never since, in over forty years in the business, has anybody offered me more than I asked for!"

Christopher Neame, son of Ronald Neame, was second assistant director on *Quatermass*. He took time to remember MGM Borehamwood. "In 1956, my father directed *The Man Who Never Was* in this wonderful studio, and, as a boy, I was an excited visitor to the set on several occasions.

Twelve years went by before my turn came to work there on a feature, which was *Quatermass and the Pit*. By this time, I'd got to grips with the first stages of production and it was abundantly clear that here was a studio that 'worked.'

"Everything was in the right place and of the right size. The sound stages were accessible and silent (if that makes sense); the machine shop did not get in the way of everyday shooting life, yet were close enough to the action to service a production efficiently; the outside lot was easily reached but well enough away from the noise of traffic; the offices, make-up, and dressing rooms were perfectly positioned in terms of facilitating a production. Furthermore, the often wearisome trade unions had a good working relationship with the management, both respecting one another's position. All this came about because Metro was built and run as a film studio with filmmakers in mind."

1967 would also see *Battle Beneath The Earth*, *The Shoes Of The Fisherman*, *The Fixer*, and *Inspector Clouseau* filmed on sound stages at MGM.

The Fixer directed by John Frankenheimer has a special memory for one of its stars, Murray Melvin. "I well remember a scene I had with darling Alan Bates, which we both found funny and had to stop ourselves from laughing, and John Frankenheimer, who shouted at us at the top of his voice, and on my request that I found that disturbing, he ordered the whole set to speak in whispers!"

Inspector Clouseau saw Alan Arkin take on the part of the famous bumbling detective. However, because the role was now closely associated with Peter Sellers, the project was not a great success, and Arkin would never reprise the role again.

The year 1968 saw MGM Borehamwood experience both success and failure in a big way. Success came with the box-office winner, *Where Eagles Dare*, starring Richard Burton and Clint Eastwood. A complicated wartime story from the pen of Alistair Maclean, and directed by Brian Hutton (his first movie), it would stand up, and still stands up, as one of the greatest action entertainment war films of all time.

By the late 1960s, Richard Burton's box-office pulling power was on the wane, and he later admitted that he only took the part for his kids, so they wouldn't always associate him with highbrow stuff.

Clint Eastwood, on the other hand, who took second billing, was only a step away from superstardom and his *Dirty Harry* fame in the 1970s.

Burton (who was being paid $1,200,000) and Eastwood (who was being paid $800,000) dubbed the movie "Where Doubles Dare" due to the time stand-ins and stuntmen doubled for action sequences.

Filming commenced in Austria in January 1968, mainly around Hohenwerfen Castle in Werfen, with additional shooting taking place in Ebensee and Aigen im Ennstal.

The cast and crew then arrived to complete filming at MGM Borehamwood in spring 1968.

Art Direction on the film (both on location and in the studio) was undertaken by Peter Mullins. "An art director, a very nice man, asked me if I could take his place to do the film. Well, I read the script and quickly handed it back to him saying, 'I can't do this. It's way beyond me. Big boy stuff, with a big budget and big responsibilities.'

"Anyway, he somehow talked me in to doing it. I then met Elliott Kastner, the producer, who was very impressed because I'd worked on *Alfie* (1966) with Michael Caine. And *Alfie*, of course, had made an awful lot of money and was very successful. So, my job on *Where Eagles Dare* was secured.

"I think I earned somewhere around £85.00 a week on it. Quite a lot of money in the late 1960s.

"At MGM Studios in Borehamwood, I had to build on the back lot a model of Hohenwerfen Castle in miniature, complete with cable cars. This model was constructed about 60 to 70 feet high. You do actually see the model several times in the movie. It does work, I think. The cable cars are a little bit jerky, but it does work.

"The Golden Hall scene with the big long table and roaring fireplace was also shot on a sound stage at MGM. This was an enormous set, and the fireplace was my little tribute to *Citizen Kane* (1941).

"The shootout in the castle was also done at MGM. For this, we first built the set, and because there is nothing behind the set you can place all dummy charges in the wall. So, we had about 300 bullet hits buried, which will, of course, blow out on demand. This took days to set up, and I remember on the Friday night as we were supposed to finish for the weekend, Brian Hutton, the director came on set and said, 'Where are all the bullet hits?'

"We said, 'Well you don't see them until you blow the charges.'

"He said, 'Well, how am I supposed to know where they are?'

So, unfortunately, we had to let the bloody things off, and then had to work the whole weekend to put the bloody thing back again.

"That said, Brian Hutton, was probably the best director I ever worked for. Like me, it was his first big picture. Sometimes when we were leaving the studio after a days work, he'd say, 'Are you coming in tomorrow?'

"I'd say, 'Yes, why?'

"He'd say, 'I don't know what the f**k I'm doing, I don't know if I will.'

But he got through it, and did a very good job. But he had very good people around him."

Mullins also took time to remember the two stars, Burton and Eastwood. "Richard Burton was obviously pissed sometimes on the set. But the moment Brian Hutton, said 'Action' he'd stand up and be word perfect. Burton was okay, though, and very professional.

"I remember he came back from lunch once, and was definitely the worse for wear, rambling on about, 'I don't know why I'm doing this rubbish.'

"Well one of the crew said, 'You're doing it because you are getting over a million dollars. So shut up and say the f**k**g words.'

"The film did make him a lot of money, though, as he got percentages etc.

"I also recall one day him doing a Shakespearian speech on set, and everyone giving him a round of applause. He was an extraordinary man.

"Eastwood, on the other hand, I found to be a rather boring man. Rather dull. He wouldn't say very much at all. I used to chat with him, but he wasn't very forthcoming. Never got to know him, really."

Dennis Fraser was grip on the film, and had a different opinion of Eastwood. "He was by far the nicest man I ever met in the industry."

Graeme Scaife, a young clapper/loader on the movie, would have his birthday on the set. He recalled, "Everyone, both cast and crew, made a fuss of me, and they got me a surprise birthday cake. It was quite surreal, really. Burton and Eastwood were there, too. Happy times.

"I had actually joined the camera department at MGM British in 1966, working for Les Smart. What a wonderful kind man he was, and he helped me so much to learn all about the cameras.

"I made many friends in that studio, as it was like one big happy family. The riggers, plasterers, carpenters, were all so very friendly, and I went from one film to another with many of them.

"At my young age, the studio seemed huge to me, and the sets that were built for *Where Eagles Dare* were incredible.

"MGM Borehamwood will always have a place in my heart, as it was my first place of work, and for the five enjoyable years I spent there, the memories will never fade."

Focus puller on the movie was Frank Elliott. "Burton and Eastwood were very nice men. I enjoyed working with them a lot. The studio (MGM) was the main studios for me. A very professional place. A lovely studio.

"Quite the opposite of Elstree Studios, or ABPC as it was known then. I didn't care for that one very much. ABPC was short for 'A British Prison Camp.' Well, it was to the crews anyway. It was a sort of scruffy place. Not very nice really."

The film's cinematographer was Arthur Ibbetson, and working as his camera operator was Paul Wilson. "I'd worked with Arthur before as his operator. He was a first-rate lighting cameraman. Knew his job to perfection. We'd just in fact finished a film together working with Charlie Chaplin. *A Countess From Hong Kong* (1967) it was called. It was Chaplin's last film, and he directed it. Not quite as happy an experience as *Where Eagles Dare*, but a job nevertheless.

"*Where Eagles Dare* had a great crew, and it was a fun movie to work on. It was a challenge, though, both on location and in the studio.

"On location you had the snow, which can cause a few problems to the camera crew. My lens kept misting up because of the intense cold, so I was unsure sometimes if I'd got the shot or not.

"In the studio, we did all the cable car stuff, which was quite difficult to set up and light. It was a huge set, too, and I did a lot of filming on top of the cable cars, which was sometimes quite high up in the rafters of the studio.

"The only other thing I recall is actor Derren Nesbitt strutting around the canteen at MGM in his black Nazi uniform. In fact, I think they had some trouble trying to get him to take it off."

Nesbitt plays SS Officer Von Happen, and during the original filming of his death scene, he was nearly blinded when the squibs placed on his chest blew upwards instead of outwards. Because of this, the scene was changed, and he was shot in the head instead.

This was not the first accident to occur. In Austria, producer Elliott Kastner and director Brian Hutton were badly burned during the filming of an action scene involving explosives.

On Thursday April 11, 1968, the following article appeared in the *Borehamwood & Elstree Post*:

"ELIZABETH TAYLOR JOINS THE PUBLICAN'S WIVES"

Elizabeth Taylor and Richard Burton had dropped in for a quiet drink at their favorite pub, The Artichoke, on Elstree Hill.

It goes on to say that whenever the Burtons are in Borehamwood they usually go to see their friends, Bill and Dorothy Williams, licensees of The Artichoke.

Mr. and Mrs. Williams had known the famous couple since 1961 when they were then running the Kings Arms on Stirling Corner.

Joining the Burton's at The Artichoke was Richard's closest friend, confidant, and co-star in *Where Eagles Dare* (playing Sergeant George Harrod), Brook Williams. "Elizabeth arrived in Austria while we were filming, and then stayed with Richard right until the end of shooting the picture at MGM Borehamwood.

"They both seemed happy at this time. I would say at their happiest. They certainly didn't have any pressures as such.

"Richard, though, had started to drink heavily. He always drank, but by now he was drinking much more than he should.

"By the time I worked with him on a film called *The Wild Geese* (1978), he was killing himself with drink, and both I and he knew it. He was actually drinking three bottles of hard liquor a day. I made him have blood tests (anonymously), and the doctor said if he carried on drinking he would be dead within two weeks.

"There were not many actors who could top him with drink. A few perhaps, but not many. Elizabeth would have a go. But having them both heavy on the bottle could be dangerous. I've been witness to one or two venomously tongued moments. They were not unknown to be violent to each other, too. But I loved them both, regardless of their faults, and they had many.

"Richard often said of his drinking that his liver should be buried separately, with honors. I think he was right.

"He died far too young of a brain haemorrhage in 1984, aged only 58, and probably due to his years of heavy smoking and hard drinking.

"Shamefully, I also nearly died from alcoholism. Knowing Richard as well as I did probably didn't help, but it certainly wasn't because of him.

"I remember while shooting in Austria on *Where Eagles Dare* I had my first true bout of being well and truly pissed.

"My character, Sergeant Harrod, had died in a parachute fall. Broken his neck, actually. So there I was lying dead in the snow. Now you have to remember this was Austria in wintertime. So, it was freezing cold.

"Well, me and Richard were waiting for the crew to set up the cameras, etc., which seemed to take hours because of the severe weather, and Richard being Richard had two bottles of Scotch on reserve, ready to warm us up. Anyway, I cannot remember how much we drank, but when it came to shoot my scene lying dead, that is actually all I could have done, because when I came to stand up after the shot, I couldn't stand at all, because I was totally pissed out of my face."

Second unit action and stunt photography on the movie had been directed by Hollywood's legendary stuntman, Yakima Canutt.

Canutt was most well-known for his famous drop from a stagecoach in John Ford's classic western *Stagecoach* (1939) starring John Wayne.

Kelvin Pike was camera operator on the Canutt sequences, and remembers particularly filming the cable car scenes in Ebensee, Austria. "That was probably one of the most frightening experiences of my career. We would sit up on those cable cars for hours. Even eat our food on them. We would also make parachutes out of our napkins, and watch them float down to the lake far below."

Pike also remembered working with Richard Burton's stunt double. "We were doing the escape scene at the end of the picture, and Alf Joint was doubling for Richard on a motorcycle. Alf though was the perfect Burton lookalike. So much so that when he was driving away from us, we told him to look over his shoulder. You wouldn't know it wasn't Burton."

Joint doubled most of Burton's action scenes, due to Burton's poor health and back trouble, while stuntman, Eddie Powell, only doubled Eastwood occasionally.

Back at the studio, on the massive cable car set, Alf Joint had to jump from one cable car roof to another, but felt he was unable to risk it, as the two cars were passing each other far too fast, and he felt he might miss the passing roof altogether or be seriously injured. The problem was eventually solved, with the cars moving slower, and Joint finally completing a remarkable looking stunt successfully.

Where Eagles Dare was a smash hit at the box-office, and more recently, Steven Spielberg, dubbed it as his favorite war movie, mainly due to its sheer "boys own" factor of unreality.

While *Where Eagles Dare* was being completed, two more war movies were being shot at MGM British. However, they would not share the same success.

Mosquito Squadron (1968) was a low-budget production starring David McCallum, while *The Mercenaries* (1968) saw Rod Taylor and Jack Cardiff reunited for a film that critics would condemn on its original release for its graphic scenes of violence and torture.

Jack Cardiff recalls directing the movie. "The story is basically about a band of mercenaries (headed by Rod Taylor) sent on a dangerous mission during the Congo Crisis.

"Therefore, before shooting the picture, I made a trip to the Congo and met reporters who had lived through all of the troubles there, and they showed me photographs of the real thing. I wish they hadn't. I remember vividly a photograph of a man with his throat cut in the bath; his head was nearly off and the bath was full of blood. The savagery was unbelievable.

"When I directed the film, I thought it would have been too awful for words to make it like the real violence, but it had to have violence in it.

"When the film came out though, the critics all thought the violence was so terrible that they couldn't bear to watch it. They were really appalled by its excessive violence. Yet war is violent. So, I could only say to those that I met that my film was nothing like the real thing; it was a quarter, a fifth, a sixteenth of the violence that really happened. None the less, it gained the reputation as a violent movie.

"Yes, it is a violent picture, but I feel a very good one. Rod Taylor was also just the right type of actor for that film, and I feel it is one of his best performances."

After the success of the MGM-filmed series of *The Prisoner* on television, its star, Patrick McGoohan, would hit the headlines.

On Thursday June 6, 1968, the *Borehamwood & Elstree Post* reported: "ACTORS 'LEAVE MY FENCE ALONE' APPEAL"

Patrick McGooham had gone into battle with Barnet Council over a screen fence he had erected at his home in the Ridgeway, Mill Hill, which the council had objected too.

The council had not given planning permission and had served Mr. McGooham an enforcement notice to have the fence demolished and the land reinstated.

McGoohan said he had the 6-foot-high fence built to stop "star gazers" from looking directly into his home. "Sightseers congregate to observe my activities in the house and grounds," he said, "as many as twenty people at a time watch and take photographs. My wife is particularly affected by people looking into the kitchen."

With big time successes like *Where Eagles Dare*, it was only a matter of time before MGM Borehamwood witnessed failure.

This came in a big way in the summer of 1968 with a remake of *Goodbye Mr. Chips*. A musical version of James Hilton's novel, it starred Peter O'Toole and Petula Clark. It took twenty-one weeks of shooting (including fourteen on location), making it an expensive production.

Thirty years earlier, MGM in Hollywood had hit the jackpot with the original version, a tearjerker with Greer Garson and Robert Donat.

This remake, however, wasn't destined to enjoy the same success, and would lose money for the studio.

The summer of 1968 also saw *Alfred the Great* go into production starring David Hemmings and Michael York.

A $6 million movie, directed by Clive Donner on an epic scale, with a vast amount of this money spent on recreating in exact detail ninth century England on celluloid. For this, it was necessary to build two 80-foot Viking longships and supply some 1,800 spears and 1,600 swords for the hundreds of extras.

To add to the budget, location filming would not take place in England but in Ireland, with production designer, Michael Stringer, given the difficult task of recreating the White Horse carving in Berkshire on a hill in County Galway.

The Berkshire White Horse, which dates before the English/Viking battles, was the scene of King Alfred's encounter with the Viking invaders.

The replica in Ireland was designed and cut 18 inches deep, 280 feet long, and 60 feet at its widest, and filled with about 17 tons of plaster.

All this hard work on production values was in vain. The cycle of British historical films, which had reached its peak with *Becket* (1964) and *Anne Of A Thousand Days* (1966), no longer attracted big audiences, so the movie was another money loss for MGM.

Also visiting the studio in 1968 were Peter Ustinov, Karl Malden, Maggie Smith, Robert Morley, and Cesar Romero to star in a crime comedy entitled *Hot Millions*, and George Sanders dropped in for the last time to play a supporting role in *The Best House In London*. The "house" was the type with a red light outside, and with Denis Norden having written the screenplay, an amusing movie was guaranteed, but sadly, neither this nor *Hot Millions* did outstanding business at the box-office.

Hollywood's rugged hard man, Robert Ryan, was at MGM British in early 1969 to play the title role in *Captain Nemo and the Underwater City*.

A movie inspired by some of the settings of Jules Verne's novel, *Twenty Thousand Leagues Under The Sea*.

On February 6, Robert Ryan, gave a rare interview at the studios to *Borehamwood & Elstree Post* reporter, Kay Holmes. She wrote, "Despite the multi-million dollar glitter which surrounds him—all the subterranean special effects—Ryan with his weather-worn face, Irish jutting out jaw, and large powerful hands, he might well be the respected rigger instead of the titled star. He casts a long six-foot three-inch shadow on the glossy magazine image. He doesn't use glib Hollywoodese. He's a loner and he likes it. Some might think him taciturn, and his sobriety has often cast him in not-so-nice roles."

Ryan's response to reporter Holmes, after taking a long look into the distance and an even longer drag on his cigarette, was as follows. "Quite often when I'm supposed to talk about my work and this business I'm in, I find I haven't got anything to say. Some people can talk and talk for hours and they don't know a damn thing about it. I've never heard a speech on acting that was any good, and I don't have much time for theatrical chit-chat.

"Acting is a sixth sense to me; it's intuitive; you either have it or you don't; you can't learn.

"Of course, you can learn how to walk on stage without falling over your feet. You can learn how to speak so an audience can hear you. But you've got to have talent.

"I believe they (MGM) pay me because they know I can do the part, and because I add some measure of safety to their investment, not because they like me or think I'm a great guy. They'll go on using me as long as they need me and not a moment longer.

"Why bother saying nice things I don't mean? It wouldn't help anyway."

Cinematographer on *Captain Nemo And The Underwater City* was Alan Hume. "It was a super movie to work on. Chuck Connors was in it. He was a great guy.

"MGM Borehamwood, where we shot it, was a very good studio in its day, probably the best in the country at that time.

"I also recall working their on the second unit shoot of a fire sequence, but cannot remember the title of the film, as it was so long ago.

"The director, American, was a very loud and noisy chap, who created a fair bit of chaos himself by his constant yelling and shouting at the actors and stuntmen. It got to the point were the fire was almost out of control. At this point, though, the first assistant director called the stand by studio fire department to put the fire out, which, thank goodness, they did. Meanwhile, the American director was still yelling and shouting."

In the summer of 1969, Sammy Davis Jr. and Jerry Lewis caused trouble locally while shooting their madcap comedy, *One More Time*.

On Thursday July 31, 1969, the *Borehamwood & Elstree Post* reported: "SAMMY DAVIS FILM SPARKS OFF A ROW"

It all happened while the production company, based at MGM Borehamwood, were filming on location nearby at the Allum Lane cemetery, Elstree. They received a storm of protests from irate residents, with one crying out, "Is nothing sacred?"

The cemetery had been transformed into a film set, with several large sun umbrellas in one corner, the remnants of a buffet lunch to the side, and cameras and bright lights hovering over a mock grave, which was garnished by several bunny girls in mourning.

Although MGM's band of fifty filmmakers had been given permission to film at the cemetery by Elstree Rural Council, many individual residents had not given the go ahead, and a flood of protests produced a wave of indignation.

Mr. Les Schooledge of Edulf Road, Borehamwood stormed in "looking for blood." He said the flowers on his mother-in-law's grave had been pushed aside and a stake driven through the grave, as a support for a mock tombstone.

Speaking of "the grotesque lot of plaster monuments," which were part of the movie set, Mr. Schooledge said, "I think there is a limit. Where does respect stop and finish?"

Mr. Reginald O'Connor of Melrose Avenue, Borehamwood, whose son is buried at the cemetery, was equally adamant. "I, and many others, were shocked to see the monstrosities of tombstones that had been erected on ground within feet of existing graves, and more so by the idea that such a procedure should have official blessing."

The Council and film company apologized, and the scheduled two-day filming at the cemetery had to be cut to one.

On Thursday, August 28, 1969, the following report appeared in the *Borehamwood & Elstree Post*:

"HARRY'S A LAUGH IN HIS FIRST FILM ROLE

MGM's Head Gardener is Jerry Lewis' Latest Discovery"

Head Gardener Harry Drury little thought when he arranged the flowers on the set of *One More Time* that he would be playing a role in it.

Jerry Lewis, who was directing the picture, considered Harry perfect for the part of the leader of Tom Thumb And His Fickle Fingers, the comedy group that provide music for the ballroom scene.

Harry, though, had never conducted in his life, and had no sense of rhythm. In fact, he was just perfect for the part in a film that bristles with dozens of visual gags.

For Harry the gardener, though, his screen success had come rather late in life. He was sixty-eight.

Other notable roles in the movie were played by character actors, Bill Maynard and Norman Mitchell. Maynard played Jenson, a sniper, out to bump off Sammy Davis and his comedy partner, Peter Lawford. "Anyone and everyone were welcome on that film set. There were big signs saying, 'This is not a closed set. Come on in.' This was because Sammy and Jerry used to do a comedy routine every day and needed an audience."

Norman Mitchell played Police Sergeant Bullock. "The first day we were shooting a bar scene at MGM with twenty or thirty people gyrating about. Jerry Lewis, an excellent comedian and a great director, said to everyone, 'I'm going to have two cameras running: one taking the master shot, and the other going at the same time for close-ups on Sammy. So, first of all, I want you all to ad-lib with your partner for five minutes. 1-2-3 action.'

"I turned to the person next to me, got my note book out, and said, 'I understand that you were committing gross indecency in Hyde Park last night!'

"A hand gripped me, and a voice shouted, 'Stop the shoot!' I turned round and saw it was Sammy. The cameras stopped, and he asked me, 'What did you say to that lady just now!?'

"I thought this was a moment of truth and I shouted at the top of my voice, 'I understand that you were committing gross indecency in Hyde Park last night!'

"Sammy rolled on the floor with laughter, 'Did you get that? The man is a comedic genius. It was right off the top of his head!' Everybody had a good laugh, but I don't think the lady was very pleased.

"When the morning's filming was over, Sammy took me to his caravan and got out what he called, 'a real bottle of bourbon' and made a great fuss of me.

"I asked him why he had junior at the end of his name. 'Because there was this great guy, an ace dancer, Sammy Davis, and I'm his son. I've been a pro since I was three.'

"He went over to the refrigerator, opened the door, and as soon as the light came on, he went into his old act, 'Hello Lamb Chop'. He tap-danced his way all round the caravan, all the trinkets he was wearing jiggling away the while. He had a Lapis Lazuli as big as an egg on his finger and a gold medallion round his neck. Outside the caravan there was a Rolls-Royce, which he'd been presented with by an American multimillionaire.

"At the end of the day's shooting, people would often hang around and watch Sammy and Jerry Lewis do their old double-act, which had some very funny athletic business. Then, Sammy would go outside and invite his uniformed chauffeur to take the back seat of the Rolls while he drove home. Sammy was so short, he practically disappeared when he got into the driving seat and he had to look through the spokes of the steering wheel to see out of the windscreen.

"One day, Jerry Lewis rode through the gates of the studio on a red one-stroke motorbike. As soon as Sammy saw the bike he wanted one. He turned to his chauffeur and said, 'Get me that model,' and two hours later, his man was back with another red motorbike, and Sammy and Jerry rode them round a ballroom set.

"The butler in the movie was an old actor, so Sammy said, 'Wouldn't it be fun if I order drinks, and he's so slow that when he gets back with them he's grown a beard.' They tried it and it was hilarious.

"My wife, Pauline, and my two children, Christopher and Jacqueline, visited me on the set, and Sammy treated them like the gentleman he was."

One small sequence in *One More Time* actually features the unaccredited appearances of Peter Cushing as Baron Frankenstein and Christopher Lee as Dracula. Both were friends of Sammy (a devout Hammer horror fan).

Soon after filming was completed, actress Fiona Lewis (who was then getting quite large supporting roles in British films) gave an interview to a newspaper in which she said that the filming had been a nightmare, and described director Jerry Lewis as the biggest egomaniac she had ever met. Interestingly, when the film opened in cinemas, Ms. Lewis and her scenes were nowhere to be seen.

Though many did consider Jerry Lewis full of his own self-importance, some others did not share that same opinion.

Ronnie Maasz was camera operator on *One More Time*, and found working with Jerry Lewis to be an enduring memory. They got on extremely well, and Ronnie had nothing but fond memories.

On release, *One More Time*, made very little impact, nor did *No Blade Of Grass,* which was made about the same time and directed by Cornel Wilde, and nor did an all-star film version of *Julius Caesar.*

John Gielgud played Caesar in the latter, and was supported by Charlton Heston (Marc Anthony), Jason Robards (Marcus Brutus), Richard Johnson, Richard Chamberlain, Diana Rigg, and Christopher Lee.

Despite his star billing, Christopher Lee worked on the movie for only a day and had hardly any lines. He said that the only direction he received from Stuart Burge was, "You realise, of course, that Artemidorus is quite, quite mad."

Working on the film as continuity was Phyllis Townshend. "I remember most of all shooting the opening sequence at MGM Borehamwood with Caesar entering Rome. We shot it on the back lot, and the assistant directors were sending the parade back around through the stages to make it look as if we had hundreds of extras.

"On the death of Caesar (Sir John Gielgud), the director, Stuart Burge, told the make-up man not to put too much blood on his robe. He then grabbed the bottle and put gallons on.

"Poor old Sir John, he never really knew what hit him. Especially when I had to do Jill Bennett's off lines with him. I certainly was no Shakespearian actress. He said, 'Speak up Dear.'

"The studio, MGM, was a beautiful studio. Very modern, with enormous stages."

Clapper/loader on *Julius Caesar* was Keith Blake. "First of all we filmed on location in Madrid, Spain, and it seemed to me that the company had chartered the oldest, cheapest plane they could find to get us there - a really decrepit Comet. We survived the flight though and filming, which went relatively well, and then we returned to Borehamwood to complete the shoot.

"After about a weeks filming at MGM, we noticed that Stuart Burge, the director, nice man that he was, hadn't changed his clothes, so we all had a whip-round for him. I went to the local Milletts and got him a whole outfit of safari gear, which, needless to say, he wore until the end of filming!

"Although there was a huge well-known cast, the one who we all loved was Jason Robards. He was always losing his fags [cigarettes], so we got the wardrobe department to make a type of bumbag for him that he could wear under his toga! This we presented to him, with cigarettes, a lighter, and a packet of three!

"One morning, Jason hadn't turned up on time. When he eventually arrived, he told us that he'd been arrested the previous night after drinking too much with a mate of his. For some reason, the police didn't believe that he was who he said he was, and more to the point that his mate was Stan Getz!"

In 1969, ABPC Studios, Borehamwood, was acquired by EMI and renamed EMI-Elstree Film Studios. Bryan Forbes was appointed head of production and managing director. The first films to be made at EMI under Forbes leadership were *And Soon The Darkness*, *The Man Who Haunted Himself* starring Roger Moore, *Hoffman* with Peter Sellers, and Hammer's *Taste The Blood Of Dracula* with Christopher Lee.

Hammer Films were now based at Borehamwood, and both Peter Cushing and Christopher Lee were seen filming in the studios, and at locations around the town on a regular basis.

On Thursday November 13, 1969, the *Borehamwood & Elstree Post* reported:

"DRACULA TAKES TO THE WOODS"

If you go down to the woods today, you're in for a big surprise, but not the teddy bear type.

If any member of the public dared to go down to Scratchwood, on the Borehamwood side of Barnet Lane, they would probably have come across a "gruesome twosome," Count Dracula, no less, and a pretty damsel.

Hammer Films were busy shooting there for a week, filming scenes for *Taste The Blood Of Dracula*.

By late 1969, things were not looking good for MGM British, even though there continued to be a steady flow of movies being made.

Country Dance with Peter O'Toole, *The Walking Stick*, and part of Billy Wilder's *The Private Life Of Sherlock Holmes* would though be among the final films to be shot on its sound stages.

On Thursday November 27, 1969, the following report appeared in the *Borehamwood & Elstree* Post:

"MGM STAY OPEN WITH MAJOR STAFF CUTBACK"

MGM's Studios were to stay open, but with a probable 50 per cent cutback in staff. About 124 employees had already been made redundant and more were expected within the week.

Rumours spread that MGM's 120-acre studios were to close were squashed, even though the future of some 780 workers at that time remained in doubt.

Mr. Paul Mills, an MGM director, said firmly that MGM's lion will not be leaving Borehamwood. He added that its roar would not be diminished.

However, on Thursday December 4, 1969, the *Borehamwood & Elstree Post* reported:

"JOBLESS TOLL RISES AT MGM"

390 employees of MGM British were expecting the sack by Christmas, as the only activity in the studios at that time was the television series *UFO*, and it was due to finish production that week.

With the future of MGM Borehamwood now uncertain, Gerry Anderson's *UFO*, which had filmed its first series there, would move its production permanently to Pinewood Studios, a more secure base.

By January 1970, things began to look bleak for the once grand film studios. MGM's new management in the US decided upon drastic action to halt the decline in the company's shares, as they were now heavily in debt. Within weeks, two thirds of their distribution in the USA were closed and 180 acres of their Hollywood studio went up for sale.

However, MGM was still some £13,000,000 in debt and the accountants began to take a closer look at their massive studio in Borehamwood.

On Thursday February 5, 1970, the following report appeared in the *Borehamwood & Elstree Post*:

"MGM RESHUFFLE AS STUDIOS GET BACK TO WORK"

The article mentioned that filming was to start again within three months, under new management, as no movies had been shot at MGM Borehamwood for several months.

Mr. Jack King had been appointed head of the studios to get things up and running again, but sadly, it was not to be.

On Thursday February 26, 1970, the *Borehamwood & Elstree Post* reported:

"MGM TO SACK 226 TO SAVE STUDIOS"

In this report, it stated that more people were to be sacked by MGM British under a massive scheme to reorganise the company and restart filming in England.

This decision meant that the present labour force would be cut from 370 to 144, meaning in many cases that some departments would be slashed to just one man.

In March 1970, the sackings began in an effort to reduce the £500,000 yearly wage bill.

While all this was happening, *Man's Fate* was about to start production. For this epic movie, huge sets had already been constructed on the back lot by production designer Elliot Scott.

Actor Joss Ackland was part of the cast. He takes up the story. "It is sad to say, but I was partly responsible for closing the MGM British Studios in Borehamwood.

"It started when the superb movie director, Fred Zinnemann, cast me in his film, *Man's Fate*, an adaptation of Andre Maurois fine novel, *Man's Estate*.

"Zinnemann offered me the role of Konig. It was a 'Harry Lime' of a character, who does not appear until late and then proceeds to ruin everyone's lives.

"I held my breath because I did not believe it would happen; maybe I would be replaced on the first day.

"Fred had worked on the script for three years. 10,000 civilian costumes had been made, 3,000 army costumes completed, Lord Mountbatten (as Chief of the Defence Staff) had set aside half of Singapore Harbour, two young Japanese boys had been cast as the young heroes, Liv Ullman was the heroine, and the leading character men were Peter Finch, David Niven, Max Von Sydow, and Clive Revill.

"We rehearsed for two weeks at MGM British, and had temporary costumes for rehearsal. On the last day before shooting started, I was doing my big scene, torturing David Niven. It was after lunch and Fred was five minutes late. What we did not know was that he was busy on the telephone trying to raise $3 million. $4 million had already been spent on costumes, sets, etc. This, though, was the clamp down on big budget movies by MGM. The phone calls were to no avail. As we continued to rehearse, the MGM British Studios was being pulled apart around us. Everyone was stiff upper lip: Liv Ullman cried a little; David Niven went off to do some shopping; Fred Zinnemann had the quiet strength of a man used to disappointment.

"I could not believe that we would not be saved at the last minute. But no cavalry appeared. Not one foot of film was ever shot. I got the role, but they eventually took away the studio—and the film."

Stephen Scott, son of MGM British production designer, Elliot Scott, also remembers the doomed film production. "My father had all the sets built on the back lot, and a great deal of money was spent, but the day before filming began, MGM pulled the film, and it never got made. It was the beginning of the end for MGM British."

Legal battles over *Man's Fate* went on for years, and the four main stars (Peter Finch, David Niven, Max Von Sydow, Clive Revill) sued MGM, eventually receiving compensation totalling £335,816.

The end came swiftly for MGM British over one weekend in the summer of 1970. The staff that remained were given their notice on a Friday, and by the following Monday, equipment was being removed, and what couldn't be removed was quickly destroyed.

Angela Martelli, who had worked as continuity at the studios since it opened, was one of the MGM employees to be given her notice. Nicolas Roeg recalls meeting her. "Angela was very upset. She said to me, 'I've given all these years of my life to MGM, so much of my time. They gave me two weeks notice. Is that what I'm worth?' It was very sad. It shocked Angela terribly."

Mr. Alan Sapper, then secretary of the A.C.T.T. Union, made an appeal to the government to try and save the studio. He said, "The closure of MGM will mean the elimination of the largest film studio in Britain." His words were lost on deaf ears.

Within days, word quickly got around the industry of the impending closure of one of England's great film studios.

Dennis Fraser, who had worked at MGM as grip for many years, remembers being told the news. "I was doing the film *Kelly's Heroes* (1970) with Clint Eastwood. It was an MGM film being shot in Yugoslavia. The producer on the movie, Sidney Beckerman, came to me and said, 'MGM British is closing.'

"I said, 'Don't be silly.'

"He said, 'When you get back to England, it'll be closed.'

He bet me a pound, and six years later I saw him again and gave him the pound. He was right."

Jimmy Dawes, who had worked as a grip at MGM Borehamwood since its opening, was also told the news in a similar fashion. "It was director David Lean, who told me the news. I was working with him on his movie *Ryan's Daughter* (1970) and he said to me, 'What are you going to do, Jimmy, with MGM British closing up?'

At this time, I knew nothing about it, but it was all going on, of course. Anyway, Freddie Young, said, 'He's coming with me.' His next film was *Nicholas And Alexandra* (1971). In the end, though, he couldn't use me, because the company making the film wanted certain people. So after that, it was a struggle. But I managed."

As MGM British was preparing for closure, an independent film *Zeppelin* was still being shot there.

Alan Hume was cinematographer on the movie. "My camera operator, Skeets Kelly, who had worked on dozens of films at MGM Borehamwood, was tragically killed while we were filming that picture, and this happened during the final days that that studio was in operation.

"We were doing a shot of old fighter aircraft passing a mock-up Zeppelin, firing blanks, of course, and the director spoke to one of the chaps who was flying the aircraft, and told him to fly the plane closer to the Zeppelin.

"The worst thing happened, of course, and the aircraft hit part of the Zeppelin, and that is how Skeets lost his life, as he was sitting on a platform with his camera outside the Zeppelin.

"It is a dreadful experience to lose one of your mates like that, and I remember going to see his wife afterwards. Devastating."

Nicolas Roeg had also worked with Skeets Kelly. "Skeets was a special kind of guy. A true professional, and extremely good at his job."

Filming on *Zeppelin* resumed within days, but MGM were desperate to move the production elsewhere. Studio workers, the ones that remained at MGM British, "blacked the set" because of a dispute with the management over future employment or compensation, but the movie would eventually have to be completed at EMI Elstree Studios.

Mr. Nat Weiss of MGM commented, "As far as we're concerned, the studios are closed and we do not intend to open them again. It would be economically impossible. If there were any possibility of using the studios again, we would have before now."

MGM agreed to merge with EMI Elstree Studios and pay £175,000 a year towards the upkeep of that complex, thus renaming it EMI-MGM Elstree Studios.

The 120 acre MGM site was then sold to a development company for 1,8000,000 pounds with further payments due according to the use of the land.

The studio, its stages, and back lot stood empty for nearly two years, by which time the sets that were still standing were beginning to decay, and the greenhouses and gardens that once blossomed with flowers were overgrown.

The studio's last connection with the movie world came in 1972, when the bulldozers moved in and demolition on the huge sound stages began.

Sally Jones was there to witness it. "I was working as continuity on the Hammer Film, *Holiday on the Buses* with Reg Varney, when a scene called for Reg to demolition a building.

"We were filming at EMI-MGM Elstree Studios, and just down the road was the empty MGM British facility, which was about to be knocked down. So, we filmed some of it. It was sad and amazing to watch as that big concrete ball swung time and time again into the side of one of the stages. Mesmerizing that this massive heavy object weighing tons didn't seem to be having any effect! MGM Borehamwood just didn't want to go. Finally, after what seemed like hours, she cracked and the studio started to crumble."

"If you care to look, you can actually see it go at the end of the film, *Holiday on the Buses*."

All the buildings were demolished, but the art deco clock tower at the entrance was left standing and leased to the local council as offices.

The back lot stayed unaltered until the late 1970s, mainly because this was greenbelt land. Here props and set pieces from *2001* lay abandoned alongside, amongst other things, one of the cable cars from *Where Eagles Dare*. Most of the standing sets, including the chateau from *The Dirty Dozen*, the Chinese village from *The Inn Of The Sixth Happiness*, and the town square from *Quatermass And The Pitt* were eventually destroyed by a series of unexplained fires.

It was during this period that Stanley Kubrick made a return visit to the back lot to shoot part of the maze sequence for *The Shining*.

Roy Walker was production designer. "We constructed the large exterior maze on what was the old MGM British back lot. We needed a massive open space with no trees, and it was ideal as it was just being cleared for housing.

"Stanley, I remember, was thrilled to be filming there, as it was where he had shot *2001* in the late 1960s. He was certainly in nostalgic mood."

A housing estate was built on the back lot site in the early 1980s and named Studio Way. The landmark art deco white clock tower could not be given a "listed building" status, was demolished in secret one evening in 1987, much to the horror of local people.

The only surviving remnants of MGM British today are a small brick wall by the main road on Elstree Way and a grass mound in the center of the housing estate where the *Ivanhoe* castle once stood.

On June 23, 1996, a plaque was placed at the site to commemorate the studio. Resident cinematographer at MGM British, Freddie Young, and colleague Freddie Francis, did the unveiling.

Francis later said, "It was a moving moment for Freddie Young, as he was there when it opened and when it closed. So, giving that site a permanent fixture to say that it actually existed was very important to him.

"Sadly, it was quite depressing, as well, as there was a housing estate there when we did the unveiling, which didn't impress Freddie very much, as the old MGM Studio had held a lot of special memories for him. All he kept saying to me was, 'It should never have been closed. How could this have been allowed to happen?'

"I myself hadn't worked at the MGM studio a great deal, but there was no mistaking how impressive a studio it was. It was similar to Denham, another great studio, long gone, and I suppose, forgotten.

"For Freddie, though, who died shortly after the unveiling, it was a solid old veteran saying goodbye to a great era in British filmmaking, when studios were studios and the movies being made in them were of a high standard.

"When MGM closed, it seemed to mark a change in the British film industry, and not for the better, and Freddie Young knew that. I do hope, for his sake rather than mine, that MGM British and the movies made there will never be forgotten."

A Cinematic Legacy

After the closure of MGM British, the newly merged EMI-MGM Elstree Studios was in full swing. Interesting and varied productions included, *The Railway Children, Dulcima* with John Mills and Carol White, and *The Go-Between* starring Julie Christie and Alan Bates, which was the winner of the Palme d'Or at Cannes in 1971.

Studio head, actor-director Bryan Forbes, green-lit these films, which were financed by EMI itself, and despite a lack of sufficient funds, they remain impressive achievements.

During 1971 and 1972, the studios were at full stretch. Thirteen films were produced in 1971, with a further eighteen films the following year.

Not getting the financial support he deserved to keep the studio moving, Bryan Forbes resigned, and the studio became a four-wall facility, hiring itself out to visiting movie companies that needed soundstage space. This led to films as diverse as *Get Carter* (1971), *Digby, The Biggest Dog in the World* (1973), and *The Legend Of Hell House* (1973) directed by John Hough, being shot there.

Cinematographer on the latter was Alan Hume. "It was a horror film, but a very good one. Sadly, it didn't do very well. It flopped at the box-office. I can't think why. But it was, and still is, one of my favorite films to photograph. I was very proud of it photographically. It was a good looking movie."

In 1973, MGM pulled out of their agreement and the studio reverted to the earlier name of EMI Elstree Studios.

Only eight films were made that year, and with a lack of self-financed commercial successes the studio was left to struggle from one movie to the next.

Andrew Mitchell, with years of practical filmmaking experience, was appointed managing director, but towards the end of 1973, EMI Elstree reached a crucial stage in its history, when it was announced that the studios, as they operated, were no longer a viable proposition and might have to be closed down.

In November 1973, the permanent staff of 518 were cut to 261 "for reasons of economy." Was history repeating itself?

Things looked up at the beginning of 1974, when one of the most ambitious movies ever to be made at the studios arrived—Agatha Christie's *Murder On The Orient Express.*

Directed by Sidney Lumet, the movie featured a galaxy of international stars, including Albert Finney, Sean Connery, Ingrid Bergman, John Gielgud, Anthony Perkins, Richard Widmark, and Lauren Bacall.

Angela Allen was continuity. "All I can say is that it was a very smooth-running film. Mainly, I think, because Sidney Lumet was directing it. The actors were also very organized, though, and very professional."

Despite the movie's great success at the box-office, EMI Elstree saw nothing of the money other than its soundstage fees, as the film was released by another company.

1975 saw further downturn in production, although a series of low-budget sex comedies including, *Confessions of a Driving Instructor* with Robin Askwith, proved popular.

1976 saw EMI Elstree occupied by Ken Russell's biopic *Valentino*, starring Rudolph Nureyev.

However, it was a low-budget science fiction film and a relatively unknown young director that were destined to turn the studios fortunes around.

George Lucas chose EMI Elstree to shoot *Star Wars* mainly because it was cheap facility and had a number of empty sound stages. When Lucas arrived on site, it was the beginning of a very special relationship between director and studio, and one that would last many years.

Before shooting *Star Wars,* Lucas offered EMI Elstree a percentage of profits instead of paying to hire. The studio declined, reasoning that the fees would be more helpful in the short term. It proved to be their biggest mistake, as filmmaking—not to mention Elstree/Borehamwood itself—would never be the same again.

At the start of filming, things did not look too bright for *Star Wars* or its director. Neither the actors nor crew could make sense of the screenplay, and most considered Lucas to be an American director "without a clue."

Frictions between Lucas and cinematographer Gilbert Taylor led the crew to believe that this would turn into a science fiction flop, be swept under the carpet, and probably go down in history as one of the worst movies ever produced, with its cardboard-looking sets and silly characters.

What they didn't realise was that Lucas was one giant step ahead of them, and that his story, settings, and characters that he had created were nothing less than pure genius.

In post production, he would also introduce some ground-breaking special visual effects that would change the look of movies forever—and *Star Wars* would become one of the most successful films of all time.

In fact, it was largely due to Lucas that at one period in the 1980s it was Borehamwood, not Hollywood, that had been home to six of the top ten grossing films up until that time.

Star Wars was completed just in time to make way for Stanley Kubrick's *The Shining* with Jack Nicholson, and Anthony Quinn in *The Greek Tycoon*.

Continuity on the latter was undertaken by June Randall. "One of my jobs as continuity is to see that everyone has the proper clothes for their character. Anyway, I happened to overhear Anthony Quinn having a go at the props people, and so I asked what it was about.

"Anthony Quinn said to me, 'You are the script girl?'

"I said, 'Yes.

"He said, 'How come you let me wear these glasses?'

"I said to him, 'First of all, these props people don't get paid tuppence to get shouted at like that. What's wrong with your bloody glasses?'

"He said, 'My character should have a different pair of glasses every day.'

"I said, 'Well why don't you just tell us you want different glasses, and we'll do it.

"So, he said, 'Who do you think you are talking to?

"I said, 'You. I don't like to see my props people getting shouted at like that.

"After that, I couldn't put a foot wrong with that man. He wanted me to do every film he did after that. I think he was just so surprised that someone had dared answer back to him."

When June Randall left the movie to take up her commitments on *The Shining*, Renee Glynne took her place as continuity. "It was the only time I met Anthony Quinn. He was a wonderful man. Outrageous and beautiful.

"The director of *The Greek Tycoon* was J. Lee Thompson. He had a psychological thing going were he used to sit and tear his call sheets into strips. He used to eat them, as well.

"As a person, he was alright, but he didn't love me. He used to make me feel very self-conscious. I personally like directors to love me, and sadly, he didn't."

An excellent Sherlock Holmes film, *Murder by Decree* with Christopher Plummer and James Mason, followed in 1978, alongside *The Empire Strikes Back*, which brought Mark Hamill, Carrie Fisher, and Harrison Ford back to the studios for what some consider to be the best of the *Star Wars* movies.

Kelvin Pike was camera operator on the latter. "Carrie Fisher was a delight to work with. I would talk with her about her mother, Debbie Reynolds. Then one day, Carrie handed the telephone to me, and a voice on the other end said, 'I hope you are looking after my daughter Mr. Pike?' It was her mother, of course. I was lost for words."

Replacing Kay Rawlings as continuity for the studio scenes on *The Empire Strikes Back* was, Pamela Francis. "I replaced Kay as she had fallen sick, and so was therefore given the opportunity to work with George Lucas.

"The crew on the original *Star Wars* film were very unpopular with George. They couldn't understand him, and he couldn't understand them.

"The *Star Wars* movies were George's train set. We always used to say that. There was no question about it. He could do what he liked with *Star Wars*.

"As a person he was always delightful. A lovely man. But he couldn't direct. He wasn't really a director.

"I remember *The Empire Strikes Back* going wildly over budget, and George getting absolutely furious. But it was probably the better of the first three original films, in my opinion."

In 1979, the studios became Thorn-EMI with the merger of the two companies, and Oliver Reed and Klaus Kinski were on site to appear in the horror film, *Venom*.

Malcolm Vinson was camera operator. "In all my years working in the film business, *Venom*, was by far the most difficult picture to work on. It didn't help that the main stars, Reed and Kinski, hated each other, and the original director, Tobe Hooper, hadn't got a clue what he was doing. He was then replaced after two weeks by Piers Haggard, but whether Tobe had had a nervous breakdown or was drinking too much, I couldn't say.

"I remember that we were to have a week of night shoots. Three weeks later, we were still working, simply because the artistes were at each other's throats.

"Sterling Hayden had a role in the movie, and smoked a Sherlock Holmes-style pipe full of dope, and by three in the afternoon, he was on some other planet.

"We'd often get important people on the phones, asking why we hadn't finished a day's work. Well, we couldn't tell them that it was because the actors were drunk or stoned.

"Klaus Kinski was a very unfriendly man and very much kept himself to himself, except, that is, when Oliver Reed was around, as he would get Klaus deliberately in a violent rage.

"Now this movie was about a deadly snake (not deadly actors), but the snake itself was another problem. Once, it was released in the studio, mayhem ensued. The sound stage door had to be opened, a car engine fired up, the Borehamwood police had to be notified, and a doctor had to be on set in case an accident occurred."

Gilbert Taylor was cinematographer. "Working on that movie is not an experience I care to remember."

David Wynn-Jones was focus puller. "Whoever had the idea to cast Oliver Reed and Klaus Kinski in the same film should be stuffed.

"Oliver had a great sense of humor, though, but Klaus was a very serious man. So Oliver liked nothing more than to wind him up, after he'd got tanked in the bar at the studios, of course. Then, he'd do the goose step in front of Klaus, shake his trailer, call him a 'Nazi' bastard, etc., until Klaus blew his top, then a huge argument would ensue.

"Sterling Hayden kept away from all the trouble, smoking on his rather large pipe, full of pot.

"It was a truly outrageous film to work on."

The high camp science fiction movie, *Flash Gordon*, followed *Venom*, and then in early 1980, George Lucas was back at the studios, but this time with Steven Spielberg in tow. The pair were set to film the first in a trilogy of movies featuring Harrison Ford playing the character Indiana Jones.

The first, *Raiders of the Lost Ark*, directed by Spielberg and produced by Lucas, would become another mega-hit for the studios.

This was followed in 1984 by *Indiana Jones and the Temple Of Doom*, and then in 1989 with *Indiana Jones and the Last Crusade*. Both were equally successful, and both teamed Spielberg, Lucas, and Ford playing the title role.

Douglas Slocombe was cinematographer on the trilogy. "Steven [Spielberg] was always a delight to work with. He always knew exactly what he wanted and had immense enthusiasm. I miss working with him a lot."

Robin Vidgeon was focus puller on the first two of the trilogy, and shares his memories of working with Steven Spielberg. "In 1977, a young director had just completed *Close Encounters of the Third Kind,* and one sequence remained unshot. So, Steven gathered all the artists needed for the scene and went off to Bombay… for a week. Passing through London, he had asked Douggie Slocombe to join him for the shoot, together with Chic Waterson, his operator, and myself, focus puller. Sound mixer John Mitchell also joined the team. For the long (first class) flight, we all talked at length on all the joys and trials of filmmaking. By the time we arrived in India, we were tired but excited to be working with this famous man. The week was exhausting. The sequence we shot was with 2,000 saffron-robed Indians being asked by Francois Truffaut where the famous five chords came from in outer space.

"Cut to the return flight to London, we were even more exhausted but still talked again during the whole flight. The BIG difference now, though, was that we all felt like a big family. And, more importantly, Steven told us that all the time he had spent in Film School he was led to believe that it was not wise to make movies in the UK, because the Brits were always taking tea breaks and were very unionized. Before we landed, he had promised us, however, that one day he would come to make films in the UK, and he kept that promise.

"Cut to 1980… *Raiders of the Lost Ark*. Together again, and Steven was just the same, totally focused, a director who always did his homework and enthused all who worked with him. My biggest joy was that whatever he threw at us, he never waited for the camera crew, and he always kept his sense of humor. Days on location around the world, or on set, went in a flash, and I always looked forward to going to work, and confront the challenges that he kept throwing at us.

"Cut to 1983… *Indiana Jones and the Temple of Doom* Another hectic schedule, but still the same Steven, a little older, like all of us, but still as sharp and almost childlike in his love and enthusiasm for the movies. I am still amazed how after working with him on two and a bit movies, he is still the only director I know who comes to set every day with every sequence and every shot in his memory. That's not to say that he is not open to suggestions that might improve the scene, he is.

"We have kept in touch over the last years, and when I was in Berlin choosing my equipment for *The Neverending Story III* (1994), which I photographed, a mechanic placed two camera bodies on the table. They looked like they had been used in a ploughed field covered in mud. When I asked what film they had just come from, I was told *Schlinder's List* (1992). They were the ones I chose, of course. When *Schindler's* won awards at the Oscars, I emailed Steven with congratulations for all concerned and told him the story about the cameras."

Danny Shelmerdine was assistant camera on *Raiders*. "What can I say about Steven Spielberg. He's a legend. I have great memories of him. He was good to work with. A very fast worker, though, but he knew what he wanted. At first, I found him to be a bit aloof, but that soon passed. He was always very complimentary after a shoot.

"Douglas Slocombe, his cinematographer, is another legend. A great technician. But a very down to earth man. It was an honour to work with him."

Working on the first two of the trilogy as continuity was Pamela Francis. "Steven started off being very very insular towards his British crew. He thought we all stopped for tea at 4:00 in the afternoon. To be honest, at first he didn't quite know what to make of us. A consummate director, though. Superb. I'm sure if he could he would make his films single handed. He just loves filmmaking.

"I also think he was happy making movies at the studios in Borehamwood. I don't think George (Lucas) ever was, though. Partly due, I think, to the fact that he had so much trouble with the crew on the first *Star Wars* movie.

"Harrison Ford didn't like Borehamwood either, or England to that fact. He was fine to work with, though. A very creative actor.

"I've always found, for some reason, American artists to be very well-schooled in the film business. They always hit their marks, etc.

"As a note of interest, the submarine mock-up used in *Raiders Of The Lost Ark* was the one used in the famous German movie *Das Boot* (1981), and the Indiana Jones costume and famous hat were designed by the wife of John Landis, Deborah Nadoolman."

Phyllis Townshend was continuity on the studio scenes for *Temple Of Doom*. "Steven Spielberg was a lovely man. He was a real film enthusiast. As a director, he knew exactly what he wanted on set, and went about it in a very quiet way."

Former MGM British production designer, Elliot Scott, was designer on the latter two of the trilogy, and his son, Stephen Scott, joined him, firstly as assistant art director, and then as art director. "I actually worked with my father three times at those Borehamwood studios. It was a very contained facility, surrounded by a very big housing estate. Space was at a premium there. It was a fine place, though, apart, that is, from the drains. I can remember now the office block we worked in, the drains used to seep up through the floor. And I also recall the boiler which made a terrible booming sound. Very bloody irritating.

"Steven Spielberg was a good man. Brilliant, absolutely brilliant. Him and George Lucas had a sort of affinity for that studio in Borehamwood, mainly because *Star Wars* was filmed there, I think."

While *Raiders of the Lost Ark* was being filmed at Thorn-EMI Studios, Vincent Price was also shooting the horror comedy, *The Monster Club*, with John Carradine and Donald Pleasence, and Jim Henson's Muppets were appearing in *The Great Muppet Caper* with Liza Minnelli.

1981 was a less hectic year with amongst others the fantasy film, *The Dark Crystal*, but 1982 was a busier year when production commenced on *Monty Python's Meaning of Life*, the epic, *Greystoke: The Legend of Tarzan, Lord of the Apes*, and *Never Say Never Again* with Sean Connery playing James Bond for the final time.

George Lucas also made a return visit to the studios to film the final entry in the original *Star Wars* trilogy entitled, *Return of the Jedi*.

Pamela Francis was continuity. "This movie was originally called *Revenge of the Jedi* and *Blue Harvest*. But it was actually called *Blue Harvest* to distract people, so they wouldn't know it was a *Star Wars* film when we were on location. So we all wore caps and shirts with *Blue Harvest* written on them. This was to stop us being mobbed, because by this time the *Star Wars* movies were big business. It was so obvious though that we were *Star Wars*, as all the props were on show.

"Richard Marquand was not really the right director for *Return of the Jedi*. Originally, they wanted David Lynch. I said to them, 'If you have David, you'll get something very very different,' as I'd known him from *The Elephant Man*, which my husband, Freddie Francis, photographed.

"Anyway, David turned George Lucas down and directed *Dune* (1984) instead."

Cinematographer on *Return of the Jedi* was, Alan Hume. "George Lucas was a nice man to work with, but quite hard, as well. A very clever man, though. But quite tough. You have to be tough though to be as successful as that. You also have to remember that his movies were way ahead of any others being made at that time."

Alan Hume also returned to the studio two years later in 1984 to photograph the science fiction movie, *Lifeforce*, directed by Tobe Hooper. "*Lifeforce* was a very good-looking film, but the story wasn't up to much. It was about some vampires, who arrive in London from space. So, it wasn't really a surprise when it did nothing at the box-office. It bombed. But it was definitely one of the best-looking movies I've worked on, and the director, Tobe, was a nice guy to work for. Even though inside I think he was a very nervous person. In fact, he used to disappear from the set, and we'd all wonder where he was. I think he may have been on drugs or drinking heavily. But regardless of this, he was a lovely guy."

Unfortunately, by 1986, the studio's future was uncertain again when Thorn-EMI decided to sell to the Golan-Globus team of Cannon Films, and thus the studios became Cannon Elstree Studios.

However, it soon became clear that Cannon had way overstretched its finances, and in trying to keep afloat, they sold off the studio's vast library of movies dating back to the 1920s.

Cannon's final hope, the filming of *Superman IV: The Quest For Peace* would turn out to be a failure in cinemas due to the extreme cutting of the budget by Golan-Globus.

Further productions in 1986, including *Who Framed Roger Rabbit?* with Bob Hoskins, and Spielberg's *Empire of The Sun*, though very successful, did nothing to save Cannon from financial straits.

When Spielberg and George Lucas returned a year later to shoot *Indians Jones and the Last Crusade*, dark clouds were gathering over the historic facility.

Cannon eventually admitted financial defeat during the early part of 1988, and announced that the studio was up for sale again, whether for filmmaking or development.

Fearing the studio would be lost, production supervisor on the latter *Indiana Jones* movie, Patricia Carr decided to set up a Save Our Studios campaign, with Paul Welsh (of Borehamwood Town Council) as chairman.

The campaign garnered worldwide media attention and included a presentation at the House Of Commons, a public meeting in Borehamwood attended by 700 residents, and a 15,000-strong petition gathered within weeks.

In October 1988, it was announced that Brent Walker had purchased the studios, and would merge it with their Goldcrest Film Company.

It all looked good, until the company sold off twelve acres—almost half of the studio's land—to Tesco, a major supermarket, and planned to redevelop the remaining fifteen acres for retail use.

In haste, Paul Welsh, continued the Save Our Studio campaign, and continued to gather much support, and even a promise from Peter Cushing, in which he said, "I am only held together nowadays by glue and blu-tack, but if you need someone to lie down in front of the bulldozers then I am your man!"

Despite all of this, though, the battle to protect the studios would last several very long and dark years.

By the early part of 1990, Brent Walker was in debt, had all but closed the studio down, and was turning away major film productions, such as *Robin Hood Prince Of Thieves* (1991).

The studio gates closed for business in 1993, and stripping the facility to raise cash, Brent Walker left the studios buildings and soundstages empty to deteriorate.

For the following three years, legal battles ensued between the local authority and Brent Walker, whose only interest was the destruction of the studios and its site.

In a stroke of luck, one of the largest soundstages in the country was saved from Walker's bulldozers when the *Star Wars* stage was bought by another studio. The entire construction was dismantled piece by piece and rebuilt to the original specifications at Shepperton Studios.

Finally, in February 1996, in an out-of-court settlement, the local authority (Hertsmere Borough Council) found itself the unlikely owners of a film studio.

The following year, Paul Welsh, for his many efforts in trying to save the studio, received an MBE, while Brent Walker and their company Goldcrest eventually went bust.

Refurbishment was the first priority for Hertsmere in getting the newly named Elstree Film Studios back on its feet. Buildings were quickly repaired and, within a few months, cameras were rolling again, and the Bill Murray comedy *The Man Who Knew Too Little*, reopened the studio in late 1996.

The century would end with the construction of "The George Lucas Stage"—a huge sound stage in honour of the producer, and officially opened by HRH Prince Charles.

Since the year 2000, the studio has had two more name changes, starting with Elstree Film & Television Studios, and then more recently becoming what it is today, Elstree Studios. As of 2014 it continues to thrive, and remains, as it always did, a vital piece of the British filmmaking landscape delivering entertainment for both the big and small screen.

In 1914, Borehamwood opened its doors to the film industry. Now, over 100 years later, it continues to do just that.

Borehamwood: The British Hollywood is sadly a thing of the past, but in its heyday the people and pubs of the town became accustomed to seeing Errol Flynn or Richard Burton having a pint, and Indiana Jones strolling along the road to the newsagents. It was a strange mixture of high glamour and a small working-class town, hand in hand.

As regards to that greatest Borehamwood studio of them all, MGM British, it is now just a faded memory. Where the many famous names of Hollywood once stood, and gave us memorable performances on celluloid, a housing estate now stands.

Maybe, though, if you were to go to the center of that housing estate on a quiet cold winter's night, and stand on the grass mound where the *Ivanhoe* castle once stood, you might just hear the ghosts of MGM past come to life, and for one night, the lion may roar again in Borehamwood.

2001: A Space Odyssey (1968). Stanley Kubrick walking through the grounds of MGM British Studios. Courtesy of Kelvin Pike.

2001: A Space Odyssey (1968). Kelvin Pike (camera operator) preparing to shoot a scene. Courtesy of Kelvin Pike.

2001: A Space Odyssey (1968). Stanley Kubrick (behind camera), Kelvin Pike, camera operator (bottom right) and Graeme Scaife, clapper (foreground) preparing to shoot a scene. Courtesy of Graeme Scaife.

2001: A Space Odyssey (1968). Kelvin Pike (camera operator) relaxes on set at MGM British. Courtesy of Kelvin Pike.

Stanley Kubrick's home between 1968/78 – Abbots Mead on Barnet Lane, Elstree. Courtesy of Derek Pykett.

Where Eagles Dare (1968). Richard Burton and Arthur Ibbetson (cinematographer) having a chat between takes at MGM British. Courtesy of Graeme Scaife.

Where Eagles Dare (1968). Brian Hutton, director (left) chats with Frank Elliott, focus puller (right) on location. Courtesy of Neil Thompson.

Where Eagles Dare (1968). Peter Mullins (art director) overlooks the miniature of Hohenwerfen Castle he designed being constructed on the back-lot at MGM British Studios. Courtesy of Peter Mullins.

Where Eagles Dare (1968). Graeme Scaife, clapper (third left) celebrating his birthday on the set at MGM British. Richard Burton, also pictured, displays his drinking skills, alongside Clint Eastwood (first left), Dennis Fraser, grip (second left) and Frank Elliott, focus puller (between Scaife and Burton). Courtesy of Graeme Scaife.

Where Eagles Dare (1968). Clint Eastwood chatting with Graeme Scaife in the grounds of
MGM British Studios, Borehamwood. Courtesy of Graeme Scaife.

Where Eagles Dare (1968). Paul Wilson (camera operator) films Clint Eastwood on a studio set at MGM British. Note the painted backdrop. Courtesy of Paul Wilson.

Where Eagles Dare (1968). Arthur Ibbetson, cinematographer (top right) lighting the set, and Paul Wilson (holding the camera). Courtesy of Neil Thompson.

Richard Burton and Elizabeth Taylor's favourite pub when visiting Borehamwood—
the Artichoke on Elstree Hill. Courtesy of Derek Pykett.

Where Eagles Dare (1968). Elizabeth Taylor visits cast and crew at MGM British Studios.
Richard Burton (her then husband) is to her right, Arthur Ibbetson, cinematographer (far
left), Paul Wilson, camera operator (behind Ibbetson), Graeme Scaife, clapper (right of
Ibbetson), Dennis Fraser, grip (left of Taylor). Courtesy of Neil Thompson.

Where Eagles Dare (1968). Yakima Canutt (left), Hollywood's legendary stuntman, on location with Peter Mullins, art director (right). Courtesy of Peter Mullins.

Where Eagles Dare (1968). Filming on a real cable-car on location in Ebensee, Austria. Kelvin Pike, camera operator, is on top of the cable-car (behind camera), and David Wynn-Jones, clapper, is seen peering out of cable-car (left side). Courtesy of Kelvin Pike.

Where Eagles Dare (1968). Kelvin Pike (camera operator) filming on top of a real cable-car on location in Austria. Courtesy of Kelvin Pike.

Where Eagles Dare (1968). Graeme Scaife (clapper) celebrates his birthday on set at MGM British. Graeme is pictured standing between Burton and Eastwood. Arthur Ibbetson (cinematographer) is far left. Paul Wilson (camera operator) is second right. Courtesy of Paul Wilson.

Where Eagles Dare (1968). The miniature of Hohenwerfen Castle, designed by Peter Mullins, on the back-lot at MGM British. Courtesy of Peter Mullins.

Goodbye Mr. Chips (1969). Unused 'production design' by Elliot Scott. The film was designed by Ken Adam. Courtesy of Stephen Scott.

Goodbye Mr. Chips (1969). Unused 'production design' by Elliot Scott. The film was designed by Ken Adam. Courtesy of Stephen Scott.

Goodbye Mr. Chips (1969). Peter O'Toole on location. Dennis Fraser (grip) is standing to his left. Courtesy of Dennis Fraser.

Julius Caesar (1970). Charlton Heston relaxes on location. Courtesy of Keith Blake.

The Walking Stick (1970). Samantha Eggar and David Hemmings rehearse a scene at MGM British Studios. Arthur Ibbetson, cinematographer (holding lamp) is lighting the set-up. Dennis Fraser (grip) is standing far left. Courtesy of Dennis Fraser.

No Blade Of Grass (1970). Cornel Wilde on set at MGM British. Dennis Fraser
(grip) stands to his right. Courtesy of Dennis Fraser.

Unused sets on the back-lot of MGM British in 1970 for the doomed film *Man's Fate*.
Courtesy of Stephen Scott.

'Production designer' Elliot Scott standing on his unused sets on the back-lot at MGM British constructed for the unmade film *Man's Fate* in 1970. Courtesy of Stephen Scott.

Bulldozers demolish one of the huge sound-stages at MGM British in 1972.
Courtesy of Roger Garrod.

One of the standing sets from Quatermass And The Pit (1968) which stood on the back-lot
at MGM British until the mid 1970's. Courtesy of Roger Garrod.

The model miniature of Hohenwerfen Castle used in the movie *Where Eagles Dare* (1968) stood on the back-lot at MGM British until the mid 1970's. Courtesy of Roger Garrod.

The MGM British administration building with its
art-deco white clock tower as it looked in the late 1970's.
It survived until 1987. Note the small brick wall at the front.
Courtesy of Roger Garrod.

The site of the MGM British administration building in 2015. The only thing that
remains is the small brick wall at the front. Courtesy of Derek Pykett.

The Shining (1980). Stanley Kubrick (left) and Kelvin Pike filming a scene.
Courtesy of Kelvin Pike.

The Shining (1980). Stanley Kubrick (right) and Kelvin Pike, camera
operator (left of Kubrick) prepare to shoot a scene at EMI-Elstree
Film Studios. Courtesy of Kelvin Pike.

The Shining (1980). June Randall (continuity) on set with Jack Nicholson.
Courtesy of June Randall.

The Shining (1980). June Randall (continuity) on set with Shelley Duvall.
Courtesy of June Randall.

The Shining (1980). Kelvin Pike (camera operator) sitting on the impressive Overlook Hotel interior set at EMI-Elstree Film Studios. Courtesy of Kelvin Pike.

The Shining (1980). Kelvin Pike relaxing on the set at EMI-Elstree Film Studios, Borehamwood. Courtesy of Kelvin Pike.

The Empire Strikes Back (1980). Carrie Fisher helps Kelvin Pike (camera operator) out behind the camera. Irvin Kershner (director) is far left. Courtesy of Kelvin Pike.

Raiders of the Lost Ark (1981). Steven Spielberg and Harrison Ford relaxing on the back-lot at Thorn-EMI Elstree Film Studios. Pamela Francis (continuity) is far left. Courtesy of Pamela Francis.

Indiana Jones and The Temple of Doom (1984). George Lucas on set at Thorn-EMI Elstree Film Studios. Courtesy of Stephen Scott.

Indiana Jones and The Temple of Doom (1984). Steven Spielberg directing Raj Singh on set at Thorn-EMI Elstree Film Studios. Phyllis Townshend (continuity) is standing to Spielberg's left with the script. Courtesy of Phyllis Townshend.

Indiana Jones and The Temple of Doom (1984). Elliot Scott 'production design'.
Courtesy of Stephen Scott.

Indiana Jones and The Temple of Doom (1984). Elliot Scott 'production design'.
Courtesy of Stephen Scott.

Lifeforce (1985). Cast and crew celebrate Frank Finlay (centre) receiving his CBE on set at Thorn-EMI Elstree Film Studios. Tobe Hooper, director (first right), Alan Hume, cinematographer (third right), Michael Gothard (fourth right) and Peter Firth (first left). Courtesy of Alan Hume.

Indiana Jones and The Last Crusade (1989). Preparing to film a scene on set at Cannon Elstree Studios. Steven Spielberg can be seen directing Sean Connery on the scaffold. Courtesy of Stephen Scott.

Indiana Jones and The Last Crusade (1989). Elliot Scott 'production design'. Courtesy of Stephen Scott.

On the site (in 2015) where *Star Wars*, *The Shining* and many other classic films were shot stands now a giant 'Tesco' superstore. Courtesy of Derek Pykett.

Once 'The Red Lion' pub in Borehamwood (now a 'McDonald's' in 2015) where many a famous film-star once drank, including, Errol Flynn, Richard Burton and Lee Marvin. Courtesy of Derek Pykett.

A blue plaque on the site of the MGM British Studios, unveiled on the 23rd of June 1996 by cinematographers, Freddie Young and Freddie Francis. Courtesy of Derek Pykett.

Afterword

Sir Sydney Samuelson (British film commissioner): "In my opinion, MGM Borehamwood was 'superior' to all the other studios. Whereas other studios were mostly what had become a hodgepodge of buildings over a period of years, MGM was designed and built as a production center with the quality and style expected of anything to do with Metro-Goldwyn-Mayer. Even Pinewood, that great place, had some shabby buildings dotted around the back lot.

In 1947, when I was about to be demobbed from the RAF, I was still in uniform but I thought I would try for a job as a junior in the camera department, so I called in at MGM. Not only was I rejected but it was made very clear to me that one doesn't just call in for a job at MGM! A formal application in writing was required, and this I provided. I received a standard reply about my application being on file, but I was never even asked to appear for an interview.

"My 'special memory' of the studio came years later, when the company I had set up became a major supplier of camera equipment and we were servicing the film *Casino Royale* with four different units working from different bases. I received a frantic phone call one Monday morning from Les Smart, who ran the MGM camera department, asking where the Panavision equipment was for the John Huston-directed unit of *Casino Royale*, who were waiting to start work on the one of the stages that very morning. I had to explain that although we were servicing four units on *Casino Royale*, none of them were for Mr. Huston at MGM. It turned out that in the confusion of getting another unit—the fifth unit—started, nobody in the production office had thought to order any camera gear.

"I was delighted to hear that Derek Pykett was writing the story of MGM British. It's about time this studio with its list of movies—great and less than great—was put on to permanent record."

Michael Winner (film director): "I have a reason to be grateful to the film studios of Elstree and Borehamwood, as this is more or less where my career began in the business.

"In fact it was Edward Danziger who gave me my first job, as First Assistant Director on the second unit of his *Mark Saber* television series at Elstree. This was 1956.

"Danziger actually had a studio at Elstree, just off the Watford Road, with his brother, Harry, and working for them really did teach me my craft. I was paid £27 a week.

"Unfortunately, I'd no idea what a First Assistant Director did! However I did soon discover that it involved a lot of shouting a yelling, so thereafter I did my job with reasonable competence, and continued, so some tell me, to shout and yell for the rest of my career as a movie director.

"I left the Danzigers when I was offered a job as Director by Sheldon Reynolds, an American making a tv series at MGM British, Borehamwood called *Dick And The Duchess* with Hazel Court and Patrick O'Neal. In fact, though, Sheldon Reynolds did most of the directing, and all I did was shout 'Action' and 'Cut,' but once again I was learning. I did eventually get a chance to direct, but was shattered when Reynolds brought in a more experienced director to take over! I thought I'd got through the day rather well, but I think the actors were helping me a little too much, so I was replaced. However, the whole experience taught me, a young man starting his life in a tough business, valuable lessons.

"In hindsight, these two studios and others like them were the training ground for many directors and technicians, it is a shame though that the two that gave me my start are now long gone.

"I never used studios myself when directing, as I preferred real locations and settings, but the above studios I remember with nothing less than affection. They certainly were happy days and are happy memories."

June Randall (continuity): "It truly breaks my heart when I think of what happened to MGM British. You wouldn't even know it ever existed now."

Danny Shelmerdine (assistant camera): "The demolition of MGM British was a grave mistake."

Roy Walker (production designer): "MGM British was a very nice studio. It was a far better facility than EMI-Elstree Studios."

Angela Allen (continuity): "It was a big mistake to demolish MGM. It should really have been EMI-Elstree. It was a stupid mistake, and it didn't take any brain power to know which was the better studio. It was a major, major error of judgement."

Peter Mullins (production designer): "It was very depressing when they demolished MGM. Everyone in the business said that they should have demolished EMI-Elstree rather than MGM. But there we go. It certainly had more to offer. A wonderful back lot, etc."

David Minty (art director): "EMI-Elstree was a terrible place with no character, whereas MGM had a lot of character, with a lot of interesting and creative characters working there. It also had a huge lot with a huge amount of land. They used to keep herds of sheep on it, and we were never sure whether the "boss" wanted to do farming or filming. As a studio, it should never have closed."

Keith Blake (assistant camera): "MGM British was the best studio in the UK. But, sadly, it was one of the first ones to be demolished."

Elaine Schreyeck (continuity): "MGM was built as a studio, and it should have stayed as a studio. It was a great place. Everyone worked so well together. As a studio, it was certainly on par with Denham, another great studios, sadly, also lost."

Jack Lowin (camera operator): "MGM British was a happy place to work."

Pamela Francis (continuity): "Everyone has always said that they got rid of the wrong studio when they demolished MGM, and kept EMI-Elstree."

Terry Ackland-Snow (production designer): "I really shouldn't say this because I now work at Pinewood, but MGM British was most definitely one of the best studios in Europe. It had a good system, and excellent security. It was also run efficiently. I was heartbroken when they closed it."

Peggy Spirito (continuity): " MGM British was like a village. I cried when they knocked it down. It was awful. It was definitely the best studio that they had in Borehamwood. Well I think so. It was a golden age.

Brian Johnson (special effects): "I do think that because *2001* took so long to film and took up nearly the entire studio losing MGM an enormous amount of money financially, that it was partly responsible for MGM going to the wall. It was criminal, though, when they demolished it. Even the art deco front went. Very sad.

Peter Sasdy (director): "MGM was a very exciting studio to work, and certainly lived up to its reputation."

Terry Pearce (assistant director): "I feel proud to say that I worked at MGM British, even though it was for only one or two days."

Christopher Neame (producer): "Although no death knell sounded on the day MGM Studios was knocked down, it should have. It would aptly signal the end of an era when British films really were great, and in their own right, too."

Michael Gough (actor): "All of the big stars passed through that studio, and in those days, they were real stars."

Trevor Coop (camera operator): "MGM British was the last 'proper' studio in this country, and over four decades on, I still miss it."

Gilbert Taylor (cinematographer): "The studios of Borehamwood and its history is a lifetime of great filmmaking and movies from the silent days through to television, to the present day. Those studios have made great Oscar-winning films still great sixty years on. How can I make a short statement over 100 years work?"

Alan Hume (cinematographer): "Borehamwood has always been a filmy place, and MGM was a major part of that."

Jack Cardiff (cinematographer): "As all of us who had the opportunity to work at MGM British depart this world, the movies shot there will continue to be shown around the world, bearing the words on their credits—

made at MGM British Studios, Borehamwood, England—and, therefore, continuing its legacy through this century and hopefully beyond."

Bryan Forbes (producer/director): "My only connection with MGM Borehamwood was when, as Chief Executive of the newly merged MGM-EMI Studios, I was given the unhappy task of telling the employees of MGM at the studios that they were being given two weeks notice and that the studios was being, cynically, closed.

"I fought vehemently against the closure, but was out-voted. James Aubrey ('the smiling cobra') was the heads of MGM Hollywood and came over to England with Doug Netter his sidekick, intent in selling off MGM's family silver.

"The MGM studio at Borehamwood was possibly the most modern in Europe at the time with, of course, the largest back lot."

"It was a sad chapter in the history of the British Film Industry of the 1970s, when that studio was demolished and both the management and the craft unions allowed it to happen."

MGM London Studios:
The Best in Europe

In the late 1950s, a brochure was produced by MGM British to sell its studio and facilities to film companies. It gives you an idea of the scale of the Borehamwood studios and why it became known as the greatest movie studio outside of Hollywood.

It also gives an intimate account of the people who worked there. Those important names who gave the studio its reputation.

This is how it read, [quoted as it was published]:

WHEN YOU START planning your next picture, whether the scale be luxurious or limited, remember we provide all the facilities and the experience you would wish to have.–Mathew Raymond, Managing Director

MGM HAS A RECORD IN THE MOTION PICTURE INDUSTRY THAT IS SECOND TO NONE. REMEMBER THE WHOLE RESOURCES OF THIS GREAT COMPANY HAVE GONE INTO THE DEVELOPMENT OF MGM LONDON STUDIOS.

MGM LONDON STUDIOS WERE BUILT FOR THE EXPRESS PURPOSE OF MAKING FIRST QUALITY FILMS FOR THE INTERNATIONAL MARKET.

NO OTHER STUDIO IN EUROPE CAN PRODUCE A MORE IMPRESSIVE RECORD OF MERIT AND FINANCIAL SUCCESS SINCE ITS OPENING IN 1948.

Sound Stages
Stage 1: 7,100 sq. ft. Clear Shooting Area.
Stage 2: 11,520 sq. ft. Clear Shooting Area.

Stage 3: 18,820 sq. ft. Clear Shooting Area. Stage 3 also has a tank under floor level, 80 ft. by 32 ft. by 11 ft. deep complete with armoured glass windows for underwater filming.

Stage 4: 11,520 sq. ft. Clear Shooting Area.

Stage 5: 7,100 sq. ft. Clear Shooting Area.

Stage 6: 11,500 sq. ft. Clear Shooting Area. Stage 6 is also fitted with two tanks under floor, 37 ft. by 20 ft. by 11 ft. deep, and 17 ft. by 9 ft. by 8 ft. deep.

Stage 7: 6,000 sq. ft. Clear Shooting Area. Stage 7 is also dual purpose. A shooting and music recording stage it is fitted with projection, footage indicator, echo and vocal chambers.

Stage 1 to 5 are 45 feet high to the rails that carry the lighting cradles. Above these are cat walks and switchboards with 15 feet headroom.

Stage 6 and 7 are 34 feet high to the rails.

All stages are soundproof, and temperature, ventilation, and humidity on the stages are under control at all times ensuring perfect working conditions—A RARE FEATURE IN EUROPEAN STUDIOS.

MGM Production Department

The MGM Production Department IS UNDER THE DIRECTION OF Miss Dora Wright who has 26 years experience in the film industry. She was production manager for a majority of the pictures made at the studios, and was Associate Producer for *I, Accuse!* and *Tom Thumb*.

Miss Wright's long experience in film production has enabled her to acquire and maintain a contact with Government and Service Departments and other valuable sources of co-operation vital to location work and research that is second to none.

Working in co-ordination with Miss Wright is First Assistant/ Unit Manager David Middlemas who has 25 years experience in film production. Middlemas was recently first assistant director on *The Inn of the Sixth Happiness* and *Tom Thumb* and has worked with pictures associated with MGM for eight years. He was given the Screen Directors Guild of America Annual Award for the Best

Assistant Director for 1958.

Office Accommodation
There are 6 executive office suites for producers and directors in the front office building. There is ample office space to accommodate five productions concurrently.

MGM Casting Department
Under the direction of Miss Irene Howard, sister of the late Leslie Howard, MGM's casting department is considered the best in Europe.

Miss Howard's wide experience includes first-hand knowledge of American, European as well as British artistes and agents.

Miss Howard has 18 years experience as a Casting Director and was at Denham Studios before joining MGM. With her long list of credits in international pictures, it is not surprising that independent producers and directors from all over the world, whether connected with MGM or not, frequently call on her expert advise.

MGM Art Department
Director of the Art Department, Elliot Scott, who has 26 years experience in the film industry, is considered one of the leading art directors in Europe.

John Ford called Scott's sets for *Mogambo*: "The best I have ever seen for any picture."

The photographic library in the art department comprises several hundred thousand illustrations.

Consequently, any form of research for producers is easily and readily made, and the department's considerable home and overseas location experience is also available to producers seeking sites or photographic or other backings.

The department has worked frequently with foreign art departments on films produced abroad.

Four suites of offices are available for art department use, each equipped for art directors, draftsmen and set dressers.

The art department has facilities for die-line printing and for photographic and document copying.

Outstanding staff scenic artists are available as are facilities for preparing set dressing and construction lists.

MGM Make-Up And Hair Dressing Department

The Make-Up and Hair Dressing Departments are the most modern in Europe, and is under the direction of Joan Johnstone who has 25 years experience in the film industry.

The Make-Up Department has 7 private cubicles for stars' use. It has, in addition, what is undoubtedly the best equipped laboratory in the world of research and the manufacture of teeth, plastic facial attachments and other specialised make-up.

The Hair Dressing Department has 7 private cubicles for stars' use, plus a shampoo room and a wig room.

In addition to the stars' private cubicles, there are make-up and hairdressing facilities in the crowd artistes' dressing rooms sufficient for the largest possible crowd. THIS PROVISION IS UNIQUE IN EUROPEAN STUDIOS.

MGM Special Effects Department

Tom Howard who has 25 years experience in film production, is in charge of the special effects department which offers facilities unrivalled by any other studios in Europe. Howard won an Academy Award for *Blithe Spirit* in 1946 and *Tom Thumb* in 1959.

Such pictures as *Ivanhoe*, *The Inn of the Sixth Happiness* and *Tom Thumb*, together with others have been the subject of worldwide acclaim, illustrating the ability and versatility of MGM's Special Effects Department.

It can also be proudly stated that certain special effects created in the motion picture *Tom Thumb* are unique. Some processes invented by Tom Howard for this picture made at MGM's London Studios have never before been achieved—even in Hollywood.

The separate sections of the department include:

BACK PROJECTION operated with the most modern blimpless projectors. The department maintains two complete equipments that can be used in interlock for dual screen projection filling screens from a few feet in width up to a maximum of 20 feet for colour and up to 30 feet for black and white.

THE PHOTOGRAPHIC EFFECTS AND MATTE PAINTING DEPARTMENTS combine multiple exposure photography in conjunction with miniatures.

Two fully motorised high speed camera equipments, running up to 8 times normal speed are maintained for use with miniatures involving fire, water and smoke.

Travelling Matte work is a speciality in which MGM's own systems for both black and white and colour film are used.

MGM Sound Department

When MGM London Studios sound department was planned in 1946, it incorporated space for use of techniques then only in the development stage. By continuing to install the most modern machines, it has remained the finest of its size in the world.

MGM London Studios were the first in Europe to record Stereophonic Sound, and the music recording facilities at MGM London are considered by some American experts to be in advance of Hollywood.

A. W. Watkins is in charge of the Sound Department. Sometime recording director of Western Electric and recording director of London Films, he also planned the acoustics and sound for Denham Studios.

MGM Camera Department

MGM London Studios were the first in Europe to produce a film in CinemaScope.

MGM London Studios were the first in Europe to produce a film in Technirama.

MGM London were the first in Europe to produce a film in Eastman Colour.

Leslie Smart, in charge of the Camera Department, has wide experience in the preparation and packing of equipment and stock for use overseas and in presenting these for customs examination before and after location.

Attached to the department, which is connected by a covered way to all seven stages, is a dark room for the processing of hand tests during shooting.

MGM Editorial Department

A glance at the list of films the studio has produced will show the style and quality of the work of editors Frank Clarke, who is in charge of the department and has 26 years experience and Ernest

Walters, 17 years experience. Sound Editor Robert Carrick has 24 years experience.

17 cutting rooms are available, each equipped with film bins, storage cupboards, two cutting benches with four-way rewinds and synchronisers and a single rewind table.

Each room has either an Acmiola or a Moviola fitted with both optical and magnetic sound-heads and an additional silent picture head.

Each room has a magnetic pull-through reader with separate amplifier.

Each room has splicing facilities.

3 code numbering machines operated by an MGM assistant serve all productions.

THE LIBRARY, which is always expanding includes –

over 4,000 picture stock shots.

over 1,300 back projection plates.

over 7,500 sound effects.

FILM STORAGE –

There are 28 approved vaults in various parts of the studios.

PROJECTOR MOVIOLA –

This is available for editing and matching purposes on the stages. It has both optical and magnetic sound heads, can be used with either CinemaScope or Wide-Screen lenses, and is fitted with reversible motors.

MGM Stills Department

Davis Boulton, in charge of the Stills Department, has 24 years experience in the film industry. He is considered the finest portrait photographer in European film studios. Was specially commended for his work on *Quo Vadis* (1951) and *Ben-Hur* (1959) and for his photography in seven European countries of 124 Van Gogh originals with a CinemaScope lens for use in the actual print of *Lust for Life* (1956).

MGM Wardrobe Department

Miss Elsie Hunt, 13 years in the industry, is in charge of the administration of the Wardrobe Department leaving Miss Dolly Smith and Charles Monet, who have over 40 years film experience between them, to operate the male and female sections.

An extensive collection of male and female costumes, modern dress, boots, shoes and ancillary effects, including jewellery, is maintained scrupulously clean in the department which is connected by covered way to all seven stages.

Long association with leading designers, costumiers and fashion houses in London, Paris, Rome, Madrid and Munich enables the department quickly to assemble the best possible wardrobe for any kind of production.

Dressing Room Accommodation

The studio maintains 10 modern furnished, very comfortable stars' dressing suites complete with private baths and/or showers and 12 similarly furnished smaller part dressing rooms, all situated in the same studio block.

The dressing rooms are connected by a covered way to all seven stages.

MGM Estate Department

MGM's studio lot is the biggest of its kind in Europe and covers 114 acres. The land is at high level so that surrounding buildings, etc, to not interfere with the photographic skyline.

The estate is run on orthodox farming lines. Consequently the fields are well drained and in good order. Such alterations as may be made for productions are immediately made good so that the estate maintains its rural character.

The estate Department supplies trees, branches and turf as required. The nursery of 2 acres supplies plants and cut flowers.

Maintained under 5,000 square feet of glass, a large and varied collection of tropical and sub-tropical plants are always readily available for use. Hundreds of large plants and trees up to 20 feet in height, are readily transportable in tubs and boxes, are also available.

The studio maintains an experienced estate and garden staff (green men) for landscape and set dressing.

Exteriors built at MGM London Studios are as outstanding in quality and design, construction and finish as are the interiors.

Tom Dawson, in charge of the Estate Department, has 24 years experience in the film industry.

MGM Construction Department

The Construction Departments are under the direction of Cyril Graysmark who has 34 years experience in the film industry.

The departments are all centrally situated. Workshops are spacious and equipped with every convenience for speedy set making and erection. SETS ARE ALWAYS PRE-FABRICATED IN THE VARIOUS SHOPS WHENEVER POSSIBLE IN ORDER TO SAVE VALUABLE STAGE SPACE.

THE SCENE DOCK –

Of tremendous economic importance to the studio, it covers a floor area of approximately 60,000 square feet and contains the largest collection of stock sets, flats, rostrums, backings and set pieces in Europe.

All stock sets and set pieces are carefully catalogued in illustrated files readily available to producers and art directors. PRUDENT USE OF THE STOCK CAN SAVE THOUSANDS OF POUNDS ON A NORMAL PRODUCTION.

MGM Property Department

Jack Ramsey, MGM Studios property master, has had 38 years experience in the film industry.

The Property Department, situated just behind the stages, maintains an extremely large stock of all kinds of furniture and fittings and set dressing articles carefully stored and indexed for easy access. Continued care and maintenance keep the stock in first-rate condition.

The long experience of Jack Ramsey and his colleague, buyer Bill Isaacs, enables them to hire or purchase additional props required, not only at short notice but at prices that are invariably the lowest.

The "prop" staff's reputation in handling and clerically controlling highly priced antique furniture and other precious effects is second to none. There has not been one insurance claim due to negligence either for damage in handling or for loss since the studio started production.

MGM Restaurant And Cafeteria

Subsidised by the Studio, the restaurant and cafeteria offer best quality food at lowest possible prices. Sam Nolan, in charge of catering, is able to supply the needs of the largest crowds likely to be called. There is room at any one sitting for 150 people in the restaurant and 500 in the cafeteria.

MGM Security
The security force is under the direction of former Detective Inspector of Police, G. Brown. Security is maintained by frequent patrols of the entire studios and estate.

MGM London Studios Operate The Following Working Conditions –
1. A five day week of 44 hours.
2. A fixed 1 hour lunch break. Other refreshment breaks are taken WITHOUT PRODUCTION STOPPING.
3. Overtime may be worked outside the normal working day and/or on Saturdays and Sundays provided agreement has been reached before production starts. A 15 minute overtime may be worked without warning in order to complete a "take." 1 hour may be worked to complete a set.
4. Location work entails the payment of travelling, hotel and out-of-pocket expenses including costs of meals and payment in lieu.
5. A normal unit, excluding producer and director, consists of 40-45 technical craft and other grades. The cost of a first-class crew of this number would approximate $3,000-$3,500 dollars for a 44-hour week.

MGM Studio Personnel
MATHEW RAYMOND	Managing Director
GEORGE CATT	Studio Manager

HEADS OF DEPARTMENTS:
C. ANDERSON	Carpenters
F. BEADLE	Transport
D. BOULTON	Stills
G. Brown	Security
V. BRYANT	Cleaning
W. BULL	Plasterers
F. CLARKE	Editorial
K. CRACK	Plant Engineer

T. DAWSON	Estate
R. DAVEY	Accounts
B. FENSHAM	Scenic
C. GRAYSMARK	Construction
MISS I. HOWARD	Casting
T. HOWARD	Special Effects
MISS E. HUNT	Wardrobe
W. ISAACS	Buyer
MISS J. JOHNSTONE	Hairdressing
P. MEAD	Pattern
G. MERRITT	Engineers
F. MIALL	Drapes
P. MILLS	Publicity, P.R., Advertising
S. NOLAN	Catering, Restaurant
L. PETTIT	Fire
J. RAMSEY	Property
E. SCOTT	Art
L. SMART	Camera
MISS E. SMITH	Telephones
S. TURNER	Stores
F. WALTERS	Electrical
A. WATKINS	Sound
R. WHITE	Personnel
H. WOOLVERIDGE	Studio Operating
MISS D. WRIGHT	Production

MGM British Studios
A Filmography

* means the film was only partly made at the studio
d   Director
p   Producer
dop   Director of Photography
pd   Production Designer
s   Screen-play
e   Editor
c   Cast

Brighton Rock (1947) *

d John Boulting   p Roy Boulting   s Graham Greene
e Peter Graham Scott   dop Harry Waxman   pd John Howell

The teenage leader of a racetrack gang uses a waitress as alibi to cover a murder, and marries her. He later decides to be rid of her, but fate takes a hand in his murder plot.

c Richard Attenborough, Hermione Baddeley, Harcourt Williams, William Hartnell, Alan Wheatley, Carol Marsh, Nigel Stock

"Very flashily done." – Leslie Halliwell, *Halliwell's Film and Video Guide*, 2000.

While I Live (1947)

d John Harlow   p Edward Dryhurst   s John Harlow, Doreen
Montgomery   e Raymond Poulton   dop Freddie Young
pd Bernard Robinson

A Cornishwoman believes a girl pianist suffering from amnesia to be the
reincarnation of her dead sister, Olwen.

c Tom Walls, Sonia Dresdel, Carol Raye, Clifford Evans, Patricia Burke,
John Warwick, Edward Lexy

"Silly melodrama." – David Quinlan, *British Sound Films*, 1984.

The Guinea Pig (1948)

d Roy Boulting   p John Boulting   s Bernard Miles, Warren
Chetham Strode   e Richard Best   dop Gilbert Taylor
pd John Howell

The story of a poor boy who wins a scholarship to a famous public
school, and finds that life there quickly becomes a living hell for him.

c Richard Attenborough, Robert Flemyng, Cecil Trouncer, Sheila Sim,
Bernard Miles, Joan Hickson

"Enjoyable school drama." – David Quinlan, *British Sound Films*, 1984.

Idol of Paris (1948)

d Leslie Arliss   p R. J. Minney   s Norman Lee, Stafford Dickens,
Henry Ostrer   e Bert Bates   dop Jack E. Cox   pd Albert Jullion

In old Paris, the daughter of a rag-and-bone man becomes queen of the
demimondaines.

c Beryl Baxter, Christine Norden, Michael Rennie, Margaretta Scott,

Henry Oscar, Miles Malleson, Andrew Cruickshank

"Unintentionally hilarious." – David Quinlan, *British Sound Films*, 1984.

Spring In Park Lane (1948)

d Herbert Wilcox   p Herbert Wilcox   s Nicholas Phipps   e
Frank Clarke   dop Mutz Greenbaum   pd William C. Andrews

A diamond merchant's niece falls for a footman who just happens to be an impoverished lord in disguise.

c Anna Neagle, Michael Wilding, Tom Walls, Nicholas Phipps, Peter Graves, Marjorie Fielding, Nigel Patrick

"Highly successful romantic comedy." – David Quinlan, *British Sound Films*, 1984.

Edward My Son (1949)

d George Cukor   p Edwin H. Knopf   s Donald Ogden Stewart
e Raymond Poulton   dop Freddie Young   pd Alfred Junge

A rich, unscrupulous man remembers the people he has made unhappy , and the son to whom he never behaved as a father should.

c Spencer Tracy, Deborah Kerr, Ian Hunter, James Donald, Mervyn Johns, Felix Aylmer

"Rather ugly-looking adaptation of a gripping piece of theatre." – Leslie Halliwell, *Halliwell's Film and Video Guide*, 2000.

Conspirator (1949)

d Victor Saville   p Arthur Hornblow Jr.   s Sally Benson, Gerard Fairlie   e Frank Clarke   dop Freddie Young   pd Alfred Junge

A guard officer, unknown to his lovely teenage bride, belongs to a subversive political party to whom he is giving military secrets.

c Robert Taylor, Elizabeth Taylor, Harold Warrender, Robert Flemyng, Honor Blackman, Marjorie Fielding, Thora Hird, Wilfrid Hyde-White, Janette Scott

"Lacklustre film has neither life nor credibility." – David Quinlan, *British Sound Films*, 1984.

Maytime In Mayfair (1949)

d Herbert Wilcox   p Herbert Wilcox, Anna Neagle   s Nicholas Phipps   e Raymond Poulton   dop Mutz Greenbaum
pd William C. Andrews

A man-about-town, Michael, inherits a dress salon and falls in love with the lady manager, Eileen.

c Anna Neagle, Michael Wilding, Nicholas Phipps, Peter Graves, Tom Walls, Thora Hird, Michael Shepley

"Witless comedy." - David Quinlan, *British Sound Films*, 1984.

Under Capricorn (1949)

d Alfred Hitchcock p Sidney Bernstein, Alfred Hitchcock
s James Bridie   e Bert Bates   dop Jack Cardiff
pd Thomas N. Morahan

In Australia in 1830 an English immigrant stays with his cousin Henrietta, who has become a dipsomaniac because of her husband's cruelty.

c Ingrid Bergman, Joseph Cotton, Michael Wilding, Margaret Leighton, Jack Watling, Cecil Parker, Francis de Wolff, Martin Benson

"Muffled Hitchcock, with principals ludicrously miscast." – Leslie Halliwell, *Halliwell's Film and Video Guide*, 2000.

The Miniver Story (1950)

d H. C. Potter   p Sidney Franklin   s Ronald Miller, George Froeschel   e Frank Clarke   dop Joseph Ruttenberg
pd Alfred Junge

In 1945 Mrs. Miniver welcomes her family back from the war, although knowing that she has only a year to live.

c Greer Garson, Walter Pidgeon, Cathy O'Donnell, Leo Genn, Reginald Owen, William (James) Fox, Anthony Bushell, Peter Finch

"Well enough made, but very hard to take." – David Quinlan, *British Sound Films*, 1984.

The Elusive Pimpernel (1950) *

d Michael Powell   p Michael Powell, Emeric Pressburger
s Michael Powell   e Reginald Mills   dop Christopher Challis
pd Hein Heckroth

A foppish 18th Century London dandy is actually the hero who rescues French aristocrats from the guillotine.

c David Niven, Margaret Leighton, Cyril Cusack, Jack Hawkins, Robert Coote, Charles Victor, Patrick Macnee, Peter Copley

"Weak and bloodless film." – David Quinlan, *British Sound Films*, 1984.

Calling Bulldog Drummond (1951)

d Victor Saville   p Hayes Goetz   s Howard Emmett Rogers, Gerard Fairlie   e Frank Clarke   dop Freddie Young pd   Alfred Junge

Ex-officer, Bulldog Drummond, is called in by Scotland Yard to track down a gang of thieves operating with military precision.

c   Walter Pidgeon, Margaret Leighton, Robert Beatty, David Tomlinson, Peggy Evans, Charles Victor, Bernard Lee, James Hayter

"Minor-league quota quickie." – David Quinlan, *British Sound Films*, 1984.

Ivanhoe (1952)

d   Richard Thorpe   p   Pandro S. Berman   s   Aeneas Mackenzie, Noel Langley   e   Frank Clarke   dop   Freddie Young
pd   Alfred Junge

In return for saving rich Jewish Merchant Isaac from robbers, Saxon knight Ivanhoe is promised the money he needs for the ransom of Richard the Lionheart.

c   Robert Taylor, Elizabeth Taylor, Joan Fontaine, Emlyn Williams, George Sanders, Robert Douglas, Finlay Currie, Felix Aylmer, Francis de Wolff, Guy Rolfe

"Tolerable, big budget spectacular." – Leslie Halliwell, *Halliwell's Film and Video Guide*, 2000.

The Hour Of 13 (1952)

d   Harold French   p   Hayes Goetz   s   Leon Gordon, Howard Emmett Rogers   e   Raymond Poulton   dop   Guy Green
pd   Alfred Junge

The murder of ten policeman in identical circumstances terrifies and shocks Edwardian London.

c Peter Lawford, Dawn Addams, Roland Culver, Derek Bond, Leslie Dwyer, Michael Hordern, Michael Goodliffe, Peter Copley

"Polished if hardly full-blooded period thriller." – David Quinlan, *British Sound Films*, 1984.

Time Bomb (1953)

d Ted Tetzlaff   p Richard Goldstone   s Kem Bennett
e Frank Clarke   dop Freddie Young   pd Alfred Junge

A saboteur places a bomb on a goods train travelling from the north of England to Portsmouth.

c Glenn Ford, Anne Vernon, Maurice Denham, Harcourt Williams, Harold Warrender, Bill Fraser, Victor Maddern, Harry Locke, Sam Kydd

"Drab thriller with some built-in excitements." – David Quinlan, *British Sound Films*, 1984.

Never Let Me Go (1953)

d Delmer Daves   p Clarence Brown   s Ronald Miller, George Froeschel   e Frank Clarke   dop Robert Krasker
pd Alfred Junge

After World War II an American correspondent marries a Russian ballerina but is later deported by the authorities.

c Clark Gable, Gene Tierney, Bernard Miles, Kenneth More, Theodore Bikel, Frederick Valk

"Far-fetched farrago with ageing stars." – David Quinlan, *British Sound Films*, 1984.

Knights Of The Round Table (1953)

d Richard Thorpe   p Pandro S. Berman   s Talbot Jennings, Noel
Langley   e Frank Clarke   dop Stephen Dade, Freddie Young
pd Alfred Junge

Lancelot, banished from Kind Arthur's court for loving Guinevere, returns to defeat the evil Modred.

c Robert Taylor, Mel Ferrer, Ava Gardner, Anne Crawford, Stanley
Baker, Felix Aylmer, Robert Urquhart, Niall MacGinnis

"Spectacular but rather heartless action film." – Leslie Halliwell, *Halliwell's Film and Video Guide*, 2000.

Mogambo (1953)

d John Ford   p Sam Zimbalist   s John Lee Mahin   e Frank
Clarke   dop Robert Surtees, Freddie Young   pd Alfred Junge

The headquarters of a Kenyan white hunter is invaded by an American
showgirl and a British archaeologist and his wife, and they all go off on a
gorilla hunt.

c Clark Gable, Ava Gardner, Grace Kelly, Donald Sinden, Laurence
Naismith, Philip Stainton

"The gorillas out-act the genial cast." – Leslie Halliwell, *Halliwell's Film
and Video Guide*, 2000.

Diplomatic Passport (1954)

d Gene Martel   p Gene Martel, Burt Balaban   s Paul Tabori
e Max Benedict   dop James Wilson   pd John Elphick

An American diplomat and his wife arrive in London and fall into the
hands of international crooks.

c Paul Carpenter, Marsha Hunt, Henry Oscar, Honor Blackman, Marne Maitland, John Bennett

"The cast stands no chance against this plot." – David Quinlan, *British Sound Films*, 1984.

Seagulls Over Sorrento (1954)

d John Boulting, Roy Boulting   p John Boulting, Roy Boulting
s Frank Harvey   e Max Benedict   dop Gilbert Taylor
pd Alfred Junge

Tensions, both comic and dramatic, rise between British and American naval scientists working at a remote research station off the Scottish coast.

c Gene Kelly, John Justin, Bernard Lee, Sidney James, Jeff Richards, Patric Doonan, Patrick Barr, David Orr

"Well-mixed blend of laughter and thrills." – David Quinlan, *British Sound Films*, 1984.

Beau Brummell (1954)

d Curtis Bernhardt   p Sam Zimbalist   s Karl Tunberg
e Fred Clarke   dop Oswald Morris   pd Alfred Junge

A Regency dandy enjoys a close relationship with the Prince of Wales, and when this is eventually withdrawn he dies in penury.

c Stewart Granger, Elizabeth Taylor, Peter Ustinov, Robert Morley, James Donald, James Hayter, Rosemary Harris, Noel Willman, Peter Bull

"Stodgy historical romance with entertaining patches." – Leslie Halliwell, *Halliwell's Film and Video Guide*, 2000.

Betrayed (1954)

d Gottfried Reinhardt   p Gottfried Reinhardt   s Ronald Miller
e John D. Dunning, Raymond Poulton   dop Freddie Young
pd Alfred Junge

In 1943 a Dutch intelligence officer works with a resistance leader who turns out to be a traitor.

c Clark Gable, Victor Mature, Lana Turner, Louis Calhern, Wifrid Hyde-White, Ian Carmichael, Niall MacGinnis, Nora Swinburne

"Slow-moving, studio-set romantic melodrama." – David Quinlan, *British Sound Films*, 1984.

The Dark Avenger (1955)

d Henry Levin   p Vaughan N. Dean   s Daniel B. Ullman
e Edward B. Jarvis   dop Guy Green   pd Terence Verity

During the Hundred Years' War, The Black Prince launches an attack on the French Count de Ville.

c Errol Flynn, Peter Finch, Joanne Dru, Yvonne Furneaux, Patrick Holt, Michael Hordern, Moultrie Kelsall, Robert Urquhart, Noel Willman, Christopher Lee

"Good-humoured historical romp." – David Quinlan, *British Sound Films*, 1984.

Gentlemen Marry Brunettes (1955)

d Richard Sale   p Richard Sale, Robert Waterfield   s Mary Loos, Richard Sale   e Grant K. Smith   dop Desmond Dickinson
pd Paul Sheriff

Two American shop girls seek rich husbands in Paris, and find that their aunts were notorious there.

c Jane Russell, Jeanne Crain, Alan Young, Scott Brady, Rudy Vallee, Eric Pohlmann, Ferdy Mayne, Leonard Sachs

"Jaded sequel to *Gentlemen Prefer Blondes*." – Leslie Halliwell, *Halliwell's Film and Video Guide*, 2000.

That Lady (1955)

d Terence Young   p Sy Bartlett   s Anthony Veiller, Sy Bartlett
e Raymond Poulton   dop Robert Krasker   pd Frank White

A noble widow at the court of Philip II of Spain loves a minister but incurs the King's jealous hatred.

c Olivia de Havilland, Gilbert Roland, Paul Scofield, Dennis Price, Anthony Dawson, Robert Harris, Peter Illing, Christopher Lee

"Tepid historical romance." – David Quinlan, *British Sound Films*, 1984.

The Adventures Of Quentin Durward (1956)

d Richard Thorpe   p Pandro S. Berman   s Robert Ardrey,
George Froeschel   e Ernest Walter   dop Christopher Challis
pd Alfred Junge

An elderly English lord sends his nephew to woo a French lady on his behalf; but the boy falls in love with her himself.

c Robert Taylor, Kay Kendall, Robert Morley, Alec Clunes, Marius Goring, Wilfrid Hyde-White, Ernest Thesiger, Duncan Lamont, George Cole, John Carson

"Quite enjoyable period romp." – David Quinlan, *British Sound Films*, 1984.

Bhowani Junction (1956)

d George Cukor   p Pandro S. Berman   s Sonya Levien, Ivan Moffat   e George Boemler, Frank Clarke   dop Freddie Young pd Gene Allen

The adventures of an Anglo-Indian girl during the last years of British India, whose life is torn between a British Officer, an Anglo-Indian railway boss, and a Sikh.

c Ava Gardner, Stewart Granger, Francis Matthews, Bill Travers, Marne Maitland, Freda Jackson, Edward Chapman

"Disappointingly anaemic semi-epic." – Leslie Halliwell, *Halliwell's Film and Video Guide*, 2000.

Alias John Preston (1956)

d David MacDonald   p Harry Danziger, Edward Danziger   s Paul Tabori   e Jack Baldwin, Cynthia Moody   dop Jack E. Cox pd Erik Blakemore

A stranger with amnesia arrives in a small community, only to find that his frequent nightmares have a sinister reason.

c Christopher Lee, Alexander Knox, Betta St. John, Patrick Holt, Sandra Dorne, John Longden, Bill Fraser, Mona Washbourne

"Watchable second feature." – David Quinlan, *British Sound Films*, 1984.

Anastasia (1956)

d Anatole Litvak   p Buddy Adler   s Arthur Laurents   e Bert Bates dop Jack Hildyard   pd Andrej Andrejew, William C. Andrews

In 1928 Paris, a group of exiled White Russians claim to have found the living daughter of the Tsar, presumed executed in 1918.

c Ingrid Bergman, Yul Brynner, Helen Hayes, Martita Hunt, Felix Aylmer, Ivan Desny, Peter Sallis

"Slick, highly theatrical entertainment for the upper classes." – Leslie Halliwell, *Halliwell's Film and Video Guide*, 2000.

Odongo (1956)

d John Gilling   p Islin Auster   s John Gilling   e Alan Osbiston, Jack Slade   dop Ted Moore   pd Elliot Scott

A collector of animals for zoos runs into various kinds of trouble during an African safari.

c Macdonald Carey, Rhonda Fleming, Juma, Eleanor Summerfield, Francis de Wolff, Earl Cameron

"Elementary jungle adventure." – Leslie Halliwell, *Halliwell's Film and Video Guide*, 2000.

Stars In Your Eyes (1956)

d Maurice Elvey   p David Dent   s Talbot Rothwell   e Robert Jordan Hill   dop S. D. Onions   pd Anthony Masters

Four music hall friends, all down on their luck, decide to put on a show at the derelict theatre one of them has inherited.

c Bonar Colleano, Dorothy Squires, Pat Kirkwood, Nat Jackley, Vera Day, Joan Sims, Hubert Gregg, Freddie Frinton

"Poor material defeats energetic cast." – David Quinlan, *British Sound Films*, 1984.

Fire Maidens From Outer Space (1956)

d Cy Roth   p George Fowler   s Cy Roth   e Lito Carruthers
dop Ian D. Struthers   pd Scott MacGregor

Space explorers find that the thirteenth moon of Jupiter is inhabited solely by sixteen beautiful girls and an aged patriarch.

c Susan Shaw, Anthony Dexter, Harry Fowler, Sydney Tafler, Owen Berry, Paul Carpenter, Richard Walter

"A strong contender for the title of worst movie ever made." – Leslie Halliwell, *Halliwell's Film and Video Guide*, 2000.

The Man Who Never Was (1956)

d Ronald Neame   p Andre Hakim   s Nigel Balchin
e Peter Taylor   dop Oswald Morris   pd Jack Hawkesworth

In 1943, the British secret service confuses the Germans by dropping a dead man into the sea with false documents.

c Clifton Webb, Robert Flemyng, Gloria Grahame, Stephen Boyd, Laurence Naismith, Josephine Griffin, Andre Morell, Michael Hordern

"Enjoyable true life war story." – Leslie Halliwell, *Halliwell's Film and Video Guide*, 2000.

Around The World In Eighty Days (1956) *

d Michael Anderson, Kevin McClory   p Michael Todd   s James Poe   e Howard Epstein   dop Lionel Lindon   pd Ken Adam

A Victorian gentleman and his valet win a bet that they can go around the world in eighty days.

c David Niven, Cantinflas, Robert Newton, Shirley MacLaine, Charles

Boyer, John Carradine, Charles Coburn, Ronald Colman, Noel Coward, John Gielgud

"Amiable large-scale pageant." – Leslie Halliwell, *Halliwell's Film and Video Guide*, 2000.

OSCAR for Best Picture

Invitation To The Dance (1956)

d Gene Kelly   p Arthur Freed   s Gene Kelly   e Adrienne Fazan   dop Freddie Young, Joseph Ruttenberg   pd Alfred Junge

Three musical short stories centred around dance and mime, with two featuring Gene Kelly.

c Gene Kelly, Igor Youskevitch, Claire Sombert, David Paltenghi, Daphne Dale, Claude Bessy, Tommy Rall, Diana Adams

"Unsuccessful ballet film." – David Quinlan, *British Sound Films*, 1984.

Zarak (1956)

d Terence Young   p Phil C. Samuel   s Richard Maibaum
e Alan Osbiston   dop Cyril J. Knowles, Ted Moore, John Wilcox
pd John Box

Zarak Khan, an Afghan outlaw finally saves a British officer at the cost of his own life.

c Victor Mature, Michael Wilding, Anita Ekberg, Bonar Colleano, Finlay Currie, Bernard Miles, Eunice Gayson, Peter Illing, Frederick Valk, Andre Morell

"Ridiculous eastern dust-rouser." – David Quinlan, *British Sound Films*, 1984.

The Man In The Sky (1957)

d Charles Crichton   p Seth Holt   s William Rose, John Eldridge
e Peter Tanner   dop Douglas Slocombe   pd Jim Morahan

A test pilot refuses to bale out when an engine catches fire; he plight is interwoven with scenes of his family, friends and associates.

c Jack Hawkins, Elizabeth Sellars, Walter Fitzgerald, Eddie Byrne, John Stratton, Victor Maddern, Lionel Jeffries, Donald Pleasence

"Thin suspense drama with some effective moments." – David Quinlan, *British Sound Films*, 1984.

The Little Hut (1957)

d Mark Robson   p F. Hugh Herbert, Mark Romson
s F. Hugh Herbert   e Ernest Walter   dop Freddie Young
pd Elliot Scott

A man, his wife and her lover are all shipwrecked and washed ashore on a desert island.

c Stewart Granger, David Niven, Ava Gardner, Walter Chiari, Finlay Currie, Jean Cadell, Henry Oscar, Richard Wattis

"Sophisticated French farce which falls resoundingly flat." – Leslie Halliwell, *Halliwell's Film and Video Guide*, 2000.

The Barretts Of Wimpole Street (1957)

d Sidney Franklin   p Sam Zimbalist   s John Dighton
e Frank Clarke   dop Freddie Young   pd Alfred Junge

Invalid Elizabeth Barrett plans to marry poet Robert Browning, against her tyrannical father's wishes.

c Jennifer Jones, Bill Travers, John Gielgud, Virginia McKenna, Vernon Gray, Jean Anderson, Leslie Phillips, Richard Thorp

"An unattractive and boring film." – David Quinlan, *British Sound Films*, 1984.

Barnacle Bill (1957)

d Charles Frend   p Michael Balcon   s T. E. B. Clarke
e Jack Harris   dop Douglas Slocombe   pd Alan Withy

The last of a long line of sailors suffers from seasickness, and takes command of a decaying Victorian pier at an English seaside resort.

c Alec Guinness, Irene Browne, Percy Herbert, Harold Goodwin, Maurice Denham, George Rose, Lionel Jeffries, Victor Maddern, Donald Pleasence

"Quite an amusing comedy." – David Quinlan, *British Sound Films*, 1984.

Fire Down Below (1957)

d Robert Parrish   p Irving Allen, Albert Broccoli   s Irwin Shaw
e Jack Slade   dop Desmond Dickinson   pd Syd Cain

Partners in a Caribbean fishing and smuggling business fall out over a woman whom they are hired to get across frontiers.

c Rita Hayworth, Robert Mitchum, Jack Lemmon, Herbert Lom, Bonar Colleano, Bernard Lee, Peter Illing, Anthony Newley

"Overheated melodrama with thin characters." – David Quinlan, *British Sound Films*, 1984.

Lucky Jim (1957)

d John Boulting   p Roy Boulting   s Jeffrey Dell, Patrick Campbell
e Max Benedict   dop Mutz Greenbaum   pd Elliot Scott

At a provincial university, an accident-prone junior lecturer has a disastrous weekend with his girlfriend and his professor.

c Ian Carmichael, Terry-Thomas, Hugh Griffith, Sharon Acker, Jean Anderson, Maureen Connell, Clive Morton, Reginald Beckwith, Kenneth Griffith, John Cairney

"Quite funny." – David Quinlan, *British Sound Films*, 1984.

The Shiralee (1957)

d Leslie Norman   p Jack Rix   s Neil Paterson, Leslie Norman
e Gordon Stone   dop Paul Beeson   pd Jim Morahan

An itinerant Australian swagman leaves his wife and takes to the road with his small daughter.

c Peter Finch, Dana Wilson, Elizabeth Sellars, George Rose, Russell Napier, Niall MacGinnins, Rosemary Harris, Sidney James, Charles Tingwell

"Touching and sympathetically handled drama." – David Quinlan, *British Sound Films*, 1984.

Action Of The Tiger (1957)

d Terence Young   p Kenneth Harper   s Robert Carson
e Frank Clarke   dop Desmond Dickinson   pd Scott MacGregor

An adventurer helps a French girl to rescue her brother from political imprisonment in Albania.

c Van Johnson, Martine Carol, Herbert Lom, Gustavo Rojo, Anthony Dawson, Helen Haye, Sean Connery, Yvonne Romain

"Dull and poorly constructed action melodrama." – David Quinlan, *British Sound Films*, 1984.

Tarzan And The Lost Safari (1957)

d Bruce Humberstone   p John Croydon   s Montgomery Pittman
e Bill Lewthwaite   dop C. M. Pennington-Richards   pd Paul Sheriff

Tarzan rescues the survivors of a plane crash who are threatened by a ruthless white hunter.

c Gordon Scott, Robert Beatty, Yolande Donlan, Betta St. John, Wilfrid Hyde-White, George Coulouris, Peter Arne

"Effective adventure." – David Quinlan, *British Sound Films*, 1984.

Davy (1957)

d Michael Relph   p Basil Dearden   s William Rose
e Peter Tanner   dop Douglas Slocombe   pd Alan Withy

A member of a successful family music hall act finds that his powerful singing voice brings him to the attention of the Royal Opera House in London.

c Harry Secombe, Ron Randell, George Relph, Alexander Knox, Susan Shaw, Bill Owen, Joan Sims, Kenneth Connor, Liz Fraser

"Unsuccessful vehicle for a popular singing comic." – David Quinlan, *British Sound Films*, 1984.

I Accuse! (1958)

d Jose Ferrer   p Sam Zimbalist   s Gore Vidal   e Frank Clarke
dop Freddie Young   pd Elliot Scott

In 1894 Paris, Alfred Dreyfus, a French Army officer, is tried for treason and sentenced to life.

c Jose Ferrer, Anton Walbrook, Emlyn Williams, David Farrar, Leo

Genn, Herbert Lom, Harry Andrews, Felix Aylmer, Donald Wolfit, George Coulouris

"A well-tried historical incident is stolidly retold." – Leslie Halliwell, *Halliwell's Film and Video Guide*, 2000.

First Man Into Space (1958)

d Robert Day   p John Croydon   s John C. Cooper, Lance Z. Hargreaves   e Peter Mayhew   dop Geoffrey Faithfull
pd Denys Pavitt

An astronaut runs into a cloud of meteor dust and returns to earth having turned into a monster lusting for blood.

c Marshall Thompson, Marla Landi, Bill Edwards, Roger Delgado, Carl Jaffe, Richard Shaw, Michael Bell

"Quatermass-like shocker with modest budget but firm control." – David Quinlan, *British Sound Films*, 1984.

Dunkirk (1958) *

d Leslie Norman   p Michael Balcon   s W. P. Lipscombe, David Divine   e Gordon Stone   dop Paul Beeson   pd Jim Morahan

In 1940 on the Normandy beaches, a small group gets detached from the main force and fights and dodges its way back to Dunkirk.

c John Mills, Richard Attenborough, Bernard Lee, Robert Urquhart, Ray Jackson, Victor Maddern, Maxine Audley, Kenneth Cope, Barry Foster, Lionel Jeffries

"Sober, small-scale approach to an epic subject." – Leslie Halliwell, *Halliwell's Film and Video Guide*, 2000.

The 7ᵗʰ Voyage Of Sinbad (1958) *

d Nathan Juran   p Charles Schneer   s Kenneth Kolb
e Edwin H. Bryant   dop Wilkie Cooper   pd Gil Parrondo

Sinbad seeks a roc's egg which will restore his fiancée from the midget size to which an evil magician has reduced her.

c Kerwin Mathews, Kathryn Grant, Torin Thatcher, Richard Eyer, Alec Mango, Danny Green, Harold Kasket

"Lively fantasy with excellent effects by Ray Harryhausen." – Leslie Halliwell, *Halliwell's Film and Video Guide*, 2000.

The Inn Of The Sixth Happiness (1958)

d Mark Robson   p Mark Robson   s Isobel Lennart
e Ernest Walter   dop Freddie Young   pd John Box, Geoffrey Drake

Galdys Aylward, an English servant girl becomes a missionary and spends many arduous years in China.

c Ingrid Bergman, Curt Jurgens, Robert Donat, Athene Seyler, Ronald Squire, Richard Wattis, Moultrie Kelsall, Burt Kwouk

"Inspiring stuff." – Leslie Halliwell, *Halliwell's Film and Video Guide*, 2000.

Nowhere To Go (1958)

d Seth Holt   p Eric Williams   s Seth Holt, Ken Tynan
e Harry Aldous   dop Paul Beeson   pd Peter Proud

A thief escapes from prison but can get no help from the underworld and is accidentally shot after being sheltered by a socialite.

c George Nader, Maggie Smith, Bernard Lee, Geoffrey Keen, Andree Melly, Bessie Love, Howard Marion-Crawford, Harry H. Corbett, Lionel Jeffries

"Glum character melodrama." – David Quinlan, *British Sound Films*, 1984.

Tom Thumb (1958)

d George Pal   p George Pal   s Ladislas Fodor   e Frank Clarke
dop Georges Perinal   pd Elliot Scott

A 2-inch-tall forest boy takes it upon himself to outwit a couple of villainous thieves.

c Russ Tamblyn, Jessie Matthews, Peter Sellers, Terry-Thomas, Alan Young, June Thorburn, Bernard Miles, Peter Butterworth

"A delightful film for children." – Leslie Halliwell, *Halliwell's Film and Video Guide*, 2000.

OSCAR for Special Effects

I Want To Live! (1958)

d Robert Wise   p Walter Wanger   s Nelson Gidding, Don Mankiewicz   e William Hornbeck   dop Lionel Lindon
pd Victor A. Gangelin

A vagrant prostitute is executed in the gas chamber despite much growing doubt as to her guilt.

c Susan Hayward, Simon Oakland, Virginia Vincent, Theodore Bikel, Wesley Lau, John Marley, Raymond Bailey

"Sober, harrowing treatment of a true life case." – David Quinlan, *British Sound Films*, 1984.

Corridors Of Blood (1958)

d Robert Day   p John Croydon   s Jean Scott Rogers

e Peter Mayhew   dop Geoffrey Faithfull   pd Anthony Masters

Seeking to discover anaesthetics, a Victorian doctor, addicted to drugs, falls prey to evil resurrection men.

c Boris Karloff, Christopher Lee, Finlay Currie, Frank Pettingell, Betta St. John, Francis Matthews, Adrienne Corri, Francis de Wolff, Nigel Green, Yvonne Romain

"Unpleasant but well-mounted semi-horror." – Leslie Halliwell, *Halliwell's Film and Video Guide*, 2000.

The Safecracker (1958)

d Ray Milland   p David E. Rose   s Paul Monash
e Ernest Walter   dop Gerald Gibbs   pd Elliot Scott

A safecracker, jailed for ten years for his part in a string of antique thefts is released to help in a commando raid during World War II.

c Ray Milland, Barry Jones, Jeanette Sterke, Victor Maddern, Ernest Clark, Cyril Raymond, Melissa Stribling, Percy Herbert, Charles Lloyd Pack, Sam Kydd

"Tense drama." – David Quinlan, *British Sound Films*, 1984.

Another Time, Another Place (1958)

d Lewis Allen   p Lewis Allen, Smedley Aston   s Stanley Mann
e Geoffrey Foot   dop Jack Hildyard   pd Thomas N. Morahan

During World War II an American newspaperwomen has an affair with a British war correspondent; when he is killed in action, she consoles his widow.

c Lana Turner, Barry Sullivan, Glynis Johns, Sean Connery, Sidney James, John le Mesurier, Robin Bailey, Bill Fraser

"Drippy romance." – David Quinlan, *British Sound Films*, 1984.

Gideon's Day (1958)

d John Ford   p Michael Killanin   s T. E. B. Clarke
e Raymond Poulton   dop Freddie Young   pd Ken Adam

Being booked for speeding by Simon, a zealous young policeman, Inspector Gideon's day gets off to a shaky start.

c Jack Hawkins, Dianne Foster, Anna Lee, Andrew Ray, Anna Massey,
Frank Lawton, Cyril Cusack, James Hayter, Ronald Howard, Miles Malleson

"Quick-paced, likable crime compendium." – David Quinlan, *British
Sound Films*, 1984.

Ice Cold In Alex (1958) *

d J. Lee Thompson   p W. A. Whittaker   s T. J. Morrison
e Richard Best   dop Gilbert Taylor   pd Robert Jones

In 1942 Libya, the commander of a motor ambulance gets his vehicle and
passengers to safety despite the hazards of minefields and a German spy.

c John Mills, Sylvia Syms, Anthony Quayle, Harry Andrews, Diane
Clare, David Lodge, Walter Gotell, Frederick Jaeger, Peter Arne

"Engrossing desert adventure with plenty of suspense." – Leslie Halliwell, *Halliwell's Film and Video Guide*, 2000.

Doctor's Dilemma (1958)

d Anthony Asquith   p Anatole de Grunwald   s Anatole de
Grunwald   e Gordon Hales   dop Robert Krasker
pd Paul Sheriff

Eminent Harley Street surgeons debate the case of a devoted wife and her tubercular artist husband.

c Leslie Caron, Dirk Bogarde, John Robinson, Alastair Sim, Felix Aylmer, Robert Morley, Michael Gwynn, Alec McCowen, Peter Sallis

"Well-acted but curiously muffled filming of Bernard Shaw's play." – David Quinlan, *British Sound Films*, 1984.

'Beat' Girl (1959)

d Edmond T. Greville   p George Willoughby   s Dail Ambler
e Gordon Pilkington   dop Walter Lassally   pd Elven Webb

Precocious teenager who hangs around Soho coffee bars, gets in with the wrong crowd and ends up going to the dogs.

c David Farrar, Noelle Adam, Christopher Lee, Gillian Hills, Adam Faith, Peter McEnery, Nigel Green, Shirley Ann Field, Oliver Reed, Carol White

"Dreary exploitation film." – David Quinlan, *British Sound Films*, 1984.

Tarzan's Greatest Adventure (1959)

d John Guillermin   p Sy Weintraub, Harvey Hayutin   s Berne Giler   e Bert Rule   dop Edward Scaife   pd Michael Stringer

Tarzan, aided by a girl, pursues a ruthless boatload of killers who are in search of a diamond mine.

c Gordon Scott, Anthony Quayle, Sara Shane, Sean Connery, Niall MacGinnis, Al Mulock, Scilla Gabel

"Brisk action-packed drama." – David Quinlan, *British Sound Films*, 1984.

House Of The Seven Hawks (1959)

d Richard Thorp   p David E. Rose   s Jo Eisinger   e Ernest
Walter   dop Edward Scaife   pd William C. Andrews

An American adventurer becomes involved in a search by criminals for
buried Nazi loot.

c Robert Taylor, Nicole Maurey, Linda Christian, Donald Wolfit, David
Kossoff, Eric Pohlmann, Paul Hardtmuth

"Cliché-ridden, thick ear, adequately produced." – David Quinlan, *British Sound Films*, 1984.

The Angry Hills (1959)

d Robert Aldrich   p Raymond Stross   s A. I. Bezzerides
e Peter Tanner   dop Stephen Dade   pd Ken Adam

An American war correspondent in 1940 Greece, comes into possession
of a list of resistance agents needed by MI5.

c Robert Mitchum, Gia Scala, Elisabeth Mueller, Stanley Baker, Donald
Wolfit, Kieron Moore, Theodore Bikel, Sebastian Cabot, Peter Illing,
Leslie Phillips

"Laboured war melodrama." – Leslie Halliwell, *Halliwell's Film and Video
Guide*, 2000.

Jazz Boat (1959)

d Ken Hughes   p Harold Huth   s Ken Hughes   e Geoffrey
Foot   dop Nicolas Roeg   pd Ray Simm

A jazz musician pretends to be a crook and leads the police to an important criminal gang.

c Anthony Newley, Anne Aubrey, David Lodge, Lionel Jeffries, Berne Winters, James Booth, Leo McKern

"Flimsy comedy." – David Quinlan, *British Sound Films*, 1984.

In The Nick (1959)

d Ken Hughes   p Harold Huth   s Ken Hughes
e Geoffrey Foot   dop Ted Moore   pd Ken Adam

The Spider Kelly gang enters a prison without bars and immediately clashes with the rival Ted Ross outfit.

c Anthony Newley, Anne Aubrey, Bernie Winters, James Booth, Harry Andrews, Derren Nesbitt, Niall MacGinnis, Ian Hendry

"Warm and witty script." – David Quinlan, *British Sound Films*, 1984.

The Rough And The Smooth (1959)

d Robert Siodmak   p George Minter   s Aubrey Erskine-Lindop, Dudley Leslie   e Gordon Pilkington   dop Otto Heller
pd Ken Adam

An archaeologist about to marry the niece of a press lord falls for a mysterious nymphomaniac.

c Tony Britton, Nadja Tiller, William Bendix, Natasha Parry, Norman Wooland, Donald Wolfit, Adrienne Corri, Joyce Carey, Michael Ward, Geoffrey Bayldon

"Preposterous melodrama about unreal people." – David Quinlan, *British Sound Films*, 1984.

Serious Charge (1959)

d Terence Young   p Mickey Delamar   s Guy Elmes, Mickey Delamar   e Reginald Beck   dop George Perinal pd Allan Harris

A troublemaker, accused by his priest of being responsible for the death of a young girl, amuses himself by accusing the priest of making homosexual advances.

c Anthony Quayle, Andrew Ray, Sarah Churchill, Irene Browne, Percy Herbert, Cliff Richard, Wilfrid Brambell

"Dull film despite earnest performances." – David Quinlan, *British Sound Films*, 1984.

Solomon And Sheba (1959)

d King Vidor   p Ted Richmond   s Anthony Veiller, Paul Dudley e Otto Ludwig   dop Freddie Young   pd Richard Day

When King David names his younger son Solomon as heir, his older son Adonijah plots revenge.

c Yul Brynner, Gina Lollobrigida, George Sanders, Marisa Pavan, David Farrar, John Crawford, Laurence Naismith, Harry Andrews, Finlay Currie, Jean Anderson

"Dullish biblical spectacle." – Leslie Halliwell, *Halliwell's Film and Video Guide*, 2000.

A Touch Of Larceny (1959)

d Guy Hamilton   p Ivan Foxwell   s Roger MacDougall, Guy Hamilton   e Alan Osbiston   dop John Wilcox pd Elliot Scott

A naval commander mysteriously disappears in the hope that he will be branded a traitor and can sue for libel.

c James Mason, Vera Miles, George Sanders, Robert Flemyng, Ernest Clark, Duncan Lamont, Peter Barkworth, Harry Andrews

"Fairly amusing light comedy with lively performances." – David Quinlan, *British Sound Films*, 1984.

The Wreck Of The Mary Deare (1959)

d Michael Anderson   p Julian Blaustein   s Eric Ambler
e Eda Warren   dop Joseph Ruttenberg   pd Paul Groesse, Hans Peters

An insurance fraud comes to light when a salvage boat Mary Deare is rescued from high seas.

c Charlton Heston, Gary Cooper, Michael Redgrave, Emlyn Williams, Cecil Parker, Alexander Knox, Virginia McKenna, Richard Harris, Peter Illing

"Curious, star-studded amalgam of seafaring action and courtroom melodrama." – Leslie Halliwell, *Halliwell's Film and Video Guide*, 2000.

Libel (1959)

d Anthony Asquith   p Anatole de Grunwald   s Anatole de Grunwald   e Frank Clarke   dop Robert Krasker   pd Paul Sheriff

Sir Mark Loddon, living in gracious luxury, is accused by a former fellow-inmate in a wartime POW camp of being an imposter.

c Dirk Bogarde, Olivia de Havilland, Paul Massie, Wilfrid Hyde-White, Robert Morley, Richard Wattis, Robert Shaw, Geoffrey Bayldon, Joyce Carey, Kenneth Griffith

"Courtroom spellbinder, quite adequately done though occasionally creaky." – David Quinlan, *British Sound Films*, 1984.

The Scapegoat (1959)

d Robert Hamer   p Dennis Van Thal   s Gore Vidal, Robert Hamer   e Jack Harris   dop Paul Beeson   pd Elliot Scott

A quiet bachelor on a French holiday is tricked into assuming the identity of a lookalike aristocrat who wants to commit a murder.

c Alec Guinness, Bette Davis, Irene Worth, Nicole Maurey, Pamela Brown, Geoffrey Keen, Eddie Byrne, Peter Sallis

"Stylish, rather over-elaborate drama." – David Quinlan, *British Sound Films*, 1984.

The Day They Robbed The Bank Of England (1960)

d John Guillermin   p Jules Buck   s Howard Clewes, Richard Maibaum   e Frank Clarke   dop George Perinal   pd Peggy Gick, Scott MacGregor

Irish patriots fighting for home rule in 1901 hire an American adventurer to help them rob the Bank of England.

c Peter O'Toole, Aldo Ray, Elizabeth Sellars, Kieron Moore, Albert Sharpe, Hugh Griffith, John le Mesurier, Miles Malleson, Andrew Keir, Geoffrey Bayldon

"Small-scale, well-detailed period caper story." – Leslie Halliwell, *Halliwell's Film and Video Guide*, 2000.

Gorgo (1960)

d Eugene Lourie   p Wilfrid Eades   s John Loring, Daniel Hyatt e Eric Boyd-Perkins   dop Freddie Young   pd Elliot Scott

A prehistoric monster is caught in Irish waters and brought to London, but rescued by its mother.

c Bill Travers, William Sylvester, Vincent Winter, Christopher Rhodes, Joseph O'Conor, Martin Benson, Maurice Kaufmann, Basil Dignam

"Amiable monster movie." – Leslie Halliwell, *Halliwell's Film and Video Guide*, 2000.

Let's Get Married (1960)

d Peter Graham Scott   p John R. Sloan   s Ken Taylor   e Ernest Walter   dop Ted Moore   pd Ken Adam

A medical student who is thrown out of his university, end up working in a laundry and rebuilds his confidence with a relationship with a fashion model.

c Anthony Newley, Anne Aubrey, Bernie Winters, James Booth, Jack Gwillim, Lionel Jeffries, John le Mesurier, Joyce Carey, Victor Maddern

"Mediocre comedy drama with songs." – Leslie Halliwell, *Halliwell's Film and Video Guide*, 2000.

The Millionairess (1960)

d Anthony Asquith   p Pierre Rouve   s Wolf Mankowitz   e Anthony Harvey   dop Jack Hildyard   pd Paul Sheriff

The richest woman in the world falls for a poor Indian doctor, who is more intent on treating patients.

c Sophia Loren, Peter Sellers, Alastair Sim, Vittorio de Sica, Dennis Price, Gary Raymond, Alfie Bass, Miriam Karlin, Noel Purcell, Graham Stark, Diana Coupland

"'Messy travesty of a Shavian comedy." – Leslie Halliwell, *Halliwell's Film and Video Guide*, 2000.

Too Hot To Handle (1960)

d Terence Young   p Selim Cattan   s Herbert Kretzmer   e
Lito Carruthers   dop Otto Heller   pd Alan Withy

Two Soho strip club owners join forces to hunt down a blackmailer in this British crime drama.

c Jayne Mansfield, Leo Genn, Carl Boehm, Danik Patisson, Christopher Lee, Patrick Holt, Barbara Windsor, Kai Fischer

"Rotten, hilarious British gangster film." – Leslie Halliwell, *Halliwell's Film and Video Guide*, 2000.

Village Of The Damned (1960)

d Wolf Rilla   p Ronald Kinnoch   s Stirling Silliphant, Wolf Rilla
e Gordon Hales   dop Geoffrey Faithfull   pd Ivan King

Children born simultaneously in an English village prove to be super-intelligent and deadly beings from another planet.

c George Sanders, Barbara Shelley, Michael Gwynn, Martin Stephens, Laurence Naismith, Jenny Laird, Peter Vaughan, Richard Vernon

"Modestly made but absorbing science fiction." – Leslie Halliwell, *Halliwell's Film and Video Guide*, 2000.

The World Of Suzie Wong (1960)

d Richard Quine   p Hugh Perceval   s John Patrick   e Bert Bates   dop Geoffrey Unsworth   pd John Box

A Hong Kong prostitute Suzie Wong falls in love with an artist Robert Lomax for whom she poses.

c William Holden, Nancy Kwan, Sylvia Syms, Michael Wilding, Laurence Naismith, Jacqui Chan, Bernard Cribbins

"Dull set-bound romantic melodrama." – Leslie Halliwell, *Halliwell's Film and Video Guide*, 2000.

Macbeth (1960)

d George Schaefer   p Phil C. Samuel, George Schaefer
s Anthony Squire   e Ralph Kemplen   dop Freddie Young
pd Edward Carrick

In Scotland in the 11th Century, Macbeth pays the price for murdering the king and seizing the throne.

c Maurice Evans, Judith Anderson, Michael Hordern, Ian Bannen, Felix Aylmer, Jeremy Brett, Trader Faulkner, Megs Jenkins, Michael Ripper, Douglas Wilmer

"Striking film version of Shakespeare's play." – Leslie Halliwell, *Halliwell's Film and Video Guide*, 2000.

Tarzan The Magnificent (1960)

d Robert Day   p Sy Weintraub   s Berne Giler   e Bert Rule
dop Edward Scaife   pd Ray Simm

Tarzan escorts a criminal through the jungle to face justice, but pursued on the way by hostile natives.

c Gordon Scott, Jock Mahoney, Betta St. John, John Carradine, Lionel Jeffries, Earl Cameron, Charles Tingwell, Christopher Carlos, Ewen Solon

"Tedious entry in the series." – Leslie Halliwell, *Halliwell's Film and Video Guide*, 2000.

Five Golden Hours (1961)

d Mario Zampi   p Mario Zampi   s Hans Wilhelm   e Bill Lewthwaite   dop Christopher Challis   pd Ivan King

A con man tries to murder three widows who have invested money in one of his schemes.

c Ernie Kovacs, Cyd Charisse, Kay Hammond, George Sanders, Dennis Price, Reginald Beckwith, Martin Benson, Ron Moody, Finlay Currie, John le Mesurier

"Ill-judged black comedy, sadly lacking style." – Leslie Halliwell, *Halliwell's Film and Video Guide*, 2000.

The Green Helmet (1961)

d Michael Forlong   p Charles Francis Vetter   s Jon Cleary   e Frank Clarke   dop Geoffrey Faithfull   pd Alan Withy

A race driver with shattered nerves makes his last job the introduction of an American car of new design.

c Bill Travers, Ed Begley, Sidney James, Nancy Walters, Ursula Jeans, Megs Jenkins, Ferdy Mayne, Harold Kasket

"Totally conventional motor-racing thriller." – Leslie Halliwell, *Halliwell's Film and Video Guide*, 2000.

Invasion Quartet (1961)

d Jay Lewis   p Ronald Kinnoch   s Jack Trevor Story, John Briley   e Ernest Walter   dop Geoffrey Faithfull   pd Elliot Scott

An ill-assorted foursome of officers and a boffin take on the dangerous mission of silencing a Nazi gun trained on Dover.

c Bill Travers, Spike Milligan, Gregoire Aslan, John le Mesurier, Thorley Walters, Maurice Denham, Millicent Martin, William Mervyn, John Wood, Eric Sykes

"Played unsatisfactorily for farce." – Leslie Halliwell, *Halliwell's Film and Video Guide*, 2000.

A Matter Of WHO (1961)

d Don Chaffey   p Walter Shenson, Milton Holmes   s Milton Holmes   e Frank Clarke   dop Erwin Hillier   pd Elliot Scott

A germ detective foe WHO (World Health Organisation) finds evidence of smallpox after a passenger dies on a plane from the Middle East.

c Terry-Thomas, Sonja Ziemann, Alex Nicol, Guy Deghy, Richard Briers, Geoffrey Keen, Martin Benson, Honor Blackman, Carol White, Michael Ripper, Vincent Ball

"Curious blend of semi-documentary with suspense and comedy." – Leslie Halliwell, *Halliwell's Film and Video Guide*, 2000.

Mr. Topaze (1961)

d Peter Sellers   p Pierre Rouve   s Pierre Rouve   e Geoffrey Foot   dop John Wilcox   pd Donald M. Ashton

An honest ex-schoolmaster becomes prosperous when he joins some shady businessman.

c Peter Sellers, Herbert Lom, Leo McKern, Nadia Gray, Martita Hunt, John Neville, Billie Whitelaw, Michael Gough, Joan Sims, John le Mesurier, Michael Sellers

"Predictable, sluggish character comedy." – Leslie Halliwell, *Halliwell's Film and Video Guide*, 2000.

Murder She Said (1961)

d George Pollock   p George H. Brown   s David Pursall, Jack Seddon   e Ernest Walter   dop Geoffrey Faithfull
pd Harry White

An elderly spinster, Miss Marple, investigates after seeing a woman strangled in a passing train.

c Margaret Rutherford, Charles Tingwell, Muriel Pavlow, Arthur Kennedy, James Robertson Justice, Thorley Walters, Ronald Howard, Conrad Phillips, Stringer Davis

"Only the star holds one's attention." – Leslie Halliwell, *Halliwell's Film and Video Guide*, 2000.

Postman's Knock (1961)

d Robert Lynn   p Ronald Kinnoch   s John Briley, Jack Trevor Story   e Geoffrey Foot   dop Gerald Moss   pd Harry White

A village postman is transferred to London, finds life and work bewildering, but captures some crooks and ends up a hero.

c Spike Milligan, Barbara Shelley, Wilfrid Lawson, Warren Mitchell, Lance Percival, Arthur Mullard, Miles Malleson, Bob Todd

"Mildly amusing star vehicle." – Leslie Halliwell, *Halliwell's Film and Video Guide*, 2000.

The Secret Partner (1961)

d Basil Dearden   p Michael Relph   s David Pursall, Jack Seddon e Raymond Poulton   dop Harry Waxman   pd Elliot Scott

A blackmailing dentist is visited by a mysterious hooded stranger who forces him to rob one of his businessman victims.

c Stewart Granger, Haya Harareet, Bernard Lee, Hugh Burden, Melissa Stribling, Norman Bird, Conrad Phillips, Basil Dignam

"Complex puzzle thriller." – Leslie Halliwell, *Halliwell's Film and Video Guide*, 2000.

Village Of Daughters (1961)

d George Pollock   p George H. Brown   s David Pursall, Jack Seddon   e Tristam Cones   dop Geoffrey Faithfull pd Edward Carrick

An unemployed commercial traveller in an Italian village finds himself choosing a bride for a successful émigré.

c Eric Sykes, Warren Mitchell, Scilla Gabel, Carol White, Gregoire Aslan, John le Mesurier, Eric Pohlmann, Peter Illing, Graham Stark, Martin Benson, Roger Delgado

"Voluble, gesticulating minor comedy." – Leslie Halliwell, *Halliwell's Film and Video Guide*, 2000.

She'll Have To Go (1962)

d Robert Asher   p Robert Asher   s Ian Stuart Black, John Waterhouse   e Gerry Hambling   dop Jack Asher   pd John Stoll

Two brothers plan to murder the woman who has inherited their home; when they meet her, both decide to marry her.

c Bob Monkhouse, Alfred Marks, Hattie Jacques, Anna Karina, Dennis Lotis, Clive Dunn, Peter Butterworth, Graham Stark, Harry Locke

"A ponderous farce." – Leslie Halliwell, *Halliwell's Film and Video Guide*, 2000.

Light In The Piazza (1962)

d Guy Green   p Arthur Freed   s Julius J. Epstein   e Frank Clarke   dop Otto Heller   pd Frank White

An American matron in Florence tries to marry off her mentally retarded daughter to a wealthy Italian.

c Olivia de Havilland, Yvette Mimieux, George Hamilton, Rossano Brazzi, Barry Sullivan, Moultrie Kelsall

"Puzzling romantic drama." – Leslie Halliwell, *Halliwell's Film and Video Guide*, 2000.

Nine Hours To Rama (1962)

d Mark Robson   p Mark Robson   s Nelson Gidding
e Ernest Walter   dop Arthur Ibbetson   pd Elliot Scott

The life of Nathuram Godse, and the events leading to his assassination of Mahatma Gandhi.

c Jose Ferrer, Diane Baker, Robert Morley, Horst Buchholz, Harry Andrews, Marne Maitland, Wolfe Morris, Francis Matthews, Jack Hedley, J. S. Casshyap

"Fictionalized, sensationalized and very dull." – Leslie Halliwell, *Halliwell's Film and Video Guide*, 2000.

Dead Man's Evidence (1962)

d Francis Searle   p Francis Searle   s Arthur La Bern
e Jim Connock   dop Ken Hodges   pd Duncan Sutherland

Spy David Baxter is sent to Ireland to investigate the death of a defected colleague apparently found dead on a beach. But is the body really him...?

c Conrad Phillips, Jane Griffiths, Veronica Hurst, Ryck Rydon, Bruce Seton, Tommy Duggan

"All talk, talk, talk and no action." – Leslie Halliwell, *Halliwell's Film and Video Guide*, 2000.

The Day Of The Triffids (1962) *

d Steve Sekely, Freddie Francis   p George Pitcher   s Philip Yordan
e Bill Lewthwaite   dop Ted Moore   pd Cedric Dawe

Almost everyone in the world is blinded by meteorites prior to being taken over by intelligent plants.

c Howard Keel, Nicole Maurey, Kieron Moore, Janette Scott, Alexander Knox, Mervyn Johns, Janina Faye, Carole Ann Ford, Ian Wilson

"Quite effective with moments of good trick work." – Leslie Halliwell, *Halliwell's Film and Video Guide*, 2000.

Satan Never Sleeps (1962)

d Leo McCarey   p Leo McCarey   s Claude Binyon   e Gordon Pilkington   dop Oswald Morris   pd Thomas N. Morahan

A priest arrives to take over a mission-post in China accompanied by a young native girl, but is soon followed by communist soldiers who seize it as a command post.

c Clifton Webb, William Holden, France Nuyen, Weaver Lee, Athene Seyler, Martin Benson, Burt Kwouk

"Very entertaining with great performances." – Leslie Halliwell, *Halliwell's Film and Video Guide*, 2000.

The Inspector (1962)

d Philip Dunne   p Mark Robson   s Nelson Gidding
e Ernest Walter   dop Arthur Ibbetson   pd Elliot Scott

In 1946 a Dutch policeman rescues a Jewish girl from an ex-Nazi and helps smuggle her to Palestine.

c Stephen Boyd, Dolores Hart, Leo McKern, Hugh Griffith, Donald Pleasence, Harry Andrews, Robert Stephens, Marius Goring, Finlay Currie, Jean Anderson

"Moments of interest, but generally dully developed and acted." – Leslie Halliwell, *Halliwell's Film and Video Guide*, 2000.

I Thank A Fool (1962)

d Robert Stevens   p Anatole de Grunwald   s Karl Tunberg
e Frank Clarke   dop Harry Waxman   pd Sean Kenny

A woman found guilty of the murder of her lover is offered a fresh start in the home of the prosecutor's family… but another nightmare situation builds up.

c Peter Finch, Susan Hayward, Diane Cilento, Cyril Cusack, Kieron Moore, Athene Seyler, Richard Wattis, Miriam Karlin, Laurence Naismith, J. G. Devlin

"*Jane Eyre* melodrama of the loonier type." – Leslie Halliwell, *Halliwell's Film and Video Guide*, 2000.

Private Potter (1962)

d Caspar Wrede   p Ben Arbeid   s Ronald Harwood   e John Pomeroy   dop Arthur Lavis   pd Jack Shampan

A young soldier, Private Potter, is court-martialled for cowardice but claims he had a vision of God.

c Tom Courtenay, Mogens Wieth, Ronald Fraser, James Maxwell, Ralph Michael, Brewster Mason, Frank Finlay, Michael Coles

"Stilted morality play." – Leslie Halliwell, *Halliwell's Film and Video Guide*, 2000.

Tarzan Goes To India (1962)

d John Guillermin   p Sy Weintraub   s Robert Hardy Andrews, John Guillermin   e Max Benedict   dop Paul Beeson pd George Provis

Summoned by an Indian Princess, Tarzan travels to India where hundreds of wild elephants are in danger from floods caused by a huge dam.

c Jock Mahoney, Mark Dana, Leo Gordon, Feroz Khan, Murad Jai, Aaron Joseph, Peter Cooke, Denis Bastian

"No more than a cheap imitation of *Elephant Boy*." – Leslie Halliwell, *Halliwell's Film and Video Guide*, 2000.

Kill Or Cure (1962)

d George Pollock   p George H. Brown   s David Pursall, Jack Seddon   e Bert Rule   dop Geoffrey Faithfull   pd Harry White

A series of mysterious murders at a nature clinic are solved by a bumbling private detective.

c Terry-Thomas, Eric Sykes, Dennis Price, Lionel Jeffries, Moira Redmond, David Lodge, Ronnie Barker, Derren Nesbitt, Harry Locke, Peter Butterworth

"Flatfooted and unprofessional murder farce whose only pace is slow." – Leslie Halliwell, *Halliwell's Film and Video Guide*, 2000.

The Dock Brief (1962)

d James Hill   p Dimitri de Grunwald   s John Mortimer, Pierre Rouve   e Ann Chegwidden   dop Edward Scaife   pd Ray Simm

An incompetent barrister defends his client on a murder charge. The client is found guilty but the sentence is quashed on the grounds of inadequate defence.

c Peter Sellers, Richard Attenborough, Beryl Reid, David Lodge, Frank Pettingell, Frank Thornton

"Flat filming of a TV play." – Leslie Halliwell, *Halliwell's Film and Video Guide*, 2000.

Lolita (1962) *

d Stanley Kubrick   p James B. Harris   s Vladimir Nabokov   e Anthony Harvey   dop Oswald Morris   pd William C. Andrews

A middle-aged lecturer falls for a 14-year old girl and marries her mother to be near her.

c James Mason, Shelley Winters, Sue Lyon, Peter Sellers, Marianne Stone, Maxine Holden, John Harrison

"Fitfully amusing." – John Elliot, *Elliot's Guide To Films On Video*, 1991.

Live Now, Pay Later (1962)

d Jay Lewis   p Jack Hanbury   s Jack Trevor Story   e Roger Cherrill   dop Jack Hildyard   pd Lionel Couch

A credit store salesman is himself heavily in debt, and his private life is in ruins; but even after a chapter of unexpected and tragic events he remains optimistic.

c Ian Hendry, John Gregson, June Ritchie, Geoffrey Keen, Liz Fraser, Peter Butterworth, Nyree Dawn Porter, Ronald Howard

"Satirical farce with some funny moments." – Leslie Halliwell, *Halliwell's Film and Video Guide*, 2000.

The Password Is Courage (1962)

d Andrew L. Stone   p Andrew L. Stone, Virginia Stone
s Andrew L. Stone   e Noreen Ackland   dop Davis Boulton
pd C. Wilfred Arnold

In Europe during World War II, Sergeant Major Charles Coward has a career of escapes and audacious anti-Nazi exploits.

c Dirk Bogarde, Maria Perschy, Alfred Lynch, Nigel Stock, Reginald Beckwith, Bernard Archard, Ferdy Mayne, Olaf Pooley, Richard Marner

"Lively, slightly over-humorous account of one man's war." – Leslie Halliwell, *Halliwell's Film and Video Guide*, 2000.

The Main Attraction (1962)

d Daniel Petrie   p John Patrick   s John Patrick   e Geoffrey Foot   dop Geoffrey Unsworth   pd William Hutchinson

In Italy, a handsome wandering singer attracts the attention of a female ventriloquist and causes emotional problems backstage at a circus.

c Pat Boone, Mai Zetterling, Nancy Kwan, Yvonne Mitchell, John le Mesurier, Kieron Moore, Warren Mitchell

"Limp melodrama." – Leslie Halliwell, *Halliwell's Film and Video Guide*, 2000.

Never Put It In Writing (1963)

d Andrew L. Stone   p Andrew L. Stone, Virginia Stone
s Andrew L. Stone   e Noreen Ackland   dop Martin Curtis
pd C. Wilfred Arnold

A young executive tries to recover from the mail an indiscreet letter he has written to his boss.

c Pat Boone, Fidelma Murphy, Reginald Beckwith, John le Mesurier, Colin Blakely, Milo O'Shea

"Frantic hit-or-miss farcical comedy." – Leslie Halliwell, *Halliwell's Film and Video Guide*, 2000.

Lancelot And Guinevere (1963)

d Cornel Wilde   p Cornel Wilde   s Richard Schayer   e Frederick Wilson   dop Harry Waxman   pd Maurice Carter

Sir Lancelot covets the wife of his beloved King Arthur, but after Arthur's death she takes the veil.

c Cornel Wilde, Jean Wallace, Brian Aherne, George Baker, John Barrie, Adrienne Corri, Iain Gregory, Reginald Beckwith, Richard Thorp, Graham Stark

"Decently made." – Leslie Halliwell, *Halliwell's Film and Video Guide*, 2000.

The VIPs (1963)

d Anthony Asquith   p Anatole de Grunwald   s Terence Rattigan
e Frank Clarke   dop Jack Hildyard   pd William Kellner

Several V.I.P. passengers at London Airport are delayed by fog and have to spend the night at a hotel.

c Richard Burton, Elizabeth Taylor, Maggie Smith, Rod Taylor, Margaret Rutherford, Louis Jourdan, Orson Welles, Dennis Price, Lance Percival, Brook Williams

"Designed to exploit the real life Burton-Taylor romance." – Leslie Halliwell, *Halliwell's Film and Video Guide*, 2000.

OSCAR for Best Actress in a Supporting Role (Margaret Rutherford)

In The Cool Of The Day (1963)

d Robert Stevens   p John Houseman   s Meade Roberts
e Thomas Stanford   dop Peter Newbrook   pd Ken Adam

The frail wife of a New York publisher dies in Greece after an affair with his colleague.

c Jane Fonda, Peter Finch, Arthur Hill, Angela Lansbury, Constance Cummings, Alexander Knox, Nigel Davenport, John le Mesurier, Alec McCowen

"A pretty glum business." – Leslie Halliwell, *Halliwell's Film and Video Guide*, 2000.

Come Fly With Me (1963)

d Henry Levin   p Anatole de Grunwald   s William Roberts
e Frank Clarke   dop Oswald Morris   pd William Kellner

Three pretty air-hostesses combine their work crossing the Atlantic with searching for a rich handsome man to marry.

c Hugh O'Brian, Dolores Hart, Karl Malden, Pamela Tiffin, Lois Nettleton, Carl Boehm, Dawn Addams, Richard Wattis, Andrew Cruickshank

"Good-looking girls and airplanes but little else make thin entertainment." – Leslie Halliwell, *Halliwell's Film and Video Guide*, 2000.

Cairo (1963)

d Wolf Rilla   p Ronald Kinnoch   s Joanne Court   e Bernard Gribble   dop Desmond Dickinson   pd Ivan King

A man called Major plans to steal King Tutankhamen's jewels from the Cairo museum.

c George Sanders, Richard Johnson, Faten Hamama, John Meillon, Eric Pohlmann, Walter Rilla

"Spiritless remake of *The Asphalt Jungle*." – Leslie Halliwell, *Halliwell's Film and Video Guide*, 2000.

Impact (1963)

d Peter Maxwell   p John I. Phillips   s Conrad Phillips, Peter Maxwell   e David Hawkins   dop Gerald Moss   pd Harry White

Crime reporter Jack Moir is framed by a crooked nightclub owner, 'The Duke'. In prison, Moir plans his revenge.

c Conrad Phillips, George Pastell, Ballard Berkeley, Linda Marlowe, Richard Klee, Anita West, Mike Pratt

"Efficient, unmemorable second feature." – Leslie Halliwell, *Halliwell's Film and Video Guide*, 2000.

Maniac (1963)

d Michael Carreras   p Jimmy Sangster   s Jimmy Sangster   e Tom Simpson   dop Wilkie Cooper   pd Bernard Robinson

Murders by oxyacetylene torch in the Camargue, with the wrong lunatic going to the asylum.

c Kerwin Mathews, Donald Houston, Nadia Gray, Justine Lord, George Pastell, Arnold Diamond, Norman Bird

"Feebly done, with a fatally slow start." – Leslie Halliwell, *Halliwell's Film and Video Guide*, 2000.

Murder At The Gallop (1963)

d George Pollock   p George H. Brown   s James B. Cavanagh
e Bert Rule   dop Arthur Ibbetson   pd Frank White

Miss Marple investigates when an old man is apparently frightened to death by a cat.

c Margaret Rutherford, Flora Robson, Robert Morley, Stringer Davis, Charles Tingwell, Duncan Lamont, James Villiers, Robert Urquhart, Finlay Currie

"A good sense of pace and lively performances." – Leslie Halliwell, *Halliwell's Film and Video Guide*, 2000.

Clash By Night (1963)

d Montgomery Tully   p Maurice J. Wilson   s Montgomery Tully
e Maurice Rootes   dop Geoffrey Faithfull   pd Frank White

A bus carrying prisoners on their way to jail, is hijacked by a gang, who want to free one of the passengers.

c Terence Longdon, Jennifer Jayne, Harry Fowler, Alan Wheatley, Peter Sallis, Vanda Godsell, Mark Dignam

"Tiresome and dated." – Leslie Halliwell, *Halliwell's Film and Video Guide*, 2000.

The Haunting (1963)

d Robert Wise   p Robert Wise   s Nelson Gidding   e Ernest
Walter   dop Davis Boulton   pd Elliot Scott

An anthropologist, a sceptic and two mediums spend the weekend in a
haunted Boston mansion.

c Richard Johnson, Claire Bloom, Russ Tamblyn, Julie Harris, Lois
Maxwell, Valentine Dyall, Rosalie Crutchley, Fay Compton, Ronald
Adam

"Quite frightening melodrama with a lot of suspense." – Leslie Halliwell,
Halliwell's Film and Video Guide, 2000.

Echo Of Diana (1963)

d Ernest Morris   p John I. Phillips   s Reginald Hearne   e
David Hawkins   dop Walter J. Harvey   pd Elliot Scott

A journalist friend investigates when the wife of a missing pilot discovers that her husband seems to have had a mistress.

c Vincent Ball, Betty McDowall, Geoffrey Toone, Clare Owen, Marianne Stone, Peter Illing, Dermot Walsh, Arthur English, Michael Balfour

"Stolidly directed spy drama." – Leslie Halliwell, *Halliwell's Film and
Video Guide*, 2000.

Children Of The Damned (1964)

d Anton M. Leader   p Ben Arbeid   s John Briley   e Ernest
Walter   dop Davis Boulton   pd Elliot Scott

Six super-intelligent children of various nations are brought to London,
and turn out to be invaders from another planet.

c Ian Hendry, Alan Badel, Barbara Ferris, Alfred Burke, Sheila Allen, Ralph Michael, Martin Miller, Harold Goldblatt, Patrick Wymark

"Moderate sequel, well made but with no new twists." – Leslie Halliwell, *Halliwell's Film and Video Guide*, 2000.

The Americanization Of Emily (1964)

d Arthur Hiller   p Martin Ransohoff   s Paddy Chayefsky
e Tom McAdoo   dop Philip H. Lathrop   pd George W. Davis, Elliot Scott

World War II: just before the Normandy landings, a war widow driver falls for an American commander who is a self-confessed coward.

c Julie Andrews, James Garner, Melvyn Douglas, James Coburn, Liz Fraser, Joyce Grenfell, Edward Binns, Keenan Wynn, Bill Fraser

"Bizarre comedy full of eccentric characters." – Leslie Halliwell, *Halliwell's Film and Video Guide*, 2000.

Night Must Fall (1964)

d Karel Reisz   p Karel Reisz, Albert Finney   s Clive Exton
e Philip Barnikel   dop Freddie Francis   pd Timothy O'Brien

A young man who is really a psychopathic murderer attaches himself to the household of a rich old lady.

c Albert Finney, Susan Hampshire, Mona Washbourne, Sheila Hancock, Michael Medwin, Joe Gladwin

"Dreary remake of the 1930's film with a mannered star performance." – Leslie Halliwell, *Halliwell's Film and Video Guide*, 2000.

Master Spy (1964)

d Montgomery Tully   p Maurice J. Wilson   s Montgomery Tully
e Eric Boyd-Perkins   dop Geoffrey Faithfull   pd Harry White

A Russian scientist defects to the West and is employed at an establishment in England, using his great knowledge of nuclear power in top secret conditions.

c Stephen Murray, June Thorburn, Alan Wheatley, John Carson, Jack Watson, Ernest Clark, Peter Gilmore, Marne Maitland, Basil Dignam

"Underrated spy drama." – Leslie Halliwell, *Halliwell's Film and Video Guide*, 2000.

Murder Ahoy (1964)

d George Pollock   p Lawrence P. Bachmann   s David Pursall, Jack Seddon   e Ernest Walter   dop Desmond Dickinson
pd William C. Andrews

Miss Marple investigates murder, and stumbles into a ring of thieves on a naval cadet training ship.

c Margaret Rutherford, Lionel Jeffries, Stringer Davis, Charles Tingwell, William Mervyn, Joan Benham, Nicholas Parsons, Miles Malleson, Francis Matthews

"All chat and no interest." – Leslie Halliwell, *Halliwell's Film and Video Guide*, 2000.

Murder Most Foul (1964)

d George Pollock   p Ben Arbeid   s David Pursall, Jack Seddon
e Ernest Walter   dop Desmond Dickinson   pd Frank White

Refusing to return a guilty verdict, juror Miss Marple makes her own murder investigation backstage at a third-rate repertory company.

c Margaret Rutherford, Ron Moody, Charles Tingwell, Andrew Cruickshank, Megs Jenkins, James Bolam, Stringer Davis, Dennis Price, Francesca Annis, Terry Scott

"Moderate Marple mystery." – Leslie Halliwell, *Halliwell's Film and Video Guide*, 2000.

A Shot In The Dark (1964)

d Blake Edwards   p Blake Edwards   s William Peter Blatty, Blake Edwards   e Bert Bates   dop   Christopher Challis pd   Michael Stringer

A woman is accused of shooting her lover; accident-prone Inspector Clouseau investigates.

c Peter Sellers, Elke Sommer, George Sanders, Herbert Lom, Tracy Reed, Graham Stark, Moira Redmond, David Lodge, Martin Benson, Burt Kwouk, Douglas Wilmer

"Moderately enjoyable." – John Elliot, *Elliot's Guide To Films On Video*, 1991.

Of Human Bondage (1964)

d Henry Hathaway, Ken Hughes   p James Woolf   s Bryan Forbes   e Russell Lloyd   dop Denys N. Coop, Oswald Morris pd John Box

A well-to-do Englishman is brought down by his infatuation with a sluttish waitress who becomes a prostitute.

c Laurence Harvey, Kim Novak, Nanette Newman, Roger Livesey, Jack Hedley, Robert Morley, Ronald Lacey, Siobhan McKenna, Anthony Booth, Brenda Fricker

"Good-looking but thoroughly dull remake of the 1930's version." – Leslie Halliwell, *Halliwell's Film and Video Guide*, 2000.

The Masque Of The Red Death (1964) *

d Roger Corman   p George Willoughby   s Charles Beaumont
e Ann Chegwidden   dop Nicolas Roeg   pd Daniel Haller

A medieval Italian prince practises devil worship while the plague rages outside, but when he holds a ball, death is an uninvited guest.

c Vincent Price, Hazel Court, Jane Asher, Patrick Magee, Nigel Green, David Weston, Robert Brown

"Striking horror piece with some effective touches." – Leslie Halliwell, *Halliwell's Film and Video Guide*, 2000.

Curse Of The Mummy's Tomb (1964) *

d Michael Carrerras   p Michael Carrerras   s Michael Carrerras
e Eric Boyd-Perkins   dop Otto Heller   pd Bernard Robinson

An Egyptian mummy taken to London goes on the rampage, and meets its own wicked brother who has been cursed to eternal life.

c Ronald Howard, Terence Morgan, Fred Clark, Jeanne Roland, George Pastell, Jack Gwillim, Michael Ripper, Harold Goodwin, Marianne Stone

"Absurd farrago." – Leslie Halliwell, *Halliwell's Film and Video Guide*, 2000.

633 Squadron (1964)

d Walter Grauman   p Cecil F. Ford   s James Clavell, Howard Koch
e Bert Bates   dop Edward Scaife   pd Michael Stringer

In 1944 Mosquito aircraft try to collapse a cliff overhanging a munitions factory in a Norwegian fjord.

c Cliff Robertson, George Chakiris, Maria Perschy, Harry Andrews, Donald Houston, Michael Goodliffe, Barbara Archer, Johnny Briggs

"Standard war heroics." – John Elliot, *Elliot's Guide To Films On Video*, 1991.

The Yellow Rolls Royce (1964)

d Anthony Asquith   p Anatole de Grunwald   s Terence Rattigan
e Frank Clarke   dop Jack Hildyard   pd Vincent Korda

Three stories about the owners of an expensive car: an aristocrat, a gangster, and a wandering millionairess.

c Rex Harrison, Jeanne Moreau, Edmund Purdom, Moira Lister, Roland Culver, Shirley MacLaine, George C. Scott, Alain Delon, Ingrid Bergman, Omar Sharif

"Lukewarm all-star concoction." – Leslie Halliwell, *Halliwell's Film and Video Guide*, 2000.

Young Cassidy (1964)

d Jack Cardiff, John Ford   p Robert D. Graff, Robert Emmett Ginna
s John Whiting   e Anne V. Coates   dop Edward Scaife
pd Michael Stringer

Biographical drama and romantic view of the early life of famous Dublin writer, Sean O'Casey.

c Rod Taylor, Maggie Smith, Edith Evans, Flora Robson, Michael Redgrave, Julie Christie, Jack MacGowran, Sian Phillips, T. P. McKenna, Fred Johnson

"Generally interesting picture of a past time." – Leslie Halliwell, *Halliwell's Film and Video Guide*, 2000.

Hysteria (1965)

d Freddie Francis   p Jimmy Sangster   s Jimmy Sangster   e James Needs   dop John Wilcox   pd Edward Carrick

An American suffering from amnesia is discharged from a London clinic and walks into a murder plot.

c Robert Webber, Lelia Goldoni, Anthony Newlands, Jennifer Jane, Maurice Denham, Peter Woodthorpe, Sue Lloyd, Marianne Stone

"Complicated and rather unsympathetic twister." – Leslie Halliwell, *Halliwell's Film and Video Guide*, 2000.

The Hill (1965)

d Sidney Lumet   p Kenneth Hyman   s Ray Rigby   e Thelma Connell   dop Oswald Morris   pd Herbert Smith

Prisoners rebel against the harsh discipline of a British military detention center in North Africa during World War II.

c Sean Connery, Harry Andrews, Michael Redgrave, Ian Bannen, Alfred Lynch, Ossie Davis, Roy Kinnear, Jack Watson, Ian Hendry, Norman Bird

"Lurid melodrama." – Leslie Halliwell, *Halliwell's Film and Video Guide*, 2000.

The Alphabet Murders (1965)

d Frank Tashlin   p Ben Arbeid   s David Pursall, Jack Seddon
e John Victor-Smith   dop Desmond Dickinson
pd William C. Andrews

Hercule Poirot solves a series of murders by an apparent lunatic choosing his victims in alphabetical order.

c Tony Randall, Robert Morley, Anita Ekberg, Maurice Denham, Guy Rolfe, James Villiers, Richard Wattis, David Lodge, Margaret Rutherford, Stringer Davis

"Ruination of a classic whodunnit." – Leslie Halliwell, *Halliwell's Film and Video Guide*, 2000.

The Liquidator (1965)

d Jack Cardiff   p Jon Pennington   s Peter Yeldham   e Ernest Walter   dop Edward Scaife   pd John Blezard

An ex-war hero is recruited by the secret service as an eliminator of individuals who are considered to be security risks.

c Rod Taylor, Trevor Howard, David Tomlinson, Jill St John, Wilfrid Hyde-White, Derek Nimmo, Eric Sykes, John le Mesurier, Jennifer Jayne, Richard Wattis

"Fairly lively *James Bond* style spoof." – Leslie Halliwell, *Halliwell's Film and Video Guide*, 2000.

Operation Crossbow (1965)

d Michael Anderson   p Carlo Ponti   s Emeric Pressburger, Derry Quinn   e Ernest Walter   dop Erwin Hillier   pd Elliot Scott

In World War II, trained scientists are parachuted into Europe to destroy the Nazi rocket-making plant in Peenemunde.

c George Peppard, Tom Courtenay, John Mills, Sophia Loren, Lilli Palmer, Anthony Quayle, Patrick Wymark, Jeremy Kemp, Trevor Howard, Richard Todd, Sylvia Syms

"Unlikely, star-packed war yarn with more passing tragedy than most." – Leslie Halliwell, *Halliwell's Film and Video Guide*, 2000.

The Secret Of My Success (1965)

d Andrew L. Stone   p Andrew L. Stone, Virginia Stone
s Andrew L. Stone   e Noreen Ackland   dop Davis Boulton
pd C. Wilfred Arnold

A village policeman follows his mother's dictum that he should not think ill of others, and accidentally goes from success to success.

c James Booth, Lionel Jeffries, Amy Dalby, Stella Stevens, Honor Blackman, Shirley Jones, Joan Hickson, Richard Vernon, Martin Benson

"Flat-footed farce; satire is not evident." – Leslie Halliwell, *Halliwell's Film and Video Guide*, 2000.

Where The Spies Are (1965)

d Val Guest   p Val Guest   s Wolf Mankowitz, Val Guest
e Bill Lenny   dop Arthur Grant   pd John Howell

A country doctor is bribed into becoming a spy by the promise of a car that he greatly covets.

c David Niven, Francoise Dorleac, Nigel Davenport, John le Mesurier, Ronald Radd, Cyril Cusack, Eric Pohlmann, Geoffrey Bayldon, Basil Dignam

"Provides occasional entertainment along its bumpy way." – Leslie Halliwell, *Halliwell's Film and Video Guide*, 2000.

Lady L (1965)

d Peter Ustinov   p Carlo Ponti   s Peter Ustinov   e Roger

Dwyre   dop Henri Alekan   pd Jean D'Eaubonne

An eighty-year-old lady recalls her romantic life from her youth working as a Paris laundress.

c Sophia Loren, David Niven, Paul Newman, Peter Ustinov, Claude Dauphin, Michel Piccoli, Cecil Parker

"Unhappy, lumbering, styleless attempt to recapture several old forms." – Leslie Halliwell, *Halliwell's Film and Video Guide*, 2000.

Eye Of The Devil (1966)

d J. Lee-Thompson   p John Calley, Ben Kadish   s Robin Estridge
e Ernest Walter   dop Erwin Hillier   pd Elliot Scott

A French nobleman is obsessed by an ancient family tradition of pagan self-sacrifice.

c David Niven, Deborah Kerr, Emlyn Williams, Flora Robson, Donald Pleasence, Edward Mulhare, David Hemmings, Sharon Tate, John le Mesurier

"A general atmosphere of gloom rather than suspense." – Leslie Halliwell, *Halliwell's Film and Video Guide*, 2000.

Blow-Up (1966) *

d Michelangelo Antonioni   p Carlo Ponti   s Michelangelo Antonioni   e Frank Clarke   dop Carlo Di Palma
pd Assheton Gorton

A London fashion photographer thinks he sees a murder, but the evidence disappears.

c David Hemmings, Sarah Miles, Vanessa Redgrave, John Castle, Jane Birkin, Gillian Hills, Peter Bowles

"A beautiful and startling film." – Leslie Halliwell, *Halliwell's Film and Video Guide*, 2000.

Hotel Paradiso (1966)

d Peter Glenville   p Peter Glenville   s Peter Glenville, Jean-Claude Carriere   e Anne V. Coates   dop Henri Decae pd Francois de Lamothe

Various romantic affairs come to a head one evening at the seedy Hotel Paradiso in Paris.

c Alec Guinness, Gina Lollobrigida, Robert Morley, Peggy Mount, Robertson Hare, Derek Fowlds, Leonard Rossiter

"Good-looking but very flatly handled film farce." - Leslie Halliwell, *Halliwell's Film and Video Guide*, 2000.

Submarine X-1 (1967)

d William Graham   p John C. Champion   s Donald S. Sandford, Guy Elmes   e John S. Smith   dop Paul Beeson pd William C. Andrews

A submarine commander in World War II trains men to attack the Lindendorf in midget submarines.

c James Caan, Norman Bowler, David Sumner, William Dysart, Nick Tate, George Pravda, Rupert Davies, Paul Hansard

"Belated quota quickie, routine in every department." – Leslie Halliwell, *Halliwell's Film and Video Guide*, 2000.

Attack On The Iron Coast (1967)

d Paul Wendkos   p John C. Champion   s Herman Hoffman e Ernest Hosler   dop Paul Beeson   pd William C. Andrews

In World War II, a Canadian commando unit destroys a German installation on the French coast.

c Lloyd Bridges, Andrew Keir, Mark Eden, Sue Lloyd, Maurice Denham, Glyn Owen, Walter Gotell, Ernest Clark

"Stagey low-budgeter with modest action sequences." – Leslie Halliwell, *Halliwell's Film and Video Guide*, 2000.

The Dirty Dozen (1967)

d Robert Aldrich   p Kenneth Hyman   s Nunnally Johnson, Lukas Heller   e Michael Luciano   dop Edward Scaife
pd William Hutchinson

In 1944, twelve convicts serving life sentences are recruited for a commando suicide mission.

c Lee Marvin, Ernest Borgnine, Robert Ryan, Charles Bronson, John Cassavetes, George Kennedy, Trini Lopez, Stuart Cooper, Telly Savalas, Donald Sutherland

"Professional, commercial but unlikable slice of wartime thick ear." – John Elliot, *Elliot's Guide To Films On Video*, 1991.

Quatermass And The Pit (1967)

d Roy Ward Baker   p Anthony Nelson Keys   s Nigel Kneale
e Spencer Reeve   dop Arthur Grant   pd Bernard Robinson, Kenneth Ryan

Prehistoric skulls are unearthed during London Underground excavations, and a weird and deadly force makes itself felt.

c Andrew Keir, James Donald, Barbara Shelley, Julian Glover, Duncan Lamont, Edwin Richfield, Peter Copley, Robert Morris, Noel Howlett, Hugh Manning

"Inventive and enjoyable science fiction." – Leslie Halliwell, *Halliwell's Film and Video Guide*, 2000.

Battle Beneath The Earth (1967)

d Montgomery Tully   p Charles Reynolds   s L. Z. Hargreaves
e Sidney Stone   dop Kenneth Talbot   pd Jim Morahan

A Chinese general goes berserk and has a system of tunnels dug, under the Pacific Ocean, all the way from Chins to the USA, where he places atomic bombs.

c Kerwin Mathews, Viviane Ventura, Robert Ayres, Peter Arne, Martin Benson, Earl Cameron, Ed Bishop

"Agreeable schoolboy science fiction." – Leslie Halliwell, *Halliwell's Film and Video Guide*, 2000.

The Fearless Vampire Killers (1967) *

d Roman Polanski   p Gene Gutowski   s Gerard Brach, Roman Polanski   e Alastair McIntyre   dop Douglas Slocombe
pd Wilfred Shingleton

A zany professor and his assistant go in search of a Transylvanian vampire in comic horror spoof.

c Jack MacGowran, Roman Polanski, Alfie Bass, Sharon Tate, Ferdy Mayne, Fiona Lewis, Ronald Lacey, Sydney Bromley, Roy Evans

"An engaging oddity." – Leslie Halliwell, *Halliwell's Film and Video Guide*, 2000.

Casino Royale (1967) *

d John Huston, Richard Talmadge, Val Guest, Robert Parrish, Joe McGrath   p Charles K. Feldman, Jerry Bresler s Wolf Mankowitz, John Law   e Bill Lenny   dop Jack Hildyard, Nicolas Roeg   pd Michael Stringer

The heads of the allied spy forces call Sir James Bond out of retirement to fight the power of SMERSH.

c David Niven, Deborah Kerr, Orson Welles, Peter Sellers, Ursula Andress, Woody Allen, William Holden, John Huston, Derek Nimmo, George Raft, Geoffrey Bayldon

"One of the most shameless wastes of time and talent in screen history." – Leslie Halliwell, *Halliwell's Film and Video Guide*, 2000.

Our Mother's House (1967)

d Jack Clayton   p Jack Clayton   s Jeremy Brooks, Haya Harareet e Tom Priestley   dop Larry Pizer   pd Reece Pemberton

When mother dies, seven children, who don't want to go to an orphanage, bury her in the garden. Then their ne'er-do-well father turns up.

c Dirk Bogarde, Margaret Brooks, Pamela Franklin, Mark Lester, Yootha Joyce, Anthony Nicholls, Phoebe Nicholls, Gerald Sim, Faith Kent

"Unpleasant melodrama." – Leslie Halliwell, *Halliwell's Film and Video Guide*, 2000.

The Fixer (1968)

d John Frankenheimer   p Edward Lewis, John Frankenheimer s Dalton Trumbo   e Henry Berman   dop Marcel Grignon pd Bela Zeichan

A Jew in Tsarist Russia denies his race but becomes a scapegoat for various crimes and is imprisoned without trial until he becomes celebrated.

c Alan Bates, Dirk Bogarde, Georgia Brown, Jack Gilford, Hugh Griffith, Elizabeth Hartman, Ian Holm, David Warner, Carol White, Murray Melvin, Michael Goodliffe

"Worthy but extremely dreary realist melodrama." – Leslie Halliwell, *Halliwell's Film and Video Guide*, 2000.

The Shoes Of The Fisherman (1968)

d Michael Anderson   p George Englund   s John Patrick, James Kennaway   e Ernest Walter   dop Erwin Hillier
pd Edward C. Carfagno, George W. Davis

After spending twenty years of his life as a political prisoner, a Russion bishop becomes pope.

c Anthony Quinn, David Janssen, Laurence Olivier, Oskar Werner, John Gielgud, Barbara Jefford, Leo McKern, Frank Finlay, Clive Revill, Niall MacGinnis

"Big budget, big stars, big hopes, but a commercial dud." – Leslie Halliwell, *Halliwell's Film and Video Guide*, 2000.

Inspector Clouseau (1968)

d Bud Yorkin   p Lewis J. Rachmil   s Tom Waldman, Frank Waldman   e John Victor-Smith   dop Arthur Ibbetson
pd Michael Stringer

An incompetent French policeman is brought to London to investigate the aftermath of the Great Train Robbery.

c Alan Arkin, Delia Boccardo, Frank Finlay, Patrick Cargill, Beryl Reid, Barry Foster, Michael Ripper, Geoffrey Bayldon, Anthony Ainley, Robert Russell

"Tiresome charade with all the jokes well telegraphed." – John Elliot, *Elliot's Guide To Films On Video*, 1991.

Where Eagles Dare (1968)

d Brian G. Hutton   p Elliott Kastner   s Alistair MacLean
e John Jympson   dop Arthur Ibbetson   pd Peter Mullins

During World War II, seven British paratroopers land in the Bavarian Alps to rescue a high-ranking officer from an impregnable castle.

c Richard Burton, Clint Eastwood, Mary Ure, Patrick Wymark, Michael Hordern, Donald Houston, Peter Barkworth, Brook Williams, Derren Nesbitt, Anton Diffring

"Archetypal schoolboy adventure, containing a sufficient variety of excitements." –Leslie Halliwell, *Halliwell's Film and Video Guide*, 2000.

Hot Millions (1968)

d Eric Till   p Mildred Freed Alberg   s Ira Wallach, Peter Ustinov
e Richar Marden   dop Kenneth Higgins   pd William C. Andrews

A Cockney con-artist and trickster just out of prison makes a fortune out of fictitious companies.

c Peter Ustinov, Maggie Smith, Bob Newhart, Karl Malden, Robert Morley, Cesar Romero, William Mervyn, Lynda Baron

"Overlong comedy with irresistible star performances." – Leslie Halliwell, *Halliwell's Film and Video Guide*, 2000.

Mosquito Squadron (1968)

d Boris Sagal   p Lewis J. Rachmil   s Donald Sanford, Joyce Perry
e John S. Smith   dop Paul Beeson   pd William C. Andrews

In 1944, the Royal Air Force attacks German V-1 flying bomb installations, headed by Squadron Leader Quint Munroe.

c David McCallum, Suzanne Neve, Charles Gray, David Buck, Dinsdale Landen, Nicky Henson, Peter Copley

"Very minor and belated war heroics." – Leslie Halliwell, *Halliwell's Film and Video Guide*, 2000.

The Mercenaries (1968)

d Jack Cardiff   p George Englund   s Quentin Werty, Adrian Spies
e Ernest Walter   dop Edward Scaife   pd Elliot Scott

In the Belgian Congo in 1960 a mercenary officer is ordered to bring back a fortune in diamonds by armoured train.

c Rod Taylor, Yvette Mimieux, Kenneth More, Jim Brown, Andre Morell, Calvin Lockhart, Guy Deghy

"An unpleasant film, notable for its amount of sadistic action." – Leslie Halliwell, *Halliwell's Film and Video Guide*, 2000.

Mrs Brown, You've Got A Lovely Daughter (1968)

d Saul Swimmer   p Allen Klein   s Thaddeus Vane   e Tristam Cones   dop Jack Hildyard   pd George Provis

A young singer from working class Manchester inherits a prize greyhound, and decides to race it.

c Peter Noone, Stanley Holloway, Mona Washbourne, Lance Percival, Marjorie Rhodes, Avis Bunnage, Lynda Baron, Joan Hickson

"Inoffensive comedy musical." – Leslie Halliwell, *Halliwell's Film and Video Guide*, 2000.

2001: A Space Odyssey (1968)

d Stanley Kubrick   p Stanley Kubrick   s Arthur C. Clarke,
Stanley Kubrick   e Ray Lovejoy   dop Geoffrey Unsworth
pd Ernest Archer, Anthony Masters

From ape through to modern space scientist, mankind has striven to
reach the unattainable.

c Gary Lockwood, Keir Dullea, William Sylvester, Leonard Rossiter,
Robert Beatty, Margaret Tyzack, Ed Bishop

"A lengthy montage of brilliant model work and obscure symbolism." –
Leslie Halliwell, *Halliwell's Film and Video Guide*, 2000.

OSCAR for Special Effects

Alfred The Great (1969)

d Clive Donner   p Bernard Smith   s Ken Taylor, James R. Webb
e Fergus McDonell   dop Alex Thomson   pd Michael Stringer

In AD 871 Alfred takes over kingship from his weak elder brother and
saves a kingdom.

c David Hemmings, Michael York, Prunella Ransome, Colin Blakely,
Julian Glover, Ian McKellen, Alan Dobie, Peter Vaughan, Vivien Merchant, Peter Blythe

"A 'realistic' youth-oriented view of history." – Leslie Halliwell, *Halliwell's
Film and Video Guide*, 2000.

The Bushbaby (1969)

d John Trent   p Robert Maxwell, John Trent   s William Stevenson
e Raymond Poulton   dop Davis Boulton   pd Jack Shampan

The young daughter of a park ranger in Tanzania is distressed to learn that she and her father must permanently return to England, separating her from her pet Bushbaby.

c Margaret Brooks, Louis Gossett Jr, Donlad Houston, Laurence Naismith, Marne Maitland, Geoffrey Bayldon, Jack Gwillim, Noel Howlett, Harold Goodwin

"Much deeper than most kids movies." – Leslie Halliwell, *Halliwell's Film and Video Guide*, 2000.

Captain Nemo And The Underwater City (1969)

d James Hill   p Steven Pallos, Bertram Ostrer   s Pip Baker, Jane Baker   e Bill Lewthwaite   dop Alan Hume
pd William C. Andrews

Six survivors from an Atlantic shipwreck are picked up by a mysterious submarine and have adventures in a spectacular underwater city.

c Robert Ryan, Chuck Connors, Bill Fraser, Kenneth Connor, Nanette Newman, John Turner, Allan Cuthbertson, Luciana Paluzzi

"General production values are stolid rather than solid." – Leslie Halliwell, *Halliwell's Film and Video Guide*, 2000.

Goodbye Mr. Chips (1969

d Herbert Ross   p Arthur P. Jacobs   s Terence Rattigan
e Ralph Kemplen   dop Oswald Morris   pd Ken Adam

A musical telling the life story of a shy schoolmaster from his very first job to his death.

c Peter O'Toole, Petula Clark, Michael Bryant, Michael Redgrave, George Baker, Jack Hedley, Sian Phillips, Ronnie Stevens

"Slow and slushy." – Leslie Halliwell, *Halliwell's Film and Video Guide*, 2000.

The Best House In London (1969)

d Philip Saville   p Philip Breen, Kurt Unger   s Denis Norden
e Peter Tanner   dop Alex Thomson   pd Wilfred Shingleton

In Victorian London, the British Government attempts a solution to the problem of prostitution by establishing the world's most fabulous brothel.

c David Hemmings, George Sanders, Joanna Pettet, Warren Mitchell, William Rushton, Bill Fraser, Maurice Denham, Wolfe Morris, Martita Hunt, Hugh Burden

"Cheerful slam-bang historical send-up." – Leslie Halliwell, *Halliwell's Film and Video Guide*, 2000.

Country Dance (1969)

d J. Lee-Thompson   p Robert Emmett Ginna   s James Kennaway
e Willy Kemplen   dop Ted Moore   pd Maurice Fowler

An eccentric alcoholic baronet's incestuous love for his sister finally breaks up her marriage.

c Peter O'Toole, Susannah York, Michael Craig, Harry Andrews, Cyril Cusack, Judy Cornwell, Brian Blessed, Robert Urquhart, Jean Anderson

"Rambling melodrama with O'Toole going mad in squire's tweeds." – Leslie Halliwell, *Halliwell's Film and Video Guide*, 2000.

One More Time (1970)
d Jerry Lewis   p Milton Ebbins   s Michael Pertwee
e Bill Butler   dop Ernest Steward   pd Jack Stevens

Two American London club owners become involved with spies, gangsters and jewel-thieves.

c Peter Lawford, Sammy Davis Jr., Esther Anderson, Maggie Wright, Percy Herbert, Bill Maynard, Norman Mitchell, Dudley Sutton, Peter Cushing, Christopher Lee

"Tedious and un-amusing film." – Leslie Halliwell, *Halliwell's Film and Video Guide*, 2000.

Julius Caesar (1970)

d Stuart Burge   p Peter Snell   s Robert Furnival   e Eric Boyd-Perkins   dop Kenneth Higgins   pd Julia Trevelyan Oman

Cassius and Brutus lead the conspirators who murder Caesar, but are themselves routed by Mark Antony.

c Charlton Heston, John Gielgud, Jason Robards Jr., Richard Johnson, Robert Vaughn, Richard Chamberlain, Diana Rigg, Michael Gough, Christopher Lee

"Ugly, ill-spoken, ham-fisted." – John Elliot, *Elliot's Guide To Films On Video*, 1991.

The Walking Stick (1970)

d Eric Till   p Alan Ladd Jr.,   s George Bluestone   e John Jympson   dop Arthur Ibbetson   pd John Howell

A repressed girl polio victim falls reluctantly in love with a painter who involves her in his criminal schemes.

c David Hemmings, Samantha Eggar, Phyllis Calvert, Ferdy Mayne, Emlyn Williams, Francesca Annis, Dudley Sutton, John Woodvine, Donald Sumpter

"Slow moving character romance." – Leslie Halliwell, *Halliwell's Film and Video Guide*, 2000.

The Private Life Of Sherlock Holmes (1970) *

d Billy Wilder   p Billy Wilder   s Billy Wilder, I. A. L. Diamond
e Ernest Walter   dop Christopher Challis   pd Alexandre Trauner

A secret Watson manuscript reveals cases in which Sherlock Holmes became involved with women.

c Robert Stephens, Christopher Lee, Colin Blakely, Genevieve Page, Catherine Lacey, Stanley Holloway, Clive Revill, Irene Handl, Peter Madden

"Wilder's least embittered film, and by far his most moving." – Leslie Halliwell, *Halliwell's Film and Video Guide*, 2000.

My Lover My Son (1970)

d John Newland   p Wilbur Stark   s William Marchant, Jenni Hall
e Peter Musgrave   dop David Muir   pd William C. Andrews

Francesca Anderson, the rich wife of an older millionaire, can't cope with the death of her lover, who is the father of her only son, James.

c Romy Schneider, Donald Houston, Dennis Waterman, Peter Sallis, Patricia Brake, William Dexter, Alexandra Bastedo, Janet Brown, Peter Gilmore

"Wonderful." – Leslie Halliwell, *Halliwell's Film and Video Guide*, 2000.

No Blade Of Grass (1970)

d Cornel Wilde   p Cornel Wilde   s Sean Forestal, Jefferson Pascal
e Eric Boyd-Perkins, Frank Clarke   dop H.A.R. Thomson
pd Elliot Scott

Industrial pollution sets a destructive virus ruining the crops of the world; anarchy spreads through Britain and one family takes refuge in the Lake District.

c Nigel Davenport, Jean Wallace, Patrick Holt, John Hamill, Lynne Frederick, Anthony Sharp, George Coulouris, Wendy Richard

"Moderately well done." – Leslie Halliwell, *Halliwell's Film and Video Guide*, 2000.

Zeppelin (1971) *

d Etienne Perier   p Owen Crump   s Arthur Rowe, Donald Churchill   e John Shirley   dop Alan Hume
pd Fernando Carrere

During the outbreak of World War I the British need to steal secrets from the zeppelin works at Friedrichshafen.

c Michael York, Elke Sommer, Peter Carsten, Marius Goring, Anton Diffring, Andrew Keir, Rupert Davies, Michael Robbins, Alan Rothwell

"Entertaining period actioner." – Leslie Halliwell, *Halliwell's Film and Video Guide*, 2000.

Danziger Studios
A Filmography

* means the film was only partly made at the studio
d   Director
p   Producer
dop   Director of Photography
pd   Production Designer
s   Screen-play
e   Editor
c   Cast

Satellite In The Sky (1956)

d Paul Dickson   p Harry Danziger, Edward Danziger   s John Mather   e Sidney Stone   dop George Perinal   pd Erik Blakemore

A rocket ship is ordered to lose a tritonium bomb in space, but the device attaches itself to the side of the ship.

c Kieron Moore, Louis Maxwell, Donald Wolfit, Bryan Forbes, Jimmy Hanley, Alan Gifford, Walter Hudd

"Boringly talkative low-budget science fiction." – Leslie Halliwell, *Halliwell's Film and Video Guide*, 2000.

Quatermass 2 (1957)

d Val Guest   p Anthony Hinds   s Nigel Kneale, Val Guest
e James Needs   dop Gerald Gibbs   pd Bernard Robinson

A research station operating under military secrecy is supposed to be making synthetic foods, but is in fact an acclimatization center for invaders from outer space.

c Brian Donlevy, John Longden, Sidney James, Bryan Forbes, William Franklyn, Charles Lloyd Pack, Percy Herbert, Michael Ripper, Vera Day, Marianne Stone

"Excellent British shocker." – Leslie Halliwell, *Halliwell's Film and Video Guide*, 2000.

Operation Murder (1957)

d Ernest Morris   p Edward Danziger, Harry Danziger   s Brian Clemens   e Anne Barker   dop James Wilson   pd George Beech

Doctor Wayne is a brilliant surgeon, but when he must perform an emergency operation, and the patient dies, he is suspected of murder.

c Tom Conway, Sandra Dorne, Patrick Holt, Rosamund John, Robert Ayres, John Stone, Alastair Hunter

"Clinical claptrap." – David Quinlan, *British Sound Films*, 1984.

Three Sundays To Live (1957)

d Ernest Morris   p Edward Danziger, Harry Danziger   s Brian Clemens   e Sidney Stone   dop James Wilson   pd George Beech

Band leader Frank Martin is accused of murdering the shady owner of the club where he's performing.

c Kieron Moore, Jane Griffiths, Basil Dignam, Sandra Dorne, Hal Ayer, John Stone, Norman Mitchell, John Longden, Ferdy Mayne

"Dreary and ridiculous." – David Quinlan, *British Sound Films*, 1984.

The Traitor (1957)

d Michael McCarthy   p E. J. Fancey   s Michael McCarthy
e Monica Kimick   dop Bert Mason   pd Herbert Smith

At the annual reunion of a resistance group, the host announces that one of their number was a traitor.

c Donald Wolfit, Robert Bray, Jane Griffiths, Carl Jaffe, Anton Diffring, Oscar Quitak, Rupert Davies, John Van Eyssen, Christopher Lee

"Heavy-handed theatrical melodrama, helped by some directional flair." – David Quinlan, *British Sound Films*, 1984.

The Depraved (1957)

d Paul Dickson   p Edward Danziger, Harry Danziger   s Brian Clemens   e Vera Campbell   dop James Wilson   pd Erik Blakemore

A US Army captain stationed in England has an affair with a married woman, and together they hatch a plan to murder her husband.

c Anne Heywood, Robert Arden, Carroll Levis, Basil Dignam, Denis Shaw, Robert Ayres, Garry Thorne

"The script does not call for good acting and it doesn't get any." – David Quinlan, *British Sound Films*, 1984.

Son Of A Stranger (1957)

d Ernest Morris   p Edward Danziger, Harry Danziger   s Stanley

Miller   e Clifford Boote   dop James Wilson   pd Erik Blakemore

A young man goes on the search for the father he never knew, and who he now believes to be a millionaire.

c James Kenney, Ann Stephens, Victor Maddern, Basil Dignam, Diana Chesney, Catherine Finn, Mona Washbourne

"Ludicrously unconvincing." – David Quinlan, *British Sound Films*, 1984.

The Betrayal (1957)

d Ernest Morris   p Edward Danziger, Harry Danziger
s Brian Clemens   e Clifford Boote   dop James Wilson
pd Erik Blakemore

Ten years after being betrayed, shot and blinded in a World War II escape bid, Michael McCall hears the voice of his betrayer again at a London party.

c Philip Friend, Diana Decker, Philip Saville, Peter Bathurst, Peter Burton, Ballard Berkeley, Harold Lang

"Almost believable offbeat thriller." – David Quinlan, *British Sound Films*, 1984.

A Woman Of Mystery (1958)

d Ernest Morris   p Edward Danziger, Harry Danziger
s Brian Clemens   e Maurice Rootes   dop James Wilson
pd Erik Blakemore

Reporter Ray Savage has no appetite for the facts behind a young girl's suicide – until he discovers it was murder.

c Dermot Walsh, Hazel Court, Jennifer Jayne, Ferdy Mayne, Ernest Clark, Diana Chesney, Paul Dickson

"Flat presentation." – David Quinlan, *British Sound Films*, 1984.

Up The Creek (1958)

d Val Guest   p Henry Halsted   s Val Guest   e Helen Wiggins
dop Arthur Grant   pd Ward Richards

A none-too-bright naval lieutenant is assigned command of a broken-down shore establishment.

c David Tomlonson, Peter Sellers, Wilfrid Hyde-White, Vera Day, Michael Goodliffe, Reginald Beckwith, Lionel Jeffries, David Lodge, Sam Kydd, Barry Lowe

"Jokes fair, atmosphere cheerful and easy-going." – Leslie Halliwell, *Halliwell's Film and Video Guide*, 2000.

On The Run (1958)

d Ernest Morris   p Edward Danziger, Harry Danziger   s Brian Clemens   e Maurice Rootes   dop James Wilson   pd Erik Blakemore

An ex-boxer on the run from gangsters for refusing to throw a fight, helps a garage owner and his daughter to improve their business.

c Neil McCallum, Susan Beaumont, William Hartnell, Gordon Tanner, Philip Saville, Gil Winfield, Hal Osmond

"Predictable thriller." – David Quinlan, *British Sound Films*, 1984.

A Woman Possessed (1958)

d Max Varnel   p Edward Danziger, Harry Danziger
s Brian Clemens   e Maurice Rootes   dop James Wilson
pd Erik Blakemore

When Doctor Winthrop returns from America with his new fiancée, his domineering mother soon makes it clear that she opposes the match.

c Margaretta Scott, Francis Matthews, Kay Callard, Alison Leggatt, Ian Fleming, Jan Holden, Denis Shaw

"Well-acted, but not-too-interesting drama." – David Quinlan, *British Sound Films*, 1984.

Moment Of Indiscretion (1958)

d Max Varnel   pEdward Danziger, Harry Danziger   s Brian Clemens   e Maurice Rootes   dop James Wilson   pd Erik Blakemore

Reluctant to disclose her whereabouts on the night of the murder of her one-time fiancé's mistress, a married woman is accused of murder.

c Ronald Howard, Lana Morris, John Van Eyssen, John Witty, Denis Shaw, Ann Lynn, John Stone, Arnold Bell

"Inept thriller." – David Quinlan, *British Sound Films*, 1984.

Links Of Justice (1958)

d Max Varnel   p Edward Danziger, Harry Danziger
s Brian Clemens   e Maurice Rootes   dop James Wilson
pd Herbert Smith

Clare, a textile magnate, keeps her profligate husband short of money to a degree that drives him and his mistress to hatch a murder plot.

c Jack Watling, Sarah Lawson, Robert Raikes, Denis Shaw. Kay Callard, Michael Kelly, Jan Holden

"Thriller has some ingenuity." – David Quinlan, *British Sound Films*, 1984.

Three Crooked Men (1958)

d Ernest Morris   p Edward Danziger, Harry Danziger   s Brian Clemens   e Maurice Rootes   dop James Wilson   pd Erik Blakemore

Three crooks plan to rob a bank through the wall of the store next door, but the owner comes back unexpectedly.

c Gordon Jackson, Sarah Lawson, Eric Pohlmann, Philip Saville, Warren Mitchell, Michael Goodliffe, Michael Mellinger

"Mixture of suspense drama and character studies; not too bad." – David Quinlan, *British Sound Films*, 1984.

The Great Van Robbery (1959)

d Max Varnel   p Edwatd Danziger, Harry Danziger   s Brian Clemens   e Maurice Rootes   dop James Wilson   pd Erik Blakemore

An Interpol detective tracks robbers who have stolen £150,000 from London, through Rio de Janeiro, Rome and Paris back to London.

c Denis Shaw, Kay Callard, Tony Quinn, Philip Saville, Vera Fusek, Tony Doonan, Bob Simmons, Geoffrey Hibbert

"Routine crooks' tour with an unusual hero." – David Quinlan, *British Sound Films*, 1984.

The Child And The Killer (1959)

d Max Varnel   p Edward Danziger, Harry Danziger
s Brian Clemens   e Maurice Rootes   dop James Wilson
pd Erik Blakemore

An on-the-run psychopathic escaped murderer sweet-talks a small boy into quietly fetching him a gun and food.

c Patricia Driscoll, Robert Arden, Richard Williams, Ryck Rydon, Gordon Sterne, John McLaren, Garry Thorne

"Some tension raised in non-dialogue scenes." – David Quinlan, *British Sound Films*, 1984.

High Jump (1959)

d Godfrey Grayson   p Edward Danziger, Harry Danziger
s Brian Clemens   e Lee Doig   dop James Wilson
pd Norman G. Arnold

A woman enlists a trapeze artist to help her with a jewel heist, but two deaths during the robbery heighten his guilt and tempt him to go to the authorities.

c Richard Wyler, Lisa Daniely, Leigh Madison, Michael Peake, Arnold Bell, Nora Gordon, Tony Doonan, Robert Raglan, Colin Tapley

"Uninteresting thriller." – David Quinlan, *British Sound Films*, 1984.

Crash Drive (1959)

d Max Varnel   p Edward Danziger, Harry Danziger   s Brian Clemens   e Lee Doig   dop James Wilson   pd Norman G. Arnold

An international racing car driver is informed he'll never drive again, then regains his will to live through the efforts of his wife and a race car manufacturer.

c Dermot Walsh, Wendy Williams, Ian Fleming, Anton Rodgers, Grace Arnold, Ann Sears, Rolf Harris

"Excellent plot very indifferently treated." – David Quinlan, *British Sound Films*, 1984.

Man Accused (1959)

d Montgomery Tully   p Edward Danziger, Harry Danziger
s Mark Grantham   e Lee Doig   dop James Wilson
pd Norman G. Arnold

Just after he has become engaged to a baronet's daughter, Bob Jenson is arrested for robbery and murder.

c Ronald Howard, Carol Marsh, Ian Fleming, Catherina Ferraz, Brian Nissen, Robert Dorning, Stuart Saunders, Colin Tapley

"Careless presentation." – David Quinlan, *British Sound Films*, 1984.

Innocent Meeting (1959)

d Godfrey Grayson   p Edward Danziger, Harry Danziger
s Brian Clemens   e Lee Doig   dop James Wilson
pd Erik Blakemore

A teenage boy on probation is falsely accused of robbery. A young girl, knowing the truth, must persuade the boy to give himself up and overcome his conviction.

c Sean Lynch, Beth Rogan, Raymond Huntley, Ian Fleming, Harold Lang, Arnold Bell, Denis Shaw

"Interesting film, well characterized." – David Quinlan, *British Sound Films*, 1984.

Web Of Suspicion (1959)

d Max Varnel   p Edward Danziger, Harry Danziger   s Brian Clemens   e Lee Doig   dop James Wilson   pd George Provis

PT instructor Bradley is forced to flee from a lynch mob after being suspected of a schoolgirl's murder.

c Philip Friend, Susan Beaumont, John Martin, Peter Sinclair, Robert Raglan, Peter Elliott, Ian Fleming, Rolf Harris

"Script has enough unintentional humor to stifle yawns." – David Quinlan, *British Sound Films*, 1984.

Top Floor Girl (1959)

d Max Varnel   p Edward Danziger, Harry Danziger   s Brian Clemens   e Lee Doig   dop James Wilson   pd Norman G. Arnold

Connie joins an advertising agency and, to further her executive ambitions, makes use of the men she meets.

c Kay Callard, Neil Hallett, Robert Raikes, Maurice Kaufmann, Brian Nissen, Diana Chesney, Liz Fraser, Anrold Bell

"The old, old story—on a budget." – David Quinlan, *British Sound Films*, 1984.

No Safety Ahead (1959)

d Max Varnel   p Edward Danziger, Harry Danziger   s Robert Hirst   e Maurice Rootes   dop James Wilson   pd Norman G. Arnold

Clem, a bank clerk, desperate for money to marry his girl, falls in with his crooked brother and joins a gang that robs a bank.

c James Kenney, Susan Beaumont, Denis Shaw, Gordon Needham, Tony Doonan, John Charlesworth, Brian Weske

"Terrible." – David Quinlan, *British Sound Films*, 1984.

A Woman's Temptation (1959)

d Godfrey Grayson   p Edward Danziger, Harry Danziger

s Brian Clemens   e Desmond Saunders   dop James Wilson
pd Norman G. Arnold

Betty, a struggling young widow, finds a wad of notes and has visions of giving her young son the expensive education of which she has always dreamed.

c Patricia Driscoll, Robert Ayres, John Pike, Neil Hallett, John Longden, Kenneth J. Warren, Robert Raglan

"Drab and dispirited." – David Quinlan, *British Sound Films*, 1984.

Date At Midnight (1959)

d Godfrey Grayson   p Edward Danziger, Harry Danziger
s Mark Grantham   e Desmond Saunders   dop James Wilson
pd Norman G. Arnold

An ace New York reporter comes to England to interview a famous criminal lawyer, but finds himself involved in a murder mystery.

c Paul Carpenter, Jean Aubrey, Harriette Johns, Ralph Michael, John Charlesworth, Philip Ray, Howard Lang, Robert Ayres

"Standard crime drama." – David Quinlan, *British Sound Films*, 1984.

Night Train To Inverness (1960)

d Ernest Morris   p Edward Danziger, Harry Danziger
s Mark Grantham   e Spencer Reeve   dop James Wilson
pd Norman G. Arnold

The diabetic son of a released prisoner is snatched by his father and taken on a train travelling to the north of Scotland.

c Norman Wooland, Jan Hylton, Dennis Waterman, Silvia Francis, Irene Arnold, Howard Lang, Kaplan Kaye

"A decent low-budget thriller." - David Quinlan, *British Sound Films*, 1984.

Sentenced For Life (1960)

d Max Varnel   p Edward Danziger, Harry Danziger
s Mark Grantham   e Spencer Reeves   dop S. D. Onions
pd Norman G. Arnold

An engineer is wrongly convicted of selling secrets to enemy agents and is sentenced to life in prison.

c Francis Matthews, Jill Williams, Basil Dignam, Jack Gwillim, Lorraine Clewes, Mark Singleton, Nyree Dawn Porter, Arnold Bell

"Very modest drama." – David Quinlan, *British Sound Films*, 1984.

Compelled (1960)

d Ramsey Herrington   p Edward Danziger, Harry Danziger
s Mark Grantham   e Desmond Saunders   dop James Wilson
pd Norman G. Arnold

An ex-con-turned-engineer is blackmailed by some crooks into taking part in a jewel heist.

c Ronald Howard, Beth Rogan, John Gabriel, Richard Shaw, Jack Melford, Mark Singleton, Colin Tapley

"Predictable." – David Quinlan, *British Sound Films*, 1984.

Escort For Hire (1960)

d Godfrey Grayson   p Edward Danziger, Harry Danziger
s Mark Grantham   e Desmond Saunders   dop James Wilson
pd Norman G. Arnold

An escort guy has to play the detective to find the murderer of the wealthy woman he had to look after.

c June Thorburn, Pete Murray, Noel Trevarthen, Jan Holden, Peter Butterworth, Mary Laura Wood, Derek Blomfield, Jill Melford

"Nothing special." – David Quinlan, *British Sound Films*, 1984.

Highway To Battle (1960)

d Ernest Morris   p Edward Danziger, Harry Danziger   s Brian Clemens

e Spencer Reeve   dop Stephen Dade   pd Norman G. Arnold

German diplomats in London try to defect because they realize the criminal views of their leader, Adolf Hitler and his gang, the Nazis.

c Gerard Heinz, Margaret Tyzack, Ferdy Mayne, Dawn Beret, Peter Reynolds, Vincent Ball, George Mikell, Hugh Cross, Jill Hyem

"Boring, talkative B picture." – David Quinlan, *British Sound Films*, 1984.

The Nudist Story (1960)

d Ramsey Herrington   p John P. Wyler   s Mark Grantham

e Spencer Reeve   dop James Wilson   pd Norman G. Arnold

Jane inherits a nudist camp which she at first regards as beneath her, but to which she is soon converted through an affair with the camp's director.

c Shelly Martin, Brian Cobby, Anthony Oliver, Natalie Lynn, Joy Hinton, Paul Kendrick, Jacqueline D'Orsay

"Very long for this sort of thing." – David Quinlan, *British Sound Films*, 1984.

The Tell-Tale Heart (1960)

d Ernest Morris   p Edward Danziger, Harry Danziger   s Brian Clemens

e Derek Parsons   dop James Wilson   pd Norman G. Arnold

When Edgar sees his girlfriend getting up close and personal with his best friend, he decides to murder him and hide his corpse under the floorboards.

c Laurence Payne, Adrienne Corri, Dermot Walsh, Selma Vaz Diaz, John Scott, John Martin, Brian Cobby, Frank Thornton

"Well made horror chiller." – David Quinlan, *British Sound Films*, 1984.

The Spider's Web (1960)

d Godfrey Grayson   p Edward Danziger, Harry Danziger
s Albert G. Miller   e Bill Lewthwaite   dop James Wilson
pd Norman G. Arnold

Famous Agatha Christie murder mystery (based on her play) with an unexpected twist in the tale.

c Glynis Johns, John Justin, Jack Hulbert, Cicely Courtneidge, Ronald Howard, David Nixon, Wendy Turner, Basil Dignam, Ferdy Mayne, Peter Butterworth

"Well made Agatha Christie." – David Quinlan, *British Sound Films*, 1984.

A Taste Of Money (1960)

d Max Varnel   p Edward Danziger, Harry Danziger
s Mark Grantham   e Desmond Saunders   dop James Wilson
pd Norman G. Arnold

An aged cashier decides to rob the insurance company where she has worked for many years.

c Jean Cadell, John Bennett, Donald Eccles, Dick Emery, Christina Gregg, Ralph Michael, Pete Murray, Robert Raglan, Mark Singleton

"Average B picture." – David Quinlan, *British Sound Films*, 1984.

An Honourable Murder (1960)

d Godfrey Grayson   p Edward Danziger, Harry Danziger
s Brian Clemens   e Desmond Saunders   dop James Wilson
pd Norman G. Arnold

Shakespeare's Julius Caesar is played in modern dress with Caesar as the chairman of a board of directors, and the conspirators are his fellow directors.

c Norman Wooland, Margaretta Scott, Lisa Daniely, Douglas Wilmer, Philip Saville, John Londen, Colin Tapley, Arnold Bell

"Not likely to get pulses racing." – David Quinlan, *British Sound Films*, 1984.

Bluebeard's Ten Honeymoons (1960)

d W. Lee Wilder   p Roy Parkinson   s Myles Wilder   e Tom Simpson   dop Stephen Dade   pd Paul Sheriff

A middle-aged man loses his head for a mercantile young temptress, and finds himself driven into a series of cold-blooded murders.

c George Sanders, Corinne Calvet, Jean Kent, Patricia Roc, Greta Gynt, Maxine Audley, Ingrid Hafner, Peter Illing, George Coulouris, Ian Fleming

Predictable thriller, with enjoyable performance by Saunders." – David Quinlan, *British Sound Films*, 1984.

Feet Of Clay (1960)

d Frank Marshall   p Brian Taylor   s Mark Grantham
e Desmond Saunders   dop James Wilson   pd Norman G. Arnold

A dangerous drug-smuggling case becomes even more dangerous when an investigating lawyer discovers that the individual behind it is a police probation officer.

c Vincent Ball, Wendy Williams, Hilda Fenemore, Robert Cawdron, Brian Smith, Angela Douglas, Jack Melford

"Fun, competent British crime film." – David Quinlan, *British Sound Films*, 1984.

Two Wives At One Wedding (1960)

d Montgomery Tully   p Brian Taylor   s Brian Clemens
e John Dunsford   dop James Wilson   pd Peter Russell

A British soldier who served in France during the war is about to marry his sweetheart, but is contacted by another woman claiming to be his wife.

c Gordon Jackson, Christina Gregg, Lisa Daniely, Andre Maranne, Humphrey Lestocq, Viola Keats, Douglas Ives, John Serret

"A little staid and very low-budget." – David Quinlan, *British Sound Films*, 1984.

Identity Unknown (1960)

d Frank Marshall   p Edward Danziger, Harry Danziger
s Brian Clemens   e Lee Doig   dop James Wilson
pd Norman G. Arnold

Two reporters develop a relationship while investigating an incident involving an aircraft.

c Richard Wyler, Pauline Yates, Patricia Plunkett, Beatrice Varley, Valentine Dyall, Kenneth Edwards, Nyree Dawn Porter, Vincent Ball

"Nothing special." – David Quinlan, *British Sound Films*, 1984.

The Court Martial Of Major Keller (1961)

d Ernest Morris   p Edward Danziger, Harry Danziger
s Brian Clemens   e Spencer Reeve   dop James Wilson
pd Norman G. Arnold

The film is based around the court martial, for murdering his colonel, of Major Keller, a British army officer during the Second World War.

c Laurence Payne, Susan Stephen, Ralph Michael, Richard Caldicot, Basil Dignam, Austin Trevor, Simon Lack, Hugh Cross, Peter Sinclair

"Courtroom drama with style." – David Quinlan, *British Sound Films*, 1984.

So Evil, So Young (1961)

d Godfrey Grayson   p Edward Danziger, Harry Danziger
s Mark Grantham   e Desmond Saunders   dop James Wilson
pd Norman G. Arnold

A young girl is framed for a robbery, and sent to a harsh reform school, where she becomes the target of a vicious warden.

c Jill Ireland, Ellen Pollock, John Charlesworth, Jocelyn Britton, Joan Haythorne, Olive McFarland, John Longden, Sheila Whittingham, Natalie Lynn

"Pretty strong 'B' picture for its time." – David Quinlan, *British Sound Films*, 1984.

The Middle Course (1961)

d Montgomery Tully   p Edward Danziger, Harry Danziger
s Brian Clemens   e Bill Lewthwaite   dop James Wilson
pd Norman G. Arnold

A small town in France, with the help of a Canadian pilot, must adopt ingenious methods to cope with occupying German forces.

c Vincent Ball, Lisa Daniely, Peter Illing, Roland Bartrop, Marne Maitland, Robert Rietty, Yvonne Andre

"A good yarn." – David Quinlan, *British Sound Films*, 1984.

The Pursuers (1961)

d Godfrey Grayson   p Philip Elton, Ralph Goddard
s Brian Clemens   e John Dunsford   dop Walter J. Harvey
pd Peter Mullins

A group of former concentration camp prisoners form an underground network to hunt down Nazi leaders.

c Cyril Shaps, Francis Matthews, Susan Denny, Sheldon Lawrence, George Murcell, John Gabriel, Tony Doonan, Steve Plytas, Reginald Marsh

"Powerful drama for its time." – David Quinlan, *British Sound Films*, 1984.

Strip Tease Murder (1961)

d Ernest Morris   p Ralph Ingram   s Paul Tabori   e Derek Parsons   dop James Wilson   pd Norman G. Arnold

A stripper, Rita, tries to blackmail her former lover, the wealthy Carlos Branco, threatening to reveal his illegal dope trade to the police.

c John Hewer, Ann Lynn, Jean Muir, Vanda Hudson, Kenneth J. Warren, Carl Duering, Michael Peake, Peter Elliott

"Not for those in search of titillation." – David Quinlan, *British Sound Films*, 1984.

Tarnished Heroes (1961)

d Ernest Morris   p Edward Danziger, Harry Danziger
s Brian Clemens   e Desmond Saunders   dop James Wilson
pd Norman G. Arnold

Set in World War II, Major Bell is given the task of blowing up a bridge that is a life line for German supplies.

c Dermot Walsh, Anton Rodgers, Patrick McAlinney, Richard Carpenter, Maurice Kaufmann, Max Butterfield, Sheila Whittingham, Brian Peck

"Good old adventure." – David Quinlan, *British Sound Films*, 1984.

Fate Takes A Hand (1961)

d Max Varnel   p Edward Danziger, Harry Danziger
s Brian Clemens   e Spencer Reeve   dop James Wilson
pd Norman G. Arnold

A mail bag stolen in a robbery fifteen years previous is found, and the post office decide that the letters should be delivered.

c Ronald Howard, Christina Gregg, Basil Dignam, Jack Watson, Peter Butterworth, Noel Trevarthen, Sheila Whiitingham, Valentine Dyall, Brian Cobby

"A rare and funny little gem." – David Quinlan, *British Sound Films*, 1984.

Transatlantic (1961)

d Ernest Morris   p Edward Danziger, Harry Danziger
s Brian Clemens   e Spencer Reeve   dop Walter J. Harvey
pd Peter Mullins

A man from the FBI and a pretty English girl solve a mystery surrounding the loss of an airliner.

c Pete Murray, June Thorburn, Bill Nagy, Neil Hallett, Jack Melford, Sheldon Lawrence, Mark Singleton

"Average 'B' picture." – David Quinlan, *British Sound Films*, 1984.

Part-Time Wife (1961)

d Max Varnel   p Edward Danziger, Harry Danziger
s H. M. McCormack   e John Dunsford   dop Walter J. Harvey
pd Peter Russell

Danziger comedy involving an insurance salesman named Tom, and a farcical marital mix-up.

c Anton Rodgers, Nyree Dawn Porter, Kenneth J. Warren, Henry McCarthy, Mark Singleton, Neil Hallett, Susan Richards, June Cunningham, Michael Peake

"Fun little movie." – David Quinlan, *British Sound Films*, 1984.

The Gentle Terror (1962)

d Frank Marshall   p Brian Taylor   s Mark Grantham
e John Dunsford   dop Stephen Dade   pd Peter Russell

The predictably boring life of a meek book-keeper, until fate transforms him into an underworld terror.

c Terence Alexander, Angela Douglas, Jill Hyem, Laidman Browne, Malcolm Webster, Victor Spinetti, George Mikell

"Average." – David Quinlan, *British Sound Films*, 1984.

The Lamp On Assassin Mews (1962)

d Godfrey Grayson   p Brian Taylor   s Mark Grantham
e John Dunsford   dop Lionel Banes   pd Peter Russell

An old couple plan to defend a treasured street lamp from those who want to remove it from its rightful place – by committing murder.

c Francis Matthews, Lisa Daniely, Ian Fleming, Amy Dalby, Ann Sears,

Anne Lawson, Derek Tansley, John Lewis, Ann Lancaster, Colin Tapley, Douglas Ives

"Oddball black comedy." – David Quinlan, *British Sound Films*, 1984.

Three Spare Wives (1962)

d Ernest Morris   p Ralph Goddard   s Eldon Howard
e Peter Pitt   dop Walter J. Harvey   pd Peter Russell

A man inherits a harem of three wives from his uncle, which he decides to bring home to his wife in England.

c Susan Stephen, John Hewer, Robin Hunter, Barbara Leake, Ferdy Mayne, Gale Sheridan, Noel Purcell

"Amusing low budget comedy." – David Quinlan, *British Sound Films*, 1984.

Return Of A Stranger (1962)

d Max Varnel   p Brian Taylor   s Brian Clemens
e Spencer Reeve   dop Walter J. Harvey   pd Norman G. Arnold

A young couple buy a terraced house with their young son, but are woken in the middle of the night by a man peeping at them from the pavement outside.

c John Ireland, Susan Stephen, Cyril Shaps, Timothy Beaton, Ian Fleming, Raymond Rollett, Frederick Piper

"Cut price *Cape Fear* from the Danziger Brothers." – David Quinlan, *British Sound Films*, 1984.

The Silent Invasion (1962)

d Max Varnel   p Edward Danziger, Harry Danziger

s Brian Clemens   e Derek Parsons   dop James Wilson
pd Norman G. Arnold

In 1940, some local men in the French town of Mereux mount an attack on a German garrison stationed there, which goes horribly wrong.

c Eric Flynn, Petra Davies, Francis de Wolff, Martin Benson, Jan Conrad, Noel Dyson, Melvyn Hayes, Warren Mitchell, John Serret

"Interesting war film." – David Quinlan, *British Sound Films*, 1984.

The Battleaxe (1962)

d Godfrey Grayson   p John Ingram   s Mark Grantham
e Derek Parsons   dop Lionel Banes   pd Peter Russell

An engaged couple's pre-marital bliss is shattered by the future bride's domineering mother.

c Jill Ireland, Joan Haythorne, Francis Matthews, Michael Beint, Olaf Pooley, Richard Caldicot, Juliette Manet

"Slightly amusing comedy from a bygone age." – David Quinlan, *British Sound Films*, 1984.

Design For Loving (1962)

d Godfrey Grayson   p John Ingram   s Mark Grantham
e John Dunsford   dop Stephen Dade   pd Peter Russell

Comedy drama about a young woman and member of the Beat Generation who becomes a top fashion model.

c June Thorburn, Pete Murray, Soraya Rafat, James Maxwell, June Cunningham, Prudence Hyman, Michael Balfour, Marjie Lawrence, Patsy Smart

"Average 'B' picture." – David Quinlan, *British Sound Films*, 1984.

She Always Gets Their Man (1962)

d Godfrey Grayson   p John Ingram   s Mark Grantham
e John Dunsford   dop Lionel Banes   pd Peter Russell

A group of young women staying at a hostel try to keep a vamp from taking a wealthy man for a ride.

c Terence Alexander, Ann Sears, Sally Smith, William Fox, Avril Elgar, Bernice Swanson, Gale Sheridan, Michael Balfour

"Amusing, efficient, well-acted British comedy." – David Quinlan, *British Sound Films*, 1984.

The Durant Affair (1962)

d Godfrey Grayson   p Philip Elton   s Eldon Howard
e John Dunsford   dop James Wilson   pd Peter Russell

Drama about a young woman who becomes an unexpected heiress to a fortune, left by a mother she never knew.

c Jane Griffiths, Conrad Phillips, Nigel Green, Francis de Wolff, Richard Caldicot, Simon Lack, Ann Lancaster, Katharine Pate

"Mildly interesting British film." – David Quinlan, *British Sound Films*, 1984.

What Every Woman Wants (1962)

d Ernest Morris   p Edward Danziger, Harry Danziger
s Mark Grantham   e John Dunsford   dop James Wilson
pd Peter Russell

A marital comedy set in the 1960's about wives trying, as best they can, to reform their husbands.

c James Fox, Hy Hazell, Dennis Lotis, Elizabeth Shepherd, Guy Middleton, Andrew Faulds, Patsy Smart, Ian Fleming, George Merritt, Brian Peck, Jack Melford

"Low-budget laughs." - David Quinlan, *British Sound Films*, 1984.

Gang War (1962)

d Frank Marshall   p Brian Langslow   s Mark Grantham
e John Dunsford   dop Stephen Dade   pd Peter Russell

Set during the early 1960's, a Chicago mobster and a Londoner try to get involved in a jukebox racket.

c Sean Kelly, Eira Heath, David Davies, Sean Sullivan, Mark Singleton, Colin Tapley, Tony Doonan, Max Faulkner

"A good British gangster movie." – David Quinlan, *British Sound Films*, 1984.

The Spanish Sword (1962)
d Ernest Morris   p Brian Taylor   s Brian Clemens
e Peter Pitt   dop Walter J. Harvey   pd Roy Stannard

A swashbuckling king's knight takes up arms and fights against a treasonous evil baron.

c Ronald Howard, June Thorburn, Trader Faulkner, Nigel Green, Robin Hunter, Derrick Sherwin, Sheila Whittingham, Paul Craig, Marjie Lawrence, Jill Hyem

"Fun medieval adventure." – David Quinlan, *British Sound Films*, 1984.

Index

Bibliography

British Sound Films, David Quinlan, 1984

Elstree, The British Hollywood, Patricia Warren, 1989

Elliot's Guide To Films On Video, John Elliot, 1991

British Film Studios, Patricia Warren, 1995

Halliwell's Film And Video Guide, Leslie Halliwell, 2000

Made in the USA
Middletown, DE
05 January 2016